THE END OF
THE COMMUNIST REVOLUTION

This work is both a history of Gorbachev's ill-fated reforms and a systematic interpretation of the entire Soviet experience. Placing perestroika firmly in its long-term historical perspective as the final stage in a broad theory of revolutionary process, Daniels examines the nature of the Soviet system and the reasons for its decline and fall. He shows how the revolutionary regime was transformed into a reactionary despotism dressed up in Marxist language, and how this postrevolutionary dictatorship reached an impasse between maintenance of its power and the requirements and frustrations of a modern society. Within the context of Leninism, Stalinism and Brezhnevism, he puts forward a new explanation of the striking events in the 1980s which led to the downfall of Gorbachev and Communism in the late Soviet Union. Analyzing the whole Soviet experience since 1917, he argues that Gorbachev's reforms did not constitute a new revolution, but a "moderate revolutionary revival," with a return to the decentralist, anti-imperialist principles that inspired the original moderate phase of the Russian revolution of 1917.

Emphasizing continuity with the past, Daniels questions conventional views of the future political and economic alternatives in the region. He stresses the developmental forces, not just in the Brezhnev era but in the long historical background, that made fundamental change sooner or later inevitable, and provides an original and integrated interpretation of Soviet history and politics that will appeal to students, specialists, and the general reader.

Robert V. Daniels is Professor Emeritus of History at the University of Vermont and a leading American Sovietologist. His many books include, *A Documentary History of Communism*, *Red October*, and *Russia – the Roots of Confrontation*. He has been on the editorial board of the *Journal of Modern History* and was President of the American Association for the Advancement of Slavic Studies in 1992.

THE END OF
THE COMMUNIST
REVOLUTION

Robert V. Daniels

London and New York

First published in 1993 by
Routledge
11 New Fetter Lane, London EC4P 4EE

Simultaneously published in the USA and Canada
by Routledge
29 West 35th Street, New York, NY 10001

Reprinted 1993, 1994

Typeset in 10/12 pt Palatino by
Florencetype Ltd, Kewstoke, Avon
Printed in Great Britain by
T J Press (Padstow) Ltd, Padstow, Cornwall

British Library Cataloguing in Publication Data
Daniels, Robert V.
End of the Communist Revolution
I. Title
947.085

Library of Congress Cataloging in Publication Data
Daniels, Robert Vincent.
The end of the Communist revolution / Robert V. Daniels.
p. cm.
Includes bibliographical references and index.
1. Communism – Soviet Union – History. 2. Perestroĭka. 3. Soviet
Union – Politics and government – 1985–1991. I. Title.
HX311.5.D36 1993
320.5′32′0947 – dc20 92-22189
ISBN 0-415-06149-0. – ISBN 0-415-06150-4 (pbk)

CONTENTS

PREFACE

This book is a product of many years of study, teaching, and reflection on matters Soviet. It was brought to a focus by the extraordinary events of 1989 and 1991, as the long-feared Communist dictatorships in the Soviet Union and Eastern Europe finally decayed and collapsed. But as the chapters that follow make clear, my exploration of the context for the end of Communism was long in preparation. The aim of the book is as much to understand that context as to explain the most recent and spectacular changes, whose causes and consequences cannot be properly comprehended apart from this background.

I am indebted to a host of colleagues and predecessors in the field of Soviet studies, whose contribution is but partially reflected where I have cited them in the notes. For support of research underlying this work I am grateful to the John Simon Guggenheim Foundation and to the Kennan Institute of Advanced Russian Studies at the Woodrow Wilson Center for Scholars in the Smithsonian Institution. The International Research and Exchange Board has made it possible for me to visit the Soviet Union periodically, to try to keep abreast of changing conditions and viewpoints there, and the Institute of the History of the USSR in Moscow has been an accommodating and helpful host. My wife, Alice M. Daniels, has not only rendered my yellow pads into a workable typescript, but has subjected the whole manuscript to a rigorous editing. Claire L'Enfant of Routledge has been a constant source of valuable comment and encouragement. The staff of the University of Vermont library have helped throughout. Chapter 8 was presented in the Middlebury College Soviet and East European Seminar series, and I am appreciative of the comments made by that lively group.

In transliterating Russian names and terms I have used a modified Library of Congress style except where more familiar forms are established. In references to the Communist era as a whole I have used the terms "Russia" and "USSR" or "Soviet Union" interchangeably; strictly speaking, the Union did not come into existence until 1924. What now to call the "republics who formerly belonged to the former Soviet Union" has not been conveniently agreed upon. "Ex-Soviet republics," or "Soviet successor-states" may have to do unless or until "CIS" becomes common currency for the "Commonwealth of Independent States."

Robert V. Daniels
Burlington, Vermont
March 1992

INTRODUCTION

The year 1991 will go down in history as one of the great turning points, on a par with 1917. The attempted coup in Moscow in August by conservative Communists, the official demise of the Communist Party, the breakup of the Soviet Union into its constituent parts and the resignation of its president on 25 December, added up to a transformation that one might well consider as revolutionary and as world-shaking as the events that led from the fall of Tsar Nicholas II to the establishment of the Bolshevik dictatorship. But the impact of these changes has not generally been matched by profundity in explaining them. Typically commentators both in Russia and in the West have hailed this great upheaval as the "failure" of a wrong-headed "experiment" that had been foisted upon the Russians and their associated minority nationalities by a bunch of utopian fanatics, who only lost their grip and abandoned their global ambitions when their economic under-pinnings rotted away. As President George Bush asserted at the United Nations in September 1991, "Communism held history captive for years."[1]

This common view reflects gross misunderstanding of what hap-pened not only between 1917 and 1985 but between 1985 and 1991. It will seem presumptuous to tell former Soviet citizens who have lived through all these changes that they do not properly comprehend them, but this may be the necessary task of the outside observer. The collapse of Communism was not a sudden plunge into revolutionary disorder like 1917; it came through step-by-step, cumulative change in the sys-tem, unwitting before 1985 and conscious after that date. The transform-ation was only accelerated and dramatized by the August Coup and its aftermath. This was the point where we might say with Hegel that the quantitative change of reform turned into the qualitative change of revolution.

In many respects we could argue that the most revolutionary moment in this process came not in 1991 but in 1989, and not just in the chain reaction of popular movements that put an end to Communist rule in

1

the former Soviet satellite countries of Eastern Europe. The year 1989 was the turning point for the Soviet Union itself, in the dismantling of one-party totalitarian rule and the first steps to create a working constitutional structure. This year also saw the beginning of the precipitous economic collapse that more than any other circumstance tore away the forms of authority still linking the reformed Soviet realm with its past. But however we measure its timing, this sequence of victorious democratic breakthroughs in the former Communist realm was one of the most extraordinary and, to believers in democratic values, gratifying developments in all of modern history.

Still, the struggle to create democratic societies in this part of the world, as well as their future potential and problems, cannot be truly appreciated without accurately understanding the system against which this reaction was directed. This goal requires an awareness of the historical experience that the Communist world underwent in its nearly three-quarters of a century, the conditions under which the Communist system arose and developed, and the changes that time brought about in its nature. Something called "Communism" prevailed as a political and economic regime in Eastern Europe for four decades and in the Soviet Union for many years before that. But this "Communism" which the Soviet peoples and the East Europeans finally put an end to was not a pre-cast machine nor a long single-minded "experiment." It was the product of a complicated and unforeseen interaction of many factors – revolutionary passion, economic and cultural impoverishment, individual ambition, and mutual antagonism *vis-à-vis* the outside world. Ultimately, the system that passed for "Communism" became the creature of one Joseph Stalin, who stood at a crucial bend in the path of the Russian Revolution, to steer it to the worst of all possible outcomes.

An explanation of the post-Communist present in terms of the Communist past is also an occasion to reconsider the realities of that past. All manner of historical orthodoxies present themselves for re-evaluation – the notion of totalitarianism, for example, which was never supposed to fall of its own weight; or theories about the authoritarianism of Russian culture and the national urge to expand; or the Cold War definition of a bipolar world. The notion of a Communist "experiment" dissolves in the solvent of historical analysis. If the Communists ever really pursued an experiment it lasted for less than a year; the rest was a series of desperate expedients to keep power in the new world they had created, followed by the long darkness of Stalin's criminal and mendacious despotism, and the rearguard action by his successors to sustain their pretenses and privileges and to keep real change to a minimum. The ideological illusions assiduously propagated by the Stalinist and neo-Stalinist regime long stood in the way of realistic appraisal of it, and they have not ceased to distort even post-Communist ideas about what the Soviet peoples have gone through and where they might go from here. The year of 1991 was the last chapter in a long process. We need now to work back through that process to see what it was really all about.

*

The plan of this book is first to appraise the changes in the Soviet Union between Mikhail Gorbachev's selection as general secretary of the Communist Party in 1985 and the breakup of 1991. This task falls naturally into two parts, the subjects of Chapters 1 and 2 respectively – the first phase of perestroika, directed from the top, and the second phase, driven by broad-based political and economic forces from below. Gorbachev's government was forced to seek remedies and models further and further back in the Soviet past, until the country had repudiated everything it had experienced since the October Revolution.

Next, the book works back through the successive layers of the actual Communist experience. Chapter 3 examines the system immediately preceding perestroika, the "era of stagnation" that followed the abortive reforms of Nikita Khrushchev. My aim here is to show how change or lack of change during those years set the stage for developments since 1985 and underlay the crisis of 1991. In Chapter 4 I look at Stalinism as the essence of Communism before perestroika. This requires a re-examination both of its professed ideology and of the basic cultural, social, and economic realities contributing to the system that held sway in the Soviet Union over most of its history. Then in Chapter 5 I take a long view of the entire Communist era as a process of revolution, that is, a natural sequence of events working itself out through a series of stages, the most enduring of which was the Stalinist postrevolutionary dictatorship. The notion of process in turn gives a new meaning to perestroika and the collapse of Communism. These events represent the terminal stage of the revolution and a return to the missed opportunities of 1917.

Chapters 6 and 7 turn outwards to consider the geographical extension of the Russian revolutionary experience. Chapter 6 treats the non-Russian minorities of the Empire, and the East European satellites. Chapter 7 takes up Communism's engagement with forces both sympathetic and hostile in the world beyond the bloc. In both realms the events of 1989–1991 emerge in a new light. We have come to the end of postrevolutionary ambitions, overlordship, and confrontations.

In the final chapter I take a more reflective approach to the changes and potentialities released in Eastern Europe and the Soviet successor states by the end of what we have called "Communism." These current and future prospects are measured against the revulsion of the ex-

Communist nations from their revolutionary legacy, and particularly from anything associated with the term "socialism." But this anti-revolutionary moment raises questions about the actual direction that modern society is taking, in contrast to the ideological myths that have been entertained about it in the West as well as in the East. Finally, my attempt at analyzing the residue of Communism leads naturally to some judgements, tentative and fallible though they may be, about the opportunities that may be at stake to improve the human condition where so much suffering has been fated in the past.

1

PERESTROIKA I:
Back to the future

12 April 1984. The Supreme Soviet of the USSR has assembled in one of its infrequent plenary meetings in the Kremlin for the purpose of granting its pro forma endorsement to the new – though actually very elderly – leader of the country, Konstantin Ustinovich Chernenko. Chernenko, of course, became the effective chief executive in February when the Politburo and Central Committee of the Communist Party of the Soviet Union gave him their nod to succeed the deceased Yuri Andropov as general secretary of the Party. The charge now to the Supreme Soviet is to confer upon Chernenko the additional office of chairman of the Presidium of the Supreme Soviet – i.e., ceremonial chief of state – an honor that both his immediate predecessors, Andropov and Brezhnev, enjoyed.

The acting chairman at this meeting is Lev Tolkunov, chairman of the lower house of the Supreme Soviet, the Council of the Union. He calls for nominations for the permanent chairmanship. Up steps an energetic, rather stocky, middle-aged individual with a prominent purplish birth-mark on his deeply receding forehead. This is the man who will soon give his name to the concluding era in the history of the Soviet Union and most of the Communist movement, Mikhail Sergeyevich Gorbachev.

At 52 the youngest member of the policy-setting Politburo, Gorbachev has already begun to attract wide attention in the Soviet Union as well as among Kremlin-watchers abroad. As party secretary in charge of the eternally frustrating area of Soviet agriculture, he is believed to be forceful, pragmatic, and forward-looking. Just how far forward will be a surprise to the entire world. For the moment, the fact that it has been arranged for Gorbachev to put Chernenko's name in nomination clues in perceptive observers at home and abroad that he has already reached high into the Kremlin's unwritten power structure, perhaps to the number-two position.

In the nominating speech that he delivers to the Supreme Soviet on behalf of Chernenko, Gorbachev does not disappoint any of these expectations. He speaks, to be sure, in the familiar scripted form:

5

> The Central Committee's plenary session has, in an atmosphere of total unanimity, deemed it necessary that Konstantin Ustinovich Chernenko, general secretary of our party's Central Committee, simultaneously hold the office of chairman of the Presidium of the USSR Supreme Soviet . . . . This decision is inseparably linked with the Communist Party's leading role in our society, as established in the USSR Constitution.

The applause Gorbachev receives may really be genuine, though he is saying what no one believes:

> Communists and all Soviet people know Konstantin Ustinovich Chernenko as a staunch fighter for Communism and peace and as a tested Leninist leader who possesses outstanding political and organizing abilities and vast life experience.[1]

But Gorbachev's words are less important than his style. He speaks with vigor and clarity, without text or notes, fulfilling the required function of extolling the virtues of his candidate, but really advertising his own qualities of a commanding, persuasive, efficient, take-charge executive.

When Gorbachev finishes his encomium, the presiding officer duly asks for other nominations. Hearing none, he puts the choice of Chernenko to a vote. As if pulled by the string of some master puppeteer, every right arm in the crowded hall rises in unison. But to be fair, the chair calls for the negatives – none – and abstentions – again none. "I therefore declare Comrade Chernenko elected chairman of the Presidium of the Supreme Soviet."

Poor Konstantin Ustinovich staggers to his feet to deliver his acceptance speech. At age 73 he is already far gone with emphysema, and can hardly utter three words in succession without gasping for breath. The contrast between him and the dynamic Gorbachev could not have been more glaringly arranged. Perceptive observers might well conclude that Number Two is well on his way to becoming Number One, if he is not already that *de facto* by some behind-the-scenes agreement. Hopeful Soviets create "a minicult of personality" around Gorbachev.[2] Meanwhile, the joke starts around Moscow, after the deaths of two leaders in quick succession and the dim chances of the next, about the Soviet citizen who tries to get into Red Square for Andropov's funeral without a pass. "Pass?" he replies to the guards who challenge him, "I don't need a pass. I have a subscription ticket."

*

Until he reached the highest level of the Soviet political hierarchy, Gorbachev had given little indication of the kind and direction of leadership that he might bring to the Soviet empire. His beginnings were

6

plebeian enough, like most of the generation of Stalinist apparatchiki who preceded him. He was born to a Russian peasant family in the village of Privolnoye in the Stavropol province in the foothills of the North Caucasus, where a crazy-quilt of tribal minorities, of diverse languages and mostly Moslem in religion, had been brought under the rule of the Tsars scarcely a hundred years before. The Gorbachevs were not ordinary villagers, to be sure. Gorbachev's paternal grandfather was one of the rare rural Communists and a backer of Joseph Stalin's militant campaign to collectivize the peasants. In 1931, the year of his grandson's birth, he was made chairman of the collective farm set up for Privolnoye. His son Sergei, Gorbachev's father, worked for a machine-tractor station, where the machinery to serve the district collective farms was centered, and in time became a local party official and fought with the Red Army from Kursk to Czechoslovakia. Mikhail Sergeyevich himself was too young to recall personally the forcible deportation of the Cossacks and the kulaks (in other words, the most successful farmers) or the famine conditions of 1932–33, though as he grew up the village experience would be well known to him. Both his grandfathers were arrested during the purges.[3] Too young to serve in the Second World War, Gorbachev went to local schools and ran farm machinery in his off-hours. He followed family tradition by joining the Communist Youth organization – the Komsomol – and at age 18 he became a candidate member of the Communist Party. Then, in 1950, came the opportunity of his life, a reflection of his native ability combined with good political credentials. He was admitted to the most prestigious of all Soviet educational institutions, Moscow State University.

At the university, Gorbachev chose the law faculty, in preference to the engineering or agronomy that was the only higher education enjoyed by any of the Soviet leaders of that era. As a politically reliable student he was selected to room next to (and undoubtedly to report on) a foreigner, one of the many young Communists from Eastern Europe and China sent to the Soviet Union for higher education in these years. Gorbachev's neighbor was Zdeněk Mlynář, a Czechoslovak who also went on to achieve prominence as a political reformer, in his case in the Prague Spring of 1968. To his classmates, Gorbachev was quiet and reserved, but privately open-minded. Mlynář thought him unlike the usual Stalinists: "The student Gorbachev doubted that there were only two types of Russians, those who adhered strictly to the party line and the criminals who did not,"[4] and described him as "always a person who saw the truth."[5] Nevertheless, Gorbachev excelled in the disciplinarian virtues demanded by the Komsomol, and "played up incredibly to those in authority," according to another classmate.[6] He became chairman of the organizational committee of the university Komsomol unit, and thereby kept open the option of a career in the Communist

7

Party apparatus, in effect the profession of controlling other people. Along the way, just before Stalin's death in 1953, he was granted full membership in the Communist Party itself, a normal step for Komsomol activists.

*

Gorbachev graduated from the university in 1955, two years into the post-Stalin "thaw," just when Nikita Khrushchev had emerged on top in the succession struggle. He promptly took the plunge into career party work by accepting an assignment in the Komsomol bureaucracy back in his home territory, in the city of Stavropol. Another long-term decision was his marriage to Raisa Titorenko, a fellow student at the university and similarly a native of the Stavropol region, who was ultimately to give the world a new conception of the consort of a Soviet leader.

Moving rapidly up the career ladder in Stavropol, Gorbachev became head of the city Komsomol in 1956, the year of Khrushchev's de-Stalinization campaign; second-in-command of the provincial Komsomol two years later; and head of it in 1960. This gave him automatic membership on the provincial committee of the Party and a seat as a delegate to the Twenty-Second Party Congress in 1961. Thus he entered the *nomenklatura*, the privileged stratum of functionaries so called from the system of central party control over important appointments in all walks of life.

Next, to move into regular party work, Gorbachev turned to the area he would most often be associated with for the next twenty years, agriculture. He accepted the post of party leader in one of the local "collective-farm and state-farm production trusts," into which every rural district in the country was to be organised according to Khrushchev's latest scheme to stimulate agriculture. But he was soon (1962) brought back into the provincial party headquarters, first as secretary in charge of organization and appointments, then in 1968 as second secretary for the province, and finally in 1970 as first secretary. This post, nominally elective but actually dependent on a "recommendation" from Moscow, made Gorbachev number-one man in Stavropol province, with entitlement to a seat on the Central Committee of the Party, to which he was duly elected at the Twenty-Fourth Party Congress in 1971. Along the way, the downfall of Khrushchev, ending his reforms and experiments and initiating the Brezhnev era of bureaucratic normality, was as little a tremor for Gorbachev as it was elsewhere in the well-oiled party machine, even though he would eventually look back on the thaw of the 1950s and early 1960s as the inspiration for his own reforms.

Gorbachev's career record is a cogent illustration of the intersecting

maze of bureaucratic ladders that made up the Soviet system of administration and control. His own path was fairly typical for a rising apparatchik, but his unusually rapid progress indicated that he had special
favor among his superiors, a crucial factor in a system where informal
personal ties, patronage, and the assurance of support in return for
benefits – a feudal system of up and down relationships in the guise of a
modern state – were decisive for personal success. The feudal attitude
extended to preferential treatment of one's home territory, and
Stavropol happened to be well situated in this respect. It was
Andropov's native province, and it had also been the wartime station of
Mikhail Suslov, the king-maker and ideological leader under both
Khrushchev and Brezhnev. Gorbachev, as it turned out, enjoyed the
decisive patronage of both of these men as he climbed toward national
leadership.

*

For eight years Gorbachev had commanded the Stavropol province
when, in 1978, chance gave him the opening to become a player on the
central political stage in Moscow. Fyodor Kulakov, the Politburo member in charge of agriculture and a former patron of Gorbachev's in
Stavropol, died – by suicide, as rumor had it. Gorbachev was the man
chosen to join the eight-member Party Secretariat in Moscow and take
over Kulakov's responsibilities. The move happened to coincide with
the most extensive political shakeup of the Brezhnev era, the moment,
according to the émigré biologist-historian Zhores Medvedev, "for the
Brezhnev faction to achieve dominance in the Politburo," and "the
beginning of a serious economic and political decline . . . , years of
crisis."[7] Nevertheless, Gorbachev prospered personally as the favorite
of key front-rank leaders, even though the shortfall in Soviet agriculture
had necessitated new grain purchases from abroad. Within a year after
his appointment to the Secretariat Gorbachev was brought into the
Politburo, the highest party authority, as one of the six "candidate" or
alternate members. A year later, in October 1980, barely two years
before the death of Brezhnev, he became one of the full members of the
Politburo, youngest of the fifteen.

By Kremlin standards of the time, Gorbachev's rise was meteoric,
carrying him ahead of half a dozen men who had been senior to him on
the Secretariat. As in all such appointments, he was nominated by the
Politburo and confirmed by the Central Committee, in other words co-
opted; presumably patronage from on high and perhaps some support
from impatient modernizers lower in the apparatus fixed on Gorbachev
as the man to push. It remains a paradox that in these most conservative
years of the Brezhnev regime, the most successful political climber was

9

the man who was shortly to repudiate that whole period as the "era of stagnation." As one of the four Politburo members who also worked under Brezhnev in the Party Secretariat, along with the ideology chief Suslov, the organization chief Andrei Kirilenko, and Brezhnev's presumptive successor Chernenko, Gorbachev became one of the few men in the Soviet hierarchy who met the traditional though unwritten qualifications for the top post of general secretary should it become vacant. He had stepped onto the launching pad for the ascent to supreme power.

*

The post-Brezhnev succession contest began even before the leader's death in November 1982. Secretary Suslov's death in January removed the king-maker's hand and invited a scramble for position. The winner was KGB chief Andropov, who prevailed upon his Politburo colleagues (how, we can only guess) to reassign him in May to the vacant position in the Secretariat, thereby placing him, despite his advanced age of 68, in contention for the leadership. With the presumptive backing of the police, the military, younger figures in the party apparatus (including Gorbachev), and everyone frustrated by the immobilism of Brezhnev's last years, Andropov was ready to step in at the moment of Brezhnev's death.

It is not quite true, as so many foreign commentators suggested at the time, that the Soviet system lacked a mechanism for replacing a deceased leader. The proper analogy is not with the American presidential succession, where the vice-president automatically takes over if the president dies, but with the European parliamentary system, where parties choose their leaders internally before the designated leader of the majority party or coalition assumes the post of prime minister. It worked the same way in the one-party system in the USSR, except that the number-one job was the general secretaryship in command of the party apparatus, to which the nominal government leaders played second fiddle at every level. The succession to Brezhnev was accomplished with a minimum of fuss: Andropov easily shunted the plodding Chernenko aside, to win the Politburo's endorsement and the Central Committee's approval to succeed to the party leadership.

Despite his post-retirement age, Andropov came in like a lion, puncturing the inflated economic claims of the Brezhnev regime and issuing a clarion call for discipline, efficiency, incentives; and against corruption, "the force of inertia and old habits," the national pastime of drunkenness.[8] "Acceleration" was his watchword. He began one by one to retire superannuated functionaries of the Brezhnev era and replace them with his own men, thereby building his personal power base according to the long-standing Soviet method that I term the "circular flow of power."

The circular flow of power was the behind-the-scenes system of political control that was created by Stalin in the course of his rise to power in the 1920s. It remained the basis of personal authority in the Soviet Union until Gorbachev broke with the whole system.[9] The general secretary controlled appointments down through the party apparatus. In turn, his men manipulated the local committees and conferences of the Party and the nominal election of representatives to the higher party bodies and the national party congress. Finally, the Central Committee, installed by each congress according to prearranged lists, ratified the co-optation of the topmost leaders to the Politburo and the Secretariat. This closed the circuit by which the general secretary assured his own dominance.

When the leader died, in this system, his personal authority passed away with him, and his successor had to rebuild it by following the method of the circular flow all over again. Following Stalin's death, Khrushchev pursued this aim successfully up to a point, though late in his tenure the neo-Stalinists in the Secretariat seem to have broken into the circle and turned it against their leader.[10] The overthrow of Khrushchev in 1964 was an object lesson, by no means lost on Gorbachev, of the mutual vulnerability of the top leader and his bureaucratic entourage.

Brezhnev, having already benefited from the conspiracy against Khrushchev, never operated the circular flow in like degree and never achieved the status of a real individual dictator. Upon his death, Andropov vigorously revived the circular flow, removing and replacing almost 10 per cent of the functionaries of Central Committee rank in that one year. He promoted three Politburo candidates to full membership, and they turned out to be the same three who backed Gorbachev in 1985 – First Deputy Prime Minister Geidar Aliev, Russian Republic Prime Minister Vitaly Vorotnikov, and Party Control Commission chairman Mikhail Solomentsev. He brought new people into the Secretariat, including two figures of special note later on – Nikolai Ryzhkov, Gorbachev's future prime minister, and Yegor Ligachev, the future leader of the conservative opposition to Gorbachev. But Andropov also had to repay the support of another Politburo member by admitting him into the Secretariat; this was Leningrad party boss Grigory Romanov, no relation to the old royal family, but reputed to be a cruel and ambitious Stalinist.[11] Romanov was clearly positioning himself for the succession, just as Andropov had the year before. Gorbachev, thought to be Andropov's choice as eventual successor, mobilized some of the critically minded intellectuals of the "sixties generation," enthusiasts of Khrushchev's thaw, and set them to work to study the country's true problems. The economist Abel Aganbegian recalled how different Gorbachev was from the old leaders: "He didn't make you feel he was a big leader and you were small . . . . He was interested in what I had to say."[12]

11

Ill-health unfortunately stalled Andropov's reform program before it got well off the ground, and death soon removed him from the scene altogether, in February 1984. This time it took the Politburo a bit longer to establish a consensus around one of the eligible candidates for the succession, Romanov, Gorbachev, or Chernenko. Chernenko, 72 and himself ailing, seemed the least likely; he would be the oldest new leader since the Revolution. Yet the threat of Romanov both to the Old Guard and to the young reformers evidently prompted an alliance of those disparate elements to keep him out of the running. The outcome seems to have been a deal, promoted by Defense Minister Dmitri Ustinov and the armed forces: Chernenko for general secretary as long as he lasted, Gorbachev as the actual number-two man and presumptive successor to Chernenko.[13] Reformers outside the inner circle were dismayed by Chernenko's selection as a step back, but took heart from the curb on Romanov and the growing reputation of Gorbachev as the man of the future. Their hopes were buttressed when Gorbachev emerged at the Supreme Soviet in April 1984 as Chernenko's designated second-in-command and *de facto* acting leader.

This did not yet determine the final outcome. While Chernenko's health deteriorated, Gorbachev staked out a bold reform agenda. In a major address to the Central Committee in December 1984 he heralded all the distinctive themes that were soon to come under his own leadership – "acceleration," "the reconstruction of economic management," "glasnost," and even "democratization."[14] Meanwhile, as we can surmise from the record, Romanov was making his big push to rally all elements of the Old Guard and beat out Gorbachev when the time came. But the time came a bit too early for him: Chernenko expired on 10 March 1985.

Once again the Politburo initiated the succession process, under the most tense of circumstances, if we can believe the reports that later filtered out of Moscow.[15] Foreign Minister Andrei Gromyko took the chair. There were two obvious contenders, members of both the Politburo and the Secretariat, Romanov and Gorbachev. Romanov tried to remove his own personality as an issue by nominating Viktor Grishin, also a Politburo member and chief of the Moscow party organisation, a position almost equivalent to membership in the Secretariat. (That was Khrushchev's job when he was nominated to be first secretary upon Stalin's death in 1953.) Unfortunately for Romanov and Grishin, one of their potential supporters, the Ukrainian boss Vladimir Shcherbitsky, was in the USA at the time, heading a Supreme Soviet delegation, and he had no way to get back to Moscow in time for the decision.[16] When Gromyko called for the vote, there was a dead tie, four to four: Romanov, Grishin, Prime Minister Nikolai Tikhonov, and Kazakhstan party chief Dinmukhamed Kunayev for the conservatives; Aliev,

Vorotnikov, Solomentsev, and Gorbachev himself for reform. Ironically, none of Gorbachev's supporters had any notable reputation for liberalism, and none could have imagined how he would eventually turn out. Gromyko, so the story goes, broke the tie and gave Gorbachev the decisive vote, along with the oft-quoted remark, "Mikhail Sergeyevich has a nice smile, but he also has iron teeth."[17] Much later, at the party conference in June 1988, Ligachev confirmed the story and took part of the credit for himself: "A completely different decision could have been made . . . . Quite different people could be sitting on this podium, and this conference might not be taking place at all."[18] Possibly the reported division in the Politburo was an informal head count, followed by an uncontested formal action to propose Gorbachev to the Central Committee, which, according to Boris Yeltsin, would have accepted no one else.[19]

In a matter of months after Gorbachev's installation, three of his opponents, Romanov, Grishin, and Tikhonov, were removed from their jobs and from the Politburo, with Kunayev following the year after. In place of these old faces, several Andropov protégés were elevated to full membership in the Politburo – Ligachev, who became effectively Gorbachev's second-in-command; Ryzhkov, the new prime minister; and KGB head Viktor Chebrikov, reflecting police support for Gorbachev's candidacy. These new men were followed by the party chief of the Georgian Republic, Eduard Shevardnadze, who was soon to replace Gromyko as foreign minister. Gromyko himself was rewarded with Chernenko's honorific position as chairman of the Presidium of the Supreme Soviet. Yeltsin, a Siberian apparatchik whom Gorbachev had just brought into the central Secretariat, replaced Grishin as boss of the party organization for the city of Moscow and won the rank of candidate member in the Politburo. Gorbachev was quickly and expertly operating the circular flow of power, to set up a team of his own men in control of the party and governmental apparatus.

*

While he was firming up his power base Gorbachev lost no time in introducing his programme of *perestroika* – "restructuring." How anxiously he appraised the country's situation at that point he only revealed when he resigned in December 1991:

> When I found myself at the helm of this state it already was clear that something was wrong in this country . . . . We were living much worse than people in the industrialized countries were living and we were increasingly lagging behind them. The reason was obvious even then. This country was suffocating in the shackles of

the bureaucratic command system. Doomed to cater to ideology, and suffer and carry out the onerous burden of the arms race, it found itself at the breaking point.[20]

His initial formulation in April 1985, at the first regular plenum of the Central Committee after he took over, was entirely confined to the performance of the Soviet economy: "It is known that, along with the successes that have been achieved in the economic development of the country, in the past few years unfavorable tendencies have intensified, and a good many difficulties have arisen."[21] Therefore, he called for "restructuring of the economic mechanism," meaning intensification of effort, acceleration of growth, stronger incentives, strict accounting, new technology – essentially Andropov's agenda to get the economy moving ahead again. Gorbachev's perseverance in the anti-alcohol campaign earned him the sobriquet of "mineralnyi sekretar" – mineral-water secretary, in place of "generalnyi sekretar."

Even Gorbachev's relatively modest beginning alarmed the entrenched bureaucrats in the party apparatus and in the central economic ministries. He gave them more cause for alarm when he started up the circular flow of power again: between his accession in March 1985 and the Twenty-Seventh Party Congress in February–March 1986, he removed and replaced no less than fifty-seven functionaries of Central Committee rank, over 20 per cent of the total, compared with only ten replacements during Chernenko's year. "These replacements had to be made," Gorbachev later explained, "because for a long time there had been no renewal of the membership of the Central Committee or the government and no constant replenishment of them with new personnel, as life demanded."[22]

Gorbachev's task was eased by the fact that the Stalinist generation of leadership – people born between 1902 and the First World War, who filled the bureaucratic vacuum left by the purges of the late 1930s – were now falling away in decrepitude or death. Thanks in part to this circumstance, the Central Committee elected at the Twenty-Seventh Congress (by the time-honored method of unanimously approving a carefully prepared slate) registered the second highest rate of turnover of any congress since Stalin's death, and an actual decrease in the average age of its members. At the same time the Secretariat was thoroughly shaken up, to give the new generation firm control at this level. Nevertheless, even the younger, newly promoted bureaucrats had a distressing tendency to turn conservative in defense of their organizational interests as perestroika unfolded.

Gorbachev's first five years were marked by a constantly escalating interaction between reform and resistance – the more reform, the more resistance; the more resistance, the deeper reform had to go. After a year in office, this process had brought him to the point of his second great innovation, *glasnost*.

The event that seems to have triggered this next stage of reform was the disaster at the Chernobyl nuclear power plant in April 1986. The initial reflex both locally and in Moscow was the old Russian fear of panic and the reflex of coverup and denial, "of stonewalling in the hope that the disaster would somehow vanish or that nobody would notice it," as the journalists Dusko Doder and Louise Branson write. They cite reports that Gorbachev was dissuaded from quicker reaction by his Politburo, and Shevardnadze confirms that the reformers lost that early "battle for the truth."[23] But sheer ignorance was a factor as well. Zhores Medvedev notes, "The officials in Moscow did not understand that they were dealing with a catastrophe of global dimensions."[24] Evacuation orders to the population nearby were too limited and too late. Only when the fallout reached other countries did the accident and its consequences become generally known, to the greater embarrassment of the Soviet leadership. In his first extensive public comment on Chernobyl, on 14 May, Gorbachev was angrily defensive, and attacked the US for "an unbridled anti-Soviet campaign" of "shameless and malignant lies."[25] Nevertheless, as Shevardnadze writes, " 'Chernobyl Day' tore the blindfold from our eyes and persuaded us that politics and morals could not diverge."[26] It was clear that Gorbachev had to find new forces and new methods to support his reform program and prod the recalcitrant bureaucracy. He found them in the intelligentsia and in the media.

Historically, for two hundred years, the Russian intelligentsia – defined as everyone who read and thought as well as the writers and professionals – had been a distinctive social entity, typically critical of existing society and suspicious of governmental authority. The Communists, particularly in Stalin's time, more than justified this suspicion, subjecting the intelligentsia to purges and controls that left it decimated and humiliated. Yet its traditions remained strong enough to come back to life during Khrushchev's thaw, and to support the dissident movement during the grey Brezhnev years that followed.

Now, in turning to the intelligentsia as an ally in the cause of reform, Gorbachev was reversing the centuries-old Russian precedent of government hostility to the thinkers. "I recall a meeting in June 1986 with the personnel of the CPSU Central Committee," he wrote the following year. "I had to ask them to adopt a new style of working with the intelligentsia. It is time to stop ordering it about."[27] Looking back on this, an editor at *Moscow News* observed,

Of all the Soviet leaders, including Lenin, Gorbachev has been the first to win himself allies among intellectuals. This sort of allies are fickle, quarrelsome and annoying for their criticism and impatience – quite unlike obedient, flattering conservatives . . . . [Nevertheless,] an alliance with intellectuals is important for many reasons. It raises society's appreciation of intellect and justice, things in such short supply in this country before 1985 . . . . Intellectuals are politically disinterested allies of Gorbachev.[28]

Gorbachev put his new approach very bluntly at a closed meeting with a group of leading writers:[29] "Restructuring is going very badly . . . . The Central Committee needs support. You can't even imagine how much we need support from an outfit like the writers . . . . We have no opposition. How then can we check up on ourselves?" – an extraordinary complaint from a Communist. His own answer was, "only through criticism and self-criticism. The main thing is, through glasnost. A society cannot exist without glasnost." Thus the Soviet Union and the outside world as well acquired a new key word – "openness," "publicity," "visibility," all convey its sense. The moment was critical, Gorbachev warned. "Society is ripe for a changeover. If we retreat, society will not let us make a comeback. We have to make the process irreversible." Finally, an echo of a familiar Jewish exhortation going back as far as the Rabbi Hillel: "If not us, who? If not now, when?"

With this sort of encouragement from the Kremlin, the spirit of glasnost spread like wildfire through the Soviet intellectual establishment. The unions of film-makers, writers, and theater people overthrew their old party-line leaders. Reformers sponsored by the new, liberal party propaganda chief Alexander Yakovlev took over a series of journals and weekly papers, notably the literary review *Novy Mir* ("New World"), the former propaganda sheet *Moscow News*, and the popular weekly *Ogonyok* ("Sparkle"). Rival papers and journals began openly to exchange polemics with one another. Banned books and suppressed films suddenly started to be published and exhibited. Even the Party's highest ideological organs, the Institute of Marxism-Leninism and the journal *Kommunist*, acquired new leadership and forswore the dogmatic past. Censorship of books before publication largely ceased, although the censorship office ("Glavlit" – Main Administration for Safeguarding State Secrets in the Press) was not formally relieved of this responsibility until 1990. Asserted Fyodor Burlatsky, one-time Khrushchev speechwriter and advisor to Gorbachev, "The press will be the method for democratic control, not control by administration but control with the help of democratic institutions."[30] Gorbachev himself went all the way: "I would equate the word restructuring with the word revolution," he told party members during a trip to the Soviet Far East in July 1986.[31] In December he backed up his words by releasing the Soviet Union's best-known dissident, Andrei Sakharov, from enforced exile in the city of Gorky.

*

Gorbachev may have been exaggerating with the word "revolution," but glasnost did have revolutionary implications for some aspects of the Soviet system. If the press and the intellectuals were to be turned loose to act as an independent force against the bureaucracy, this meant that the kind of control exercised by the Party over all forms of political and cultural expression must be abandoned. Consequently, the official Marxist-Leninist ideology, enforced from on high for decades and manipulated to justify the power and policies of the ruling elite, no longer had any compulsion behind it. Quite the contrary: Yakovlev, moving up to the Politburo in 1987 to become Gorbachev's chief lieutenant in the cause of reform, blasted "dogmatism" and "authoritarian thinking elevated to a political, moral, and intellectual principle."[32] The new leadership wanted to find out about public opinion rather than manufacture it, and a Center for the Study of Public Opinion, originally conceived under Andropov, was finally activated.[33] In his own statements Gorbachev played down the familiar Marxist categories of the class struggle, and declared, "The interests of societal development and pan-human values take priority over the interests of any particular class."[34] "Socialist pluralism" was the new formula.[35]

All these ramifications of glasnost meant that Soviet life was finally being de-ideologized and relieved of the mind-numbing burden of an official orthodoxy in all realms of thought. In turn, de-ideologizing indicated that the regime was giving up one of its main instruments of political control. This fact alone made it clear that perestroika as it was now unfolding could not possibly remain a purely cosmetic reform to give the regime a better image at home and abroad. Gorbachev was beginning to cut away the foundations of the very system of power that had made him supreme leader.

As ideological strictures fell away, the study of Soviet history was reborn. Since Stalin's rise the Soviet public had been subjected to an officially manipulated and profoundly mendacious view of the past, above all of the system's own history since the Revolution. George Orwell's satires of the Stalinist rewriting of history were no exaggeration. When Khrushchev attacked Stalin's personal record he called part of this picture into question, specifically the years of maximum terror in the late 1930s. However, he did not go into deeper issues in the Stalinist system nor did he surrender the principle of the Party's last word about historical truth.

While Gorbachev at first expressed reservations about digging up the past at a time when "we have to go forward,"[36] by early 1987 he realized that his reforms could not proceed without a foundation of historical honesty:

> The roots of the present situation go back far into the past . . . . There should be no forgotten names or blank spots in either history or literature . . . . History must be seen as it is. Everything happened, there were mistakes – grave mistakes – but the country moved forward.[37]

Writers, film-makers, and economists jumped at the chance that glasnost and new liberal editors gave them to break through old falsifications and probe the record of Stalinism in a far more searching way than Khrushchev had ever allowed. In 1987, long-suppressed books and films on Stalin and his terror finally saw the light of day, notably Anatoly Rybakov's novel *Children of the Arbat* and Tenghiz Abuladze's film *Repentance*. A long essay by the economist Nikolai Shmelyov in *Novy Mir*, "Loans and Debts," openly challenged the principles of Stalin's command economy. The playwright Mikhail Shatrov, in *The Brest Peace*, broke one of Stalinism's most obsessive taboos by representing Leon Trotsky as an ordinary historical figure instead of the devil incarnate. Nikita Khrushchev, an unperson in life and in death since his overthrow in 1964, was unofficially but fully rehabilitated in a variety of publications, including the recollections of his son Sergei.[38]

In this work of disinterring the truth the professional historians lagged behind, particularly the senior people with long records of publications in the service of the official line. Nevertheless, by 1988 public discussion of the issues of Stalinism and neo-Stalinism had become as open, honest, and intense as any intellectual controversy in the democratic West. So glaring were the contrasts between the historical revelations in the news media and the old line still embedded in school textbooks, that the authorities had to cancel the 1988 high school final exams in Soviet history.

None of these manifestations of glasnost in Soviet public life rested well with the professional bureaucracy of the Communist Party. By the time perestroika had reached the two-year mark, behind-the-scenes opposition to Gorbachev was beginning to assume serious proportions. This was not a movement of the old Brezhnevite politicians resisting any and all change – those people were already being weeded out by age or demotion. Everybody spoke in favor of perestroika; the issue was what the term really meant. In its early sense, reviving Andropov's call for sobriety and discipline, perestroika was the traditional Russian answer to a crisis, i.e., intensification of central authority and control. The adherents of this conception of reform, the people who put Gorbachev into power to begin with, had plenty of representatives in the higher organs of the Party. Seeing Gorbachev turn to the intelligentsia, even to former dissidents, and to the strategy of liberating the natural forces of Soviet society from the "command-administrative system," they found a rallying point in Second Secretary Ligachev, who spoke out more and more forcefully against "runaway reform, deprecation of the Soviet past, and neglect of socialist morality."[39]

Outside the party structure, glasnost allowed the emergence in 1987 and 1988 of a vast range of "informal organizations" and political discussion circles. To some Soviet commentators this was a sign of the revival of the "civil society" that their reading of Western critics had led them to aim for. Some of the new groups, such as the "Group for the Establishment of Trust between East and West" and the "Democratic Union" were projections of formerly underground dissident activity that still found themselves victimized by the police. Others, presumably enjoying protection among high-ranking party conservatives, gave form to an ardent Russian nationalist movement, exemplified by the "Pamyat" ("Memory") organization with its authoritarian, anti-intellectual, anti-Semitic, and anti-Western sentiments.

*

Faced with active as well as passive resistance from the officials who should have been carrying out his will, Gorbachev turned, of necessity, to fashion a third leg for what now became a tripod of reform. This was *demokratizatsiya* in political life, following perestroika in the economy and glasnost in the media and intellectual life. Initially, demokratizatsiya applied only to the Communist Party, to mobilize the rank-and-file members to offset the power of the party bureaucracy. In this effort Gorbachev had the fate of Khrushchev very much on his mind, as he reminded the writers: "Our enemies [i.e. Western commentators] . . . write about the apparatus that broke Khrushchev's neck and about the apparatus that will now break the neck of our new leadership."[40]

Gorbachev sounded the opening gun in the new campaign for democratization at the January 1987 plenum of the Central Committee, as he railed against stagnation and corruption, and in the name of "revolutionary change" called for genuine grassroots election of party officials instead of the customary top-down appointment. The meeting was a major turning point, marking both the acceleration of the reform spirit and the emergence of vigorous conservative opposition. Andrei Sakharov, scarcely back from his Gorky exile, called the plenum "an extraordinarily important event"; Gorbachev, he felt, "is going further down the road of democratic changes in our country . . . . Now it is not possible to stand in one place."[41]

The depth of division in the Party was underscored by Gorbachev's

19

failure at the January plenum to get the unambiguous endorsement of intra-party democracy that he wanted. In his closing speech he had to concede that the meeting "demonstrated once more, quite a few problems accumulated in our society."[42] He was able to buttress his position in the leadership bodies by bringing party secretary Yakovlev into the Politburo as a candidate member, and by adding his old school friend Anatoly Lukianov to the Secretariat. In addition, he broached the idea of convening a party conference – a sort of smaller-scale, mid-term congress, never convoked since 1941 – to advance the reform agenda. A few days after the plenum, Academician Tatiana Zaslavskaya, a leading theoretician of perestroika, warned, "A struggle of enormous intensity is being waged 'for' and 'against' . . . restructuring."[43]

*

For some time – from early 1987 until the fall of 1988 – the newly crystallized conservative opposition seems to have achieved a certain political equilibrium with the forces of perestroika and glasnost. No dramatic political change took place, apart from the promotion in June 1987 of three members of the Secretariat to full Politburo rank (Yakovlev, for ideology; Nikolai Sliunkov, for industry; and Viktor Nikonov, for agriculture). This move gave Gorbachev a working majority in the Politburo, though Yeltsin was conspicuously passed over even though his Moscow job presumably entitled him to move up. Gorbachev continued to dominate the realm of public policy, and glasnost thrived in the press. "1987 and 1988 were a new 'golden age,' " writes Walter Laqueur. "These were years of enormous spiritual ferment and creative openness."[44] Major steps were finally taken to try to shake up the ever more sluggish economy, above all with the Law on State Enterprise, approved by the Central Committee and the Supreme Soviet in June 1987 and put into effect in January 1988. This legislation was intended to put a wide variety of state enterprises on a commercial accounting basis, and to facilitate the establishment of individual and "cooperative" businesses. Unfortunately, the law "failed to provide the enterprise with sufficient freedom from the stranglehold of the ministries and higher economic organs," in the words of the British economist Walter Joyce.[45] Never in the following years of extraordinary political change was the Soviet government able to put an effective economic reform into place and stop the more and more obvious deterioration in the national economy.

Meanwhile, under the banner of the "New Thinking," Gorbachev pressed ahead to resolve the country's confrontational Cold War relationships with the West. To the tune of much speculation about the conservative threat, he went into seclusion in August and September

1987 to write his own manifesto, the book *Perestroika: New Thinking for Our Country and the World*, reviewing the progress of reform and detente, and inviting the world to move "from suspicion and hostility to confidence, from a 'balance of fear' to a balance of reason and good-will."[46] Putting "universal human values" ahead of the old ideology of class struggle, he declared in a subsequent speech in Poland, "What is the worth of technical progress, if at the same pace as it advances ethical norms decrease and morality becomes decrepit?"[47] This, needless to say, was a direct repudiation of Lenin's revolutionary relativism in ethics.

By the fall of 1987, Ligachev and KGB chief Chebrikov were speaking openly against the excesses of glasnost and the negative treatment of the Stalinist past, and the conservatives seemed ready to force the issue. A signal victory for the Old Guard, or so it seemed at the time, was the removal of the dedicated but intemperate reformer Yeltsin from his Moscow job and from the ranks of the candidate members of the Politburo. Yeltsin had clashed openly with Ligachev and, no doubt miffed because he had not been elevated to full member of the Politburo, made the mistake of criticizing Gorbachev to his face for the slow pace of perestroika and for allowing "what I can only call adulation of the general secretary."[48]

Just afterwards came Gorbachev's long discourse on Soviet history on the occasion of the seventieth anniversary of the Revolution. This statement advanced far beyond the old official line but fell disappointingly short of what Soviet publicists were already saying in print about the crimes of Stalin and the ongoing burden of his despotic system. Still, Ivan Frolov, Gorbachev's ideological assistant and later editor of *Pravda*, looked back on the speech as a milestone, a document "that for the first time talked on such a high political level about whole periods of the development of our history and about such people as Nikolai Ivanovich Bukharin . . . or the whole period of activity associated with the name of Nikita Sergeyevich Khrushchev . . . . Everything started there."[49] Both the Yeltsin episode and the historical speech proved only to be examples of Gorbachev's tactical style, *reculer pour mieux sauter*, short steps back in preparation for much greater leaps forward that would soon transform the Soviet Union into an utterly different political realm.

Trips and holidays have always been dangerous times for Soviet leaders. In March 1988 the conservatives took advantage of Gorbachev's absence in Yugoslavia to launch what some observers consider an attempted *coup d'état*.[50] Their call to arms was a long letter, ostensibly written by a Leningrad schoolteacher, Nina Andreyeva, and published in the conservative-leaning newspaper *Sovetskaya Rossiya*.[51]

This document was a broad and explicit attack on glasnost in all its forms, from the tolerance of "decadent" Western mass culture to the renewed anti-Stalin campaign. It denounced the alleged abandonment of "socialist values" and "proletarian collectivism" and urged the faithful to close ranks against those who denied "the leading role of the party and the working class in building socialism and in perestroika." Only after an agonizing delay of nearly a month, while Gorbachev's impending overthrow was being rumored, did the leadership reply in a *Pravda* editorial (written by Yakovlev) condemning the Andreyeva letter as "a manifesto of anti-perestroika forces."[52] This was not enough to allay the deep sense of foreboding among the Soviet intelligentsia that Gorbachev would be forced to retreat or risk being overthrown like Khrushchev. Warned one letter-writer, "A plenum at which M. S. Gorbachev could be ousted . . . is still a real possibility."[53]

*

The conservative challenge evidently gave Gorbachev second thoughts about his power base, and drove him to radically new conclusions. The forthcoming party conference, set for June 1988, appeared likely to be dominated by the conservative apparatus through their time-tested methods of rigging the selection of delegates. Gorbachev therefore decided to go over the heads of the local secretaries and appeal to the millions of functionaries, executives, and workers who made up the party rank and file, to support pro-reform delegates in genuine party elections. Thus the strength of the conservative opposition now compelled him to attack the whole system of the circular flow of power and break it up before it could be used against him by his enemies as it was against Khrushchev. Gorbachev's approach would turn the political clock back before Stalin's rise in the 1920s, and validate the arguments directed in those years by Trotsky and the Left Opposition against the bureaucratization of the Party and "the system of appointment" of "the secretarial hierarchy . . . the apparatus which creates party opinion and party decisions."[54]

Gorbachev's challenge to the local party apparatus in the selection of delegates to the party conference was not generally successful, even though it generated much uproar and public demonstrations in some localities where local officials had countermanded the results of party elections. The first deputy head of the Central Committee's Department of Party Organizational Work admitted euphemistically, "True, not all party committees were sufficiently prepared to resolve these matters in an atmosphere of openness and widespread glasnost."[55] Many of the new intellectual lights of perestroika whom Gorbachev pushed to be delegates, people such as the sociologist Zaslavskaya, the economist Shmelyov, and the playwright Shatrov, were screened out by the apparatus. By all indications, a good majority of the conference was a product of the old system of prearranged selection of bureaucratic office-holders.[56] Gorbachev complained at the conference, "From now on the corps of deputies should be formed not according to 'schedules of allocations' but above all on the basis of the lively, free expression of the voters' will."[57]

Fortunately for Gorbachev, the conservative opposition were inhibited by their sense of party discipline, which made them reluctant to defy the leader openly. Chairing the conference personally, he was able to control both the agenda and the procedure. Thus, despite the conservative preponderance among the delegates, the Nineteenth Party Conference was a wide open meeting, unlike anything the Soviet Union had seen since Lenin's days, as those reformers who managed to get elected as delegates, along with many aggrieved back-benchers, sounded off about the nation's problems and prospects. Yeltsin and Ligachev, both delegates, roundly denounced each other in open forum. "The Palace of Congresses [built under Khrushchev] has never known such discussions," said Gorbachev in his concluding speech, "and I think we will not err from the truth by saying that nothing of the kind has occurred in this country for nearly six decades."[58] Indeed, he could have said seven decades.

In any case, the Nineteenth Conference was an epochal confrontation between two political cultures contending for the future of Soviet Russia. One was the old secretive, conspiratorial, xenophobic Muscovite political culture shared by the Stalinist bureaucracy and the peasantry from which it stemmed.[59] The other was the political culture embodied in the Westernized intelligentsia since the eighteenth century, committed to a free, rational, and cosmopolitan public life. It was to this culture that Gorbachev linked his fate.

Gorbachev was not able to get the party conference to shake up the membership of the Central Committee as he presumably had hoped to do, but he had virtually a free hand in winning endorsement of his economic reforms and his proposed constitutional changes. The latter were designed to shift power and responsibility, both central and local, from the party hierarchy to the system of elected soviets, all to be capped by a strong president (presumably himself). This plan would circumvent the party apparatus and give the civil government a status *vis-à-vis* the Party that it had not enjoyed since the Russian Civil War. It would open the door for genuine popular participation in politics, and would give Gorbachev and the reform movement a base entirely outside the party bureaucracy.

Two other steps that Gorbachev took in 1988 to broaden the base of popular support for perestroika were his well-publicized reconciliation with the Orthodox Church at the time of the celebration of the millenium of Christianity in Russia, and his assertion of the principle of

23

zakonnost, the law-governed state.[60] He turned Soviet precedent upside down by urging in his book, "Let's strictly observe the principle: everything which is not prohibited by law is allowed."[61] At the same time he relaxed the uniquely unpopular anti-alcohol campaign. Another mark of Gorbachev's willingness to break with the past was the Geneva Agreement of April 1988 on Afghanistan, providing that Soviet combat forces be withdrawn by early 1989. Meanwhile, the spreading historical exposé of Stalin's crimes, particularly in the collectivization and the 1932–33 famine, was highlighted by the legal rehabilitation of Stalin's rival of the late 1920s, Nikolai Bukharin. Some writers began to sense a parallel with the Prague Spring twenty years before. "Both reforms are based on the same principle," wrote the man who had been *Izvestiya*'s correspondent in Czechoslovakia at the time of the Soviet intervention.[62]

*

It is logical to suppose, as did the Soviet public following the 1988 party conference, that the conservatives would see their last chances ebbing away, and make a desperate attempt to reverse the democratic trend. But Gorbachev moved first with his own pre-emptive strike. Faced with delaying tactics over the implementation of his constitutional proposals, he suddenly acted in the oldest Russian style of a palace conspiracy. Late in September he put the military on alert and called extraordinary meetings of the Central Committee and the Supreme Soviet to execute what Roy Medvedev called "a *coup de main*," with "the most dramatic show of force yet to take place inside the new leadership."[63] The plenum took its cue and retired Gromyko and Solomentsev from the Politburo, along with two Brezhnevite candidate members (Demichev and Dolgikh); dismantled the Party Secretariat; demoted Ligachev from ideological secretary to the unenviable portfolio of agriculture; and moved Chebrikov out of the KGB to the incongruous responsibility of legal reform. Further, the plenum installed Gorbachev's new ideologist Vadim Medvedev (no relation to Roy and Zhores) in the Politburo, and brought three new candidate members into that body, including the first woman to serve at this rank in thirty years, Alexandra Biriukova. (With the removal of Gromyko and Solomentsev, following Geidar Aliev the year before, Gorbachev had not only eliminated from the Politburo the men who voted against him in 1985; but he had got rid of all but one, Vorotnikov, of those who voted *for* him. Shcherbitsky, whose absence at that time may have been decisive, held on until 1989, when his health was failing anyway.) The following day, 1 October 1988, the Supreme Soviet enacted the new constitutional structure and installed Gorbachev in place of Gromyko as president in addition to his duties as general secretary. Asserted Vadim Medvedev of the new prospects, "We are now in this country undertaking a historic attempt at creating an essentially new system of power and administration."[64]

All of the extraordinary changes in the Soviet Union and Eastern Europe in the course of the next three years followed logically and directly from the "September Revolution," as Soviet intellectuals termed that crucial shakeup. Despite the reformers' misgivings that Gorbachev was concentrating excessive power in his own person, the political process in the Soviet Union had finally been wrenched free of the party bureaucracy. The liberating events of 1989 were made possible by this fact, even though the political monopoly of the Communist Party in the Soviet Union was not formally surrendered until the Supreme Soviet agreed in March 1990 to the removal of the infamous Article 6 from the Soviet constitution.

*

The new constitutional provisions of 1988 showed the marks both of innovation and of compromise. A separation of powers between the executive and legislative branches was provided for, more or less on the French model, with a strong chief executive ("chairman of the Supreme Soviet," later on "president"), together with a prime minister ("chairman of the Council of Ministers") who would preside over the cabinet and represent the executive to the parliamentarians. The legislative arrangement was unique, and reflected the transitional nature of the Gorbachev constitution: authority was to be divided between a Congress of People's Deputies of 2,250 members, elected through a complex system, and the new Supreme Soviet of 542 members, to be chosen by the Congress from among its own numbers and renewed by one-fifth annually. The Supreme Soviet would be the working legislative body, staying in session most of the year, unlike the old one that met only briefly a couple of times a year to rubber-stamp prearranged decisions like the Gorbachev constitutional reforms themselves. The Congress, meeting twice a year, would retain the power to elect the president, to enact constitutional changes, and to lay down general policy guidelines.

The electoral arrangements for the Congress were designed to inhibit runaway reform and thus placate the conservatives. A third of the deputies, 750, would not be elected by the general citizenry, but instead were allocated to various so-called "social organizations." One hundred of these seats were reserved for the Communist Party, another 100 for the trade unions, and lesser allotments for diverse entities ranging from the Academy of Sciences (thirty) and Writers Union (ten) to the All-Union Voluntary Temperance Society and the All-Union Society of

Stamp Collectors (one each). This provision of organizational representation was an unpopular limitation of the democratic base of the
Congress, but it did facilitate the election of a remarkable number of
leading intellectuals, scientists, writers, historians, etc., from their
respective organizations. "Only much later did I realise why Gorbachev
manufactured such a complex and utterly undemocratic but ingenious,
electoral system," wrote Anatoly Sobchak, shortly to become mayor of
Leningrad.[65] Even Andrei Sakharov won a seat as a representative of the
Academy of Sciences, after a rank-and-file revolt forced the Academy
Old Guard to allow his nomination. Among the Communist Party's 100
deputies, voted *en bloc* by the Central Committee, were the top Moscow
leadership and some leading intellectuals, but most of the allotment
went to token workers and peasants, the kind of people who had
formerly been included by prearrangement in the Supreme Soviet but
were now rarely elected in the territorial districts. Local Communist
Party chiefs had to fend for themselves in their own areas, with interest-
ing results.

The remaining two-thirds of the Congress seats, to be elected by the
people as a whole, were apportioned geographically: 750 were to be
chosen in single-member ridings of equal population (like the old Soviet
of the Union) and 750 were allocated to the various nationality components of the USSR (paralleling the old Soviet of Nationalities – 32 for
each union republic, regardless of population differences; 11 for each
"autonomous republic," in addition to the entitlement of the union
republic of which they were a part; and similarly for the small "autonomous regions" and "national districts," five and one respectively).

In December 1988, the campaign was offically opened to elect the
Congress. A further constraint on the new democracy, however, was
the nomination process, filtered through "district pre-election assemb-
lies" that were often manipulated by the local party officials. Nearly half
of the almost 10,000 initial aspirants were weeded out, but the outcome
varied widely from one locality to another. In many rural areas and in
the Central Asian republics, the party apparatus managed to exclude all
but the official candidate – usually the local party leader – from the
ballot. Elsewhere two or even more candidates won the right to compete. The campaign electrified Soviet citizens with a spectacle not seen
since 1917, of aspirants for office publicly debating with one another –
and being covered by the press and televison. The entire country awoke
to the new degree of freedom that Gorbachev's revolution had brought
them.

The elections on 26 March, supplemented two weeks later by run-off
elections in ridings where no candidate had obtained 50 per cent of the
vote, showed how fast the country was changing politically. Where the
apparatus was strong, the sole official candidate was usually proclaimed

the winner, but in a few cases the one person on the ballot was actually defeated when a majority of the voters (availing themselves of a genuinely secret ballot for the first time since the Revolution) crossed that name off and called for "none of the above." This even happened to a candidate member of the Politburo, Yuri Solovyov, the party boss in Leningrad, as well as to apparatus leaders in a number of other cities. "Popular fronts" standing against the official Communist candidates carried the day in the Baltic republics and many other areas. Boris Yeltsin, enjoying the popularity of an anti-apparatus rebel, staged a spectacular political comeback by winning 90 per cent of the vote against the Party's chosen candidate in a Moscow riding. Intellectuals – writers, professors, institute researchers – were so prominent among the winners of contested elections that one might speak of the intelligentsia as the new ruling class. Even where the apparatus prevailed, it no longer enjoyed automatic compliance with its decisions, but was reduced to the petty tactics of the "machine politics" known to large American cities in the past, ranging from tearing down opposition posters and disrupting meetings to fraudulent balloting and falsified vote-counting.

*

Mikhail Gorbachev was, by any calculation, an extraordinary historical figure. Aided in the early stage of his rule by instruments of central authority that the legacy of the past had placed at his disposal, he managed in a short span of time to create, in the words of the American sovietologist Joel Moses, "an unprecedented and comprehensive political alternative to the past six decades of Soviet history."[66] More by instinct than by experience, Gorbachev proved to be a master politician in every kind of political arena – in bureaucratic infighting, in parliamentary debate, in the street with the crowds, in summit meetings with the world's chiefs of state. Equally striking were his openness to new ideas, his willingness to try new policies (or very old, discarded ones), and his tolerance of opponents even though he often had harsh words for them. He usually sensed when it was best to move or best to compromise, and thus gradually worked his way out of dependence on the party apparatus. He never fully satisfied the most ardent reformers, but let them forge ahead to clear the ground that he would then occupy when he was ready. He would speak sharply against the Left and then strike against the Right.

Did Gorbachev have the end clearly in view when he started dismantling the edifice of totalitarian power? For some time the conventional wisdom in the West was that he only wanted to modernize his system so as to make it a more formidable adversary. Ivan Frolov conceded in retrospect, "Many of the ideas of restructuring did not appear immediately after 1985. They had been ripening in our society for a long time but were latent, so to speak."[67] Gorbachev was often criticized for trying to amass more power in his own hands. After the 1991 coup he told Len Karpinsky of *Moscow News*, "That is a patently absurd assessment; if that were the case I wouldn't have launched perestroika. As I see it," he added candidly, "no one else in the world had, or has, more power than I had in 1985."[68] The paradox, as Robert Kaiser of *The Washington Post* writes, is "how a lifelong Communist and successful party official," a man of "authoritarian instincts," thin-skinned and even "narcissistic," "could change in less than six years from a modest reformer to the revolutionary leader who ended seventy-three years of Communist Party rule in Russia, and then lost his way . . . . He had started a revoluton he could not control."[69] The French political scientist Cornelius Castoriadis spoke as early as 1987 of "the Gorbachev illusion . . . that you can order people to be self-acting while . . . you can retain the absolutist power of the bureaucracy."[70]

Everything indicates that Gorbachev formulated his political aims only one step at a time. He gave people the impression of "schizophrenia . . . with Gorbachev the reformer at odds with Gorbachev the apparatchik," as Richard Owen of *The Times* put it.[71] The eminent Russian scientist Yevgeny Velikhov told Kaiser that Gorbachev seemed to be guided not by a plan but only by "a direction."[72] The general secretary conceded as much at the Twenty-Eighth Congress:

> Yes, life has turned out to be much richer than we imagined when we launched the revolutionary transformations. Glasnost, democratization, and the entry of millions of people into the arena of historic creativity gave the development of society its own objective logic, which gave rise to much that was unexpected – both positive and negative.[73]

Gorbachev was sufficiently flexible and sufficiently fearless to forge ahead where the logic of reform pointed. He thereby overturned all the powers and principles by which the country had been governed since 1917. It is hard to think of any instance in history where a leader brought about changes of such scope without terrible violence. Even Yeltsin acknowledged this:

> What he has achieved will, of course, go down in the history of mankind . . . . He could have draped himself with orders and medals; the people would have hymned him in verse and song, which is always enjoyable. Yet Gorbachev chose to go another way. He started by climbing a mountain whose summit is not even visible.[74]

2

PERESTROIKA II
Death on the operating table

19 August 1991. Five nervous, uncharismatic men file into the conference room at the Foreign Ministry's lavish modern press centre on Moscow's Sadovoye Ring Boulevard at five in the afternoon, and take their places on the dais. They are Vice-President Gennady Yanaev, who has held this newly created office since January; Interior Minister Boris Pugo, installed the previous December; Party Secretary Oleg Baklanov, in charge of the military-industrial complex; "Peasants' Union" leader V. A. Starodubtsev (really representing kolkhoz – collective farm – chairmen); and A. I. Tiziakov, head of the Association of State Enterprise Directors. Together with three other top officials, absent at the moment – Prime Minister Valentin Pavlov, Minister of Defense Dmitri Yazov, and KGB chief Vladimir Kriuchkov – these representatives of the highest organs of power in the Soviet Union have constituted themselves the "State Committee on the State of Emergency." Perceiving the crumbling of all authority around them, and fearful of the disintegration of the Soviet Union, these "conservatives" have just put the Soviet president under house arrest, ordered troops to secure the city of Moscow, and assumed emergency powers.

The alleged justification for this astounding takeover, announced through all the media at daybreak, is "the inability of Mikhail Sergeyevich Gorbachev to perform the duties of President of the USSR due to the state of his health." Along with this lie the conspirators declare their aim of "overcoming . . . the chaos and anarchy that are threatening the lives and security of the citizens of the Soviet Union." Accordingly, they proclaim a state of emergency, ban demonstrations, muzzle all but the most reliable media outlets, and promise heroic measures to restore the food supply. "We intend," they assert, "to restore immediately legality and law and order, to put an end to bloodshed, to declare a merciless war against the criminal world, and to eradicate shameful phenomena that discredit our society."[1] They never mention Communism, or even socialism.

This is the first occasion in recorded history of a coup by press conference. Not altogether sure of themselves, the Committee on the Emergency seek international legitimacy. Facing the Soviet and international press corps, Yanaev reiterates the themes of the Union and the economy, while averring support for Gorbachev's reforms. As soon as their turn comes, the press get to the real point: first question, put directly in Russian by Carroll Bogert of *Newsweek*, "Where is Mikhail Sergeyevich Gorbachev? What is he sick with? Specifically, concretely, what disease does he have? And against whom are the tanks that we see on the streets of Moscow today directed?"[2] Neither this nor the many following questions elicit credible responses. The plotters cannot win belief, and they are already in disarray. Kriuchkov is at KGB headquarters working the phones to try to mobilize his KGB troops to get on with the coup; but Marshal Yazov, a reluctant participant, is in hiding; Prime Minister Pavlov is drunk.[3]

While these extraordinary events are taking place in Moscow, President Gorbachev is virtually a prisoner at his official holiday residence at Cape Foros near Yalta in the Crimea. The afternoon before, he has been visited by a high-level delegation, including Baklanov of the yet to be announced Committee on the Emergency, party secretary Oleg Shenin, Army ground forces commander General Valentin Varennikov, and Gorbachev's personal chief of staff, Valery Boldin. The surprised president picks up a phone to call Moscow and find out what this is all about, only to find it dead. In fact all his communications have been cut on Kriuchkov's orders, and KGB troops and boats, put in place three days before, have sealed off the area, isolating Gorbachev with his family and bodyguards. The visitors present an ultimatum: sign a decree on emergency powers, or resign in favor of Vice-President Yanaev.

"Who sent you?" Gorbachev demands to know.

"The Committee."

"What committee?"

"The committee on the emergency situation in the country."

"Who created this committee?" Gorbachev retorts. "I didn't create it, the Supreme Soviet didn't create it, so who created it?" He won't budge: "Both you and those who sent you are adventurists. You will destroy yourselves – well, the hell with you, that's your own affair – but you will also destroy the country and everything we are doing."[4] He warns them:

Tomorrow you will declare a state of emergency. What then? Can you plan for at least one day ahead . . . ? The country will reject these measures . . . . The people are not a battalion of soldiers to whom you can issue the command "right turn" or "left turn, march" and they will all do as you tell them . . . . The people are no longer ready to put up with your dictatorship or with the loss of everything we have gained in recent years.[5]

Gorbachev's bodyguards, still at liberty inside the house, find an old radio that brings in foreign broadcasts, and thus he learns the official lie that he is ill. He fears assassination by poisoning and bars any food from outside the house. For history he manages to make a videotape to document his forcible detention and the lie about his health, the basis of "an unconstitutional *coup d'état*."[6]

As Yazov and Kriuchkov tell their interrogators after the coup fails, the plotters have banked entirely on Gorbachev's "voluntary resignation,"[7] no doubt on the strength of his swing to the right between the fall of 1990 and the spring of 1991. They have decided to act only the day before; in Yazov's words, "There was no conspiracy with a plan . . . . We had not thought anything through either for the short or the long run."[8] Informed of Gorbachev's refusal to cooperate, they meet in the Kremlin on Sunday at midnight to decide what to do. They drink coffee and whiskey, to excess, and Pavlov collapses with an attack of high blood pressure. Discarding a plan to convene the Supreme Soviet to remove the president, they take Kriuchkov's cue to launch an old-fashioned coup under the Committee on the Emergency.[9]

The takeover preparations by these heirs of the Bolsheviks are ludicrously inadequate. Kriuchkov admits to his interrogator, "We were simply too late . . . . What we wanted to do at 4 a.m. on the 19th didn't work."[10] Moscow and the Baltic capitals are virtually the only points where troops move out in force. Central broadcasting is easily controlled for the moment, and independent newspapers in Moscow can't publish, but elsewhere it's business as usual. Nobody cuts off foreign journalists' dispatches. Blank arrest warrants have been secretly printed – reportedly 300,000 for Moscow alone – and Kriuchkov has issued a list of individuals to be taken into custody, but hardly any precautionary arrests have actually been carried out.

Inexplicably, the plotters have taken no steps to neutralize the governments of the several republics to which *de facto* power has been gravitating, above all the government of the Russian Republic which has already become a rival of the Union leadership right there in Moscow. "They can't even organize a *coup d'état* properly," comments former interior minister Vadim Bakatin, a Gorbachev loyalist.[11] As many people observe, the plotters are not ruthless enough – those types have already been eliminated from the Soviet scene.[12]

The coup finds Russian President Boris Yeltsin, together with his prime minister Ivan Silayev and the chairman of the Russian parliament, Ruslan Khasbulatov, at the country palace of Arkhangelskoe which the Russian government has taken over. At the news, they phone Moscow to call an emergency session of the parliamentary presidium, and then they compose an appeal to the nation denouncing the coup. A KGB detachment sent to Arkhangelskoe to arrest them fails to act.[13] To avoid the danger of being arrested all at once by the troops ringing the city, Yeltsin and his associates depart in separate cars for the "White House," the headquarters of the Russian Republic on the bank of the Moscow River a mile west of the Kremlin. Meanwhile, showing how deeply the spirit of democracy has taken hold, thousands demonstrate in the streets of Moscow, and flock to the defense of the "White House." There they throw up makeshift barricades as in revolutionary days of yore. In the words of *Novy Mir* editor Sergei Zalygin, "People think differently now. They are no longer willing to do what they're told without question."[14]

Khasbulatov is the first of the Russian leadership to reach the White House, around 10.30 a.m. He calls the presidium to order and reads the appeal: "What we are dealing with is a right-wing, reactionary, unconstitutional coup . . . . [We] declare the so-called committee that has come to power illegal." The statement exhorts the public, the military, and local governments to spurn the plotters; demands that Gorbachev be freed to speak and that the Congress of People's Deputies be convened; and calls for a general strike.[15] The presidium endorses the appeal and summons an emergency session of the full Supreme Soviet of Russia, but only by a vote of 12 to 5, which prompts loud indignation against the minority.[16] Yeltsin arrives at this point and wins the acclaim of the world when, in full view of Western television cameras, he climbs onto a tank, like Lenin on his armored car in 1917, to read the appeal to the people and shout defiance of the plotters. Though the conspirators control the central Soviet media, Yeltsin's message is relayed abroad and beamed back in by Western radio. Hedging against the possibility that the White House may be overwhelmed, the Russian leadership commissions a shadow government hidden in the woods near Yeltsin's home city of Sverdlovsk in the Urals.

While the crowd at the White House fraternizes with the troops, Yeltsin works through his military aides to sow doubt in the minds of the army command. Some of the tank units deployed around the White House go over to Yeltsin – a telltale sign. The air force under Marshal Yevgeny Shaposhnikov refuses to support the coup; he threatens to shoot down army helicopters and even to bomb the Kremlin, and paratroopers under air force command arrive to help defend Yeltsin's government. From the outset the putsch is crippled by what Lenin called "dual power." The Italian journalist Giulietto Chiesa reports, "The putschists appear uncertain, they don't seem to have a plan, they don't have any prospects without letting flow a river of blood, without repeating a Tiananmen of monstrous proportions"[17] – and Defense

Minister Yazov, as it turns out, lacks the stomach for that. "I don't want bloodshed," he tells an early-morning meeting of his top commanders. "His mood seemed depressed," Air Marshal Shaposhnikov later recounts.[18] Kriuchkov decides Monday evening to take matters into his own hands and orders his elite Alpha Group to prepare to attack the White House, but somewhere down the chain of command his orders are ignored.[19]

Not until the second day of the coup, Tuesday, 20 August, do the conspirators order a curfew and seriously prepare to liquidate the rival Russian government. By this time the crowd around the White House has reached six figures, and vehicles are added to the barricades. Yeltsin manages to get through by phone to Prime Minister Major and President Bush, and gets their assurances of support for Gorbachev and himself, while declarations against the coup are coming in from all over the country and from all walks of life. Russia's Vice-President Colonel Alexander Rutskoi and Defense Minister General Konstantin Kobets prepare the defense of the White House against an assault that is expected for 2 a.m. on the 21st, but it never comes: Yanaev and Yazov completely lose their nerve, and Kriuchkov can't even be sure of his KGB troops. Kobets is a military academy classmate of the Moscow commandant General N. V. Kalinin, and persuades him over the phone to pull his main forces back. The coup nevertheless claims three martyrs, killed in a tragic clash when armored personnel carriers, actually moving away from the White House, are trapped by demonstrators in the Sadovoye Ring underpass beneath Kalinin Prospekt.

By the time a full session of the Russian Supreme Soviet convenes at 11 a.m. on the 21st, it is clear that the coup is collapsing. When Yazov hesitates, General Varennikov orders all troops to withdraw from Moscow. Desperate, Kriuchkov, Yazov, Baklanov, and Tiziakov, accompanied by Supreme Soviet chairman Lukianov and the Party's deputy general secretary Vladimir Ivashko, take off for the Crimea, "not to try to pressure Gorbachev one last time, but to beg for mercy," according to *Komsomolskaya Pravda* correspondent Igor Sichka.[20] The Russian government immediately decides to send its own team, headed by Rutskoi with a detachment of police, ready to fight to free Gorbachev if necessary. When the plotters arrive at Gorbachev's dacha, he demands that his phones be reconnected. They are, and this marks the exact point when power reverts from the Committee on the Emergency to the legitimate government.

By the time Rutskoi's group reaches the dacha, Gorbachev is already in charge. They all head immediately back to Moscow, with Kriuchkov on Gorbachev's plane as a hostage against sabotage. As they land in Moscow, all the coup leaders, those returning from Foros and those remaining in the capital, are put under arrest (except for Pugo, who commits suicide). Though still visibly shaken, Gorbachev steps before the television cameras at Vnukovo Airport and prides himself on the failure of the coup: "Everything we have done since 1985 has borne real fruit."[21] Later, in his book on the August events, he reflects further: "It was said that I arrived back to a different country. I agree. I can add that the man who returned from the Crimea to a different country now looks at everything – the past, the present and the future – with different eyes."[22]

*

The events of August 1991 followed inexorably from the systemic crisis that descended upon the Soviet Union after the glory days of perestroika. Unfortunately, these troubles were inherent in Gorbachev's conception of a peaceful and organic reorientation of the political system from totalitarianism to democracy. "We are now frequently reproached for having proceeded almost blindly, by the trial-and-error method, without any clear notion of our objective," Gorbachev said shortly before the coup.

> But every step was extremely difficult . . . and any innovation was perceived as all but an attack on the pillars of socialism . . . . The reforms that we had hoped would solve the accumulated problems in a short time were accompanied by complex, contradictory processes that have worsened the crisis. Society's illness has proved to be much more serious than could have been surmised.[23]

Through 1988 Gorbachev succeeded brilliantly in knocking down barriers to political freedom without going so far as to provoke the Communist Party conservatives into overt and violent resistance. But he was the victim of his own success. With the election of the Congress of People's Deputies in March 1989, a deeper, qualitative change took hold in the process of reform. Up to then perestroika had proceeded from above, at the prodding of the leader, against the resistance of the bureaucracy. After that date it became a widening spontaneous movement from below. Gorbachev now had to steer between the conservative bureaucrats and the popular movements led by radical democrats and nationalists. He lost control of the whole course of change in the Soviet Union.

Between 1985 and 1989 Gorbachev was seeking salvation from neo-Stalinism by working back through the successive stages and models of Soviet history. By 1989 the Soviet government had embraced the economic and social pluralism of the New Economic Policy of the 1920s, as a guideline if not as an accomplished reality. In politics the Communist Party had been led all the way back to its relatively open model of 1918, allowing free factional debate. Dusko Doder and Louise Branson thought that "Gorbachev's views resembled those held by the Menshevik leader Martov rather than those of Lenin."[24] Relations between the Russian centre and the minority republics had become freer than at any time since the formation of the USSR in 1922.

The one great hurdle remaining in the path of reform after 1989 was to undo the work of the October Revolution in launching the Communist dictatorship. In theory this obstacle was surmounted in March 1990 when the Congress of People's Deputies amended the constitution to repeal Article 6 providing for the "leading role" of the Communist Party. In practice the leap was not fully accomplished until the August Coup of 1991 and the complete disbandment of the Party. What had begun with a coup, appropriately had to end with a coup.

Three rushing currents fed the torrent of change on top of which Gorbachev tried to stay afloat at the turn of the decade. One was the demand to perfect democracy and the rule of law. Gorbachev had no problem with this, provided it did not move so fast as to undermine his own authority. Second was the unyielding impasse in the Soviet economy, unresolved by perestroika, and threatening to turn into absolute collapse. Third, and most disturbing to Gorbachev, was the urge for independence among the non-Russian republics, finally released by democratization from their decades of subservience to Moscow. Complicating all these issues was the emergence of a bitter personal rivalry, as Boris Yeltsin returned from the political shadows to find a power base in the Russian Republic from which he could challenge Gorbachev's claim to lead the Soviet Union into the future.

*

The Congress of People's Deputies convened in May 1989 with its apparatus majority strongly leavened by insurgent forces, to select the new Supreme Soviet and to debate the country's future course. In the nation at large the advent of the Congress meant a quantum leap in the spirit of democracy and freedom. Debates in the Congress on the most fundamental questions of national life were televised live, and attracted such intense public interest that industrial production is said to have dropped 20 per cent because so many workers were watching the broadcasts of the proceedings.

Gorbachev presided over the Congress with a heavy hand, and he usually got his way in the voting, but the important point is that a genuine and wide-ranging clash of opinions actually took place. Another novelty was the activity of many People's Deputies who traveled to trouble spots around the country under cover of their parliamentary immunity to serve as ombudsmen, so to speak, to rectify local grievances. The whole spectacle of the Congress cast serious doubt on familiar sovietological assumptions about the secretive and authoritarian political culture of old Russia, and instead called up memories of the democratic excitement of 1905 and 1917. As in the early phase of every revolution, fear and conformity evaporated, among the public as well as among the politicians. Soviet political life would never be the same again.

The most important function of the Congress, apart from confirming Gorbachev as its president (without opposition), was to select the members of the new Supreme Soviet. In this task it seemed to take a step backward. Rather than choose Supreme Soviet members to represent proportionally all the various currents of thought, which would have legitimized a *de facto* multi-party system then and there, the Congress followed a complex system whereby the body as a whole voted on the lists of candidates proposed by each regional delegation, often without alternative choices. Moscow was an exception, putting up a full competitive group of names, only to see Boris Yeltsin and most of its noted reform intellectuals (save Andrei Sakharov and Roy Medvedev) vetoed by the Congress as a whole. Yeltsin made it only when another deputy withdrew to create a vacancy for him.

The surprising thing about the new Supreme Soviet was that despite its comfortable majority of apparatus selectees, it nonetheless responded to the powers and role of a genuine parliament by behaving like one as well. Members debated the government's legislation at length and in detail, often imposing key liberalizing amendments (for example, to repeal the allocation of seats to "social organizations" in future congresses). They adopted the committee system and immediately made it work with great effectiveness, notably in implementing the American practice of interrogating and sometimes even rejecting candidates for government ministries. Committee chairmanships were deemed so influential that in some cases regional party leaders resigned those posts in order to devote themselves to their committees. Investigating questions from the prosecution of corruption to the reconsideration of Stalin's diplomacy, the Supreme Soviet made itself a solid constitutional foundation for glasnost. It demonstrated that, thanks to Gorbachev's bloodless constitutional revolution, power in the Soviet Union had genuinely been made subject to checks and balances and was no longer the preserve of the party hierarchy.

One of the most spectacular results of the new democracy was Yeltsin's political resurrection, beginning a duel to the political death between two Communist careerists over the corpse of the movement. Yeltsin and Gorbachev came from remarkably similar backgrounds; both were peasant boys from distant provinces, born in the same year, 1931; both entered the career service of the Communist Party apparatus, even though Yeltsin's father, like Gorbachev's grandfathers, had suffered under Stalin. In personality and style, however, the two rising apparatchiki differed sharply. Gorbachev, with his legal background at Moscow State University, was the more intellectual, more deliberative, more the manoeuvring tactician. Yeltsin was bluff and impulsive, with "a prickly sensitivity to real or imagined insults," in the view of his biographer, John Morrison.[25] The émigré writer Vladimir Bukovsky has reported his first impression of Yeltsin on television: "a typical Bolshevik, a Bolshevik straight out of central casting. Stubborn, overbearing, self-assured, honest, irresistible, a human engine without brakes."[26]

Specializing in the supervision of construction work, Yeltsin entered the party apparatus later than Gorbachev, and reached the position of first secretary in his home province of Sverdlovsk only in 1976, just two years before his future rival left Stavropol for Moscow. In Sverdlovsk Yeltsin earned a reputation as a tough anti-corruption taskmaster. Gorbachev and Ligachev, working together in the initial, Andropovite, disciplinarian phase of perestroika, brought him into the central Secretariat and then installed him as party secretary for Moscow with the rank of candidate member of the Politburo.

In Moscow, Yeltsin bumptiously overreached in his mission to root out the corrupt Old Guard, and Ligachev and the party conservatives began to conspire against him. Their resistance may account for Yeltsin's being passed over when promotions were being made to full member of the Politburo in June 1987. Nevertheless, this blow to his pride seems to have governed his relations with Gorbachev ever since. Later on he repeatedly referred back to 1987 as the point where Gorbachev "began to go wrong" and "began . . . deceiving the people."[27]

While the experiment in democratic government in the spring of 1989 was remarkably successful, Gorbachev did not immediately give up on the Party as an instrument of power. In April 1989, he was able to persuade the Central Committee to do what the party conference the year before would not do, that is, to accept the resignations of the "dead souls" on the Central Committee (members who had already been removed from the bureaucratic positions that had entitled them to membership in the first place). Then in September he tightened up the Politburo again, finally dropping the Ukrainian boss Shcherbitsky, the ex-KGB chief Chebrikov, and the undistinguished party secretary Nikonov.

These successes against the conservatives came just in time, for the climate of glasnost had allowed the strains in the Soviet economy and among the nationalities to reach crisis proportions, and the Communist system in Eastern Europe was precipitously collapsing. The most prominent advocates and beneficiaries of perestroika, above all in the Baltic

37

republics, were turning against Gorbachev for lagging in reform, while conservative Russian nationalists expressed more and more openly their authoritarian, anti-foreign, and anti-Semitic premises. People of all persuasions bemoaned what they perceived to be an absolute downturn in the Soviet economy, with galling shortages of food and essential consumer goods. The great irony of perestroika was that the more Gorbachev opened the political arena to free expression and free choice, the more he was criticized himself, from all sides, and the more his popularity slumped. He put the blame on his predecessors: "It was an extremely grim legacy that we inherited."[28] The Soviet Union entered into a national *crise de conscience*.

*

In spite of the deteriorating climate of opinion, implementation of the constitutional revolution continued. In February 1990 the Central Committee agreed to surrender the Communist Party's constitutionally privileged position. However, at the same session of the Congress of People's Deputies that ratified this great step, Gorbachev disappointed the reformers by having the Congress rather than the voters elect him to the new, more strongly defined presidency of the USSR. Endeavoring to firm up his power base in the government against the party apparatus, Gorbachev was groping toward an American-style (or more accurately, French-style) separation of powers between the legislative and executive branches of government, but he hesitated to expose himself to the whims of the electorate – a fatal misjudgement, as things turned out.

Immediately after this crucial session of the Congress came elections to the new supreme soviets of the Russian Republic, the Ukraine, and Belorussia, with no set-aside of seats for the Communist Party or anyone else. In Russia the reformers organised a *de facto* opposition party, "Democratic Russia," defied the central authorities with unsanctioned mass rallies, and made spectacular gains, sufficient by a close margin to propel Yeltsin into the presidency of the Russian Supreme Soviet. He narrowly defeated the apparatus candidate, Ivan Polozkov of Krasnodar province, a notorious opponent of the economic reforms. The democratic socialist Boris Kagarlitsky sardonically attributed Yeltsin's success to "the absence of any concrete programme because in this way he is able to consolidate or organise around him a very wide social base, very different sectors of the population, promising everything to everybody."[29]

At the same time, the party apparatus in the Russian Republic, dominated by conservative provincial functionaries, pulled away from Gorbachev in Polozkov's direction. Asserting their right to have a party organization for the Russian Republic like the other fourteen union republics, the Russian delegates chosen to attend the Twenty-Eighth Party Congress held their own preliminary convention in Moscow and elected Polozkov first secretary of the Communist Party of Russia. The conservative Party and the reformist government in the republic were totally polarized.

When the all-union party congress finally convened in July 1990, it resembled the 1988 conference, with a majority of conservative delegates issuing from the selection process, but they were now demoralized conservatives who allowed Gorbachev to have his way with the Party. They could not dispute the accomplishments he claimed:

> The political system is being radically transformed; genuine democracy is being established, with free elections, a multiparty system, and human rights; and real people's power is being revived . . . . The atmosphere of ideological *diktat* has been replaced by free thinking, glasnost, and the openness of society to information.[30]

The delegates gave their nod to the outline of a new party program extolling the virtues of humanism and pluralism, ratified the abolition of the Party's constitutional leading role, and acceded to Gorbachev's proposal to revamp the Party's leadership organs.

Here the Gorbachev revolution showed its true depth. The Politburo as it had existed since 1919, the small group of officials who sat with the leader to make basic decisions in all manner of state policies, foreign as well as domestic, was effectively dissolved. Gorbachev had already set up a counterpart entity in the civil government, the Presidential Council. This was a sort of inner cabinet, appointed by him and not subject to legislative confirmation, that included the men responsible for foreign, military, internal security, and economic affairs, and a couple of representatives of both the liberal and conservative wings of public opinion. The Party was left with an expanded, diluted, and far less powerful Politburo, including the party chiefs of all fifteen union republics but none of the leading lights except Gorbachev himself and his protégé Ivashko, who beat Ligachev for the newly created post of deputy general secretary. As Gorbachev made explicit after the 1991 putsch, he kept the top party office for himself to prevent the conservatives from using it against him, but only at the price of added unpopularity. The functions of the new Politburo were restricted to the internal business of the party organisation. Shortly afterward, the Party gave up *nomenklatura* control over top personnel appointments everywhere outside the party apparatus itself. Abandoning the conservative fight, Yegor Ligachev announced his own retirement from the leadership.

Despite these changes, the congress majority of orthodox apparatus people seemed to be out of touch with the country's mood and problems. Yeltsin and other reform leaders who had been swept into power locally in the March elections demonstratively resigned their party memberships. This was another blow to the chances of any reform current succeeding within the framework of the Communist Party. Compelled to compete in genuine elections with vastly more popular opponents, the Communist Party of the Soviet Union already seemed destined for eventual extinction.

*

The most disruptive effect of Gorbachev's democratization program was the rise of uncompromising independence movements among the non-Russian nationalities. The breadth and depth of this force were such that we will return to it in a later chapter on nationality and nationalism within the context of the Communist revolution as a whole. National separatism was the Achilles' heel of political reform in the Soviet Union. Given freedom, the first aim of the minorities was bound to be self-determination. Faced with the disintegration of their empire, the Russian leaders of the Union were bound to hesitate and divide over the future of political reform.

Even before the 1989 elections, trouble had broken out between the Azerbaidzhanis and the Armenians over the Armenian enclave of Nagorno-Karabakh inside Azerbaidzhan. This sort of conflict among the lesser nationalities continued endemically once the individual republics were given their head politically. But a much more difficult challenge for the central government was portended by nationalist demonstrations in Tbilisi in Georgia in April 1989, occasioning intervention by central troops with some twenty deaths resulting. This was the first serious blot on the escutcheon of perestroika, and responsibility for it was (and remains) unclear. Gorbachev might have deemed the action unavoidable to keep the reform process under control, or it could have been a provocation by the conservatives controlling the police and the military, to embarrass Gorbachev and make clear to the republics the limits of the center's patience. In the latter case Gorbachev may have felt it inexpedient to protest publicly and betray his lack of control over the organs of governmental force.

Following Tbilisi the focus of separatist agitation shifted to the Baltic republics, the newest and least assimilated constituent parts of the Soviet Union. There and elsewhere nationalist sentiment surged with the political opportunity afforded by the republic elections in the early months of 1990. Anti-Communist popular fronts trounced the party apparatus in many republics, and the newly elected governments proceeded to proclaim their "sovereignty" or even their independence. In many cases republics tried to nullify legislation of the central government that they found distasteful – the "war of laws," so-called. Localism now became a serious impediment to any concerted action to revive or sustain the economy of the Union.

These troubles with the republics shook Gorbachev's reformist resolve and primed the party conservatives for strong counteraction. What was apparently a trial move came in January 1991, when army and Interior Ministry troops moved into the Lithuanian capital of Vilnius, seized the television and other public buildings, and killed a dozen protesters. Like Tbilisi in 1989, responsibility was never fixed in Moscow. In any case, someone must have concluded that the action was excessive or counter-productive, and the troops left the Lithuanian government in place. But the incident further discredited Gorbachev, among democrats and separatists because it had been undertaken, and among conservatives because it had not been carried to a victorious conclusion.

If any one factor was most to blame for the ultimate failure of Gorbachev's approach to reform, it was the obdurate nationality problem. It is doubtful whether any meaningful form of the Soviet Union could have been preserved under conditions of democratic choice, but no matter what autonomy he had to yield to the republics, Gorbachev could not reconcile himself to the absolute departure of any part of the Soviet realm. By contrast, Yeltsin began eagerly to exploit the nationality issue as soon as he achieved the leadership of the Russian Republic in 1990. By declaring Russian "sovereignty" and endorsing like claims on the part of the minority republics, he did everything he could to undermine the authority of the Union government and with it Gorbachev's power. This challenge, and his own reluctance to compromise on the preservation of the Union, turned Gorbachev back at the end of 1990 to the embrace of the party conservatives, even though their set aim by that time was to get rid of him and the whole range of freedoms that he had introduced. The denouement represented by the August Coup became unavoidable, sooner or later. Gorbachev's reconciliation with national autonomy in a new Union Treaty and the Novo-Ogarevo agreements of April 1991 simply gave the signal for the last gasp of neo-Stalinist imperialism.

*

Accompanying the progress of democratization and self-determination like a rolling counterpoint, shaking the Gorbachev government even as it undertook to relax its powers, was the crisis in the Soviet economy. Apart from generalized slogans and exhortations for perestroika, acceleration, and overcoming the legacy of the "command-administrative system," Gorbachev had come in with no radical long-term economic agenda. "One of the more obvious problems," commented Ed Hewett of the Brookings Institution in 1988, "is the absence of a theory of transition. The Soviets do not have a theory, and I don't think we know much more than they do."[31]

Reform disrupted the old economic system of plans and orders, but did not go far and fast enough to supplant it with a new system of competitive rewards. The result was the progressive deterioration of Soviet economic performance that set in after the first few years of perestroika. Yuri Masliukov, chairman of the State Planning Commission (Gosplan), complained,

> There was an overestimation of the possibilities of economic-accountability methods of management, in the absence of developed market relations and basic economic legislation . . . . The state managerial structures, for all practical purposes, lost control . . . . Everyone wanted to produce less but to live better.[32]

It seems that most Soviet citizens, inured to a system of compulsion for seventy years of Communist rule and for centuries of serfdom before that, responded to the relaxation of totalitarian controls with a relaxation of their own efforts. Unable to overcome this cultural burden, Soviet economic growth ground to a halt and production in some areas actually slipped, while the disintegrating system of distribution left Soviet consumers to face critical shortages of everyday necessities. Yet the recurring refrain from the Kremlin was to beg for more time and more effort to make perestroika a success. This only created the impression of helpless floundering, just when constitutional reform and nationality tensions heightened the need for a stable economic foundation.

Through 1988 the Soviet economy just held its own, with real gross domestic product growing at around 2 per cent a year against a population increase of 1 per cent and an expansion of available consumer goods and services of less than 1 per cent. Income increases in actual roubles, reaching the rate of 13 per cent in 1989, automatically resulted in shortages and queues.[33] By the end of 1989, simultaneously with the breakthrough in democratic political institutions, economic performance actually began to decline, and by the end of 1990 the economy was in free fall. Reformers and conservatives alike held Gorbachev accountable, with good reason. Economic distress guaranteed that when political reform turned into political crisis in 1991, there would be little or no support for Gorbachev's position of preserving and reforming the Communist Party and the Soviet Union.

The economic crisis was a paradox in several ways. Initially it was the economic impasse that prompted Gorbachev's perestroika. But the prerequisite for economic reform was political reform, to break the grip of the bureaucracy in the Party and the ministries and allow economic

growth to revive. The resulting struggle distracted the efforts of perestroika, and attention to the economy was secondary and delayed.

More fundamentally, Soviet economic power – formidable by all the
basic indicators of output – was not organized and directed to supply
human needs, certainly not in any adequate, equitable, and reliable
fashion. These goals were all distorted in what Gorbachev himself
admitted to be "the most militarized economy in the world."[34] The signs
of trouble were evident well in advance of the true crisis; both Soviet and
Western commentators spoke of an economic collapse when the problem was still only that of stagnation – the inability to grow and to get
production properly distributed. By the time the true downturn set in,
in 1990, it had an aura of inevitability about it.

Talk of the "collapsing Soviet economy" conveys images of a huge
factory with the walls buckling and the roof caving in. This is a metaphor for disruption in the relations of cooperation and exchange that
enable people to keep working and supplying their mutual needs at a
modern level of technique and effectiveness. The Soviet economy and
its East European clones had always been plagued with bottlenecks and
shortages. Such troubles were inevitable in a system that tried inflexibly
to plan the intensive utilization of all resources, primarily in the service
of military power, without allowing the necessary reserves. (A
Hungarian economist, János Kornai, wrote a parody of classical economics that made shortages instead of profits the driving force in the
socialist economy.[35]) Only the coercive state and ubiquitous intervention by the Communist Party apparatus kept the system moving.
The old economic structure could not simultaneously release and mobilize the energies of its workers. Once perestroika removed the heavy
hand of central control, especially after the economic departments of the
Party were abolished in 1988, individuals and enterprises were under
little effective pressure to play their part, and the whole economic
network of mutual interdependence began to unravel.

Theories of the Soviet economic downturn are almost as numerous as
theorists. To the Gorbachevian reformers the trouble was rooted in the
old 'command-administrative system" and its failure to reward effort
and initiative. Tatiana Zaslavskaya saw "disillusionment with socialism"
carrying all moral values down into the dust. "The people . . . realize
that the difficult historical path they have travelled for seventy years was
all a mistake and ultimately led us up a blind alley."[36] "The restructuring
that began in April 1985 came roughly twenty years too late," Deputy
General Secretary Ivashko said in 1990, referring to the breakoff of
Khrushchev's reforms. "If we had taken this path back then, we would
be living differently now."[37] With the passage of time, however, this
argument wore thin, like the onus that the Stalinist regime had put on
"survivals of capitalism" decades after the Revolution.

Blaming the past failed to account for the deterioration that became critical only four or five years into perestroika. A more plausible argument, favored by Soviet conservatives right up to the August Coup, attributed the crisis to the reforms themselves, as an unwarranted disruption of a functioning system. "The crisis of power has had a catastrophic effect on the economy. The chaotic, ungoverned slide toward a market has caused an explosion of selfishness – regional, departmental, group and personal," the Committee on the State of Emergency alleged.[38] On the opposite wing, radical reformers insisted that the trouble stemmed from delay in the introduction of market-oriented reforms, and saw the cure in quick "shock therapy" such as Poland undertook in 1989–1990. Most commentators were reluctant to consider the possibility that the Russian political and economic culture, not created but only retarded by the Soviet experience, was not mature enough to sustain an efficient modern economy under conditions of political freedom.

Other factors in the crisis are more definite, notably the fiscal practices of the Soviet government. By the 1970s, the regime had already got into the habit of covering its deficits with the printing press, and under perestroika all the controls that held the rouble in check suddenly fell away. "The initial problem of the Gorbachev regime," observes the Swedish economist Anders Åslund, "seems to have been that the previously firm fiscal conservatism was replaced by extraordinary laxity in 1985. The crucial years of financial folly were 1985–86," with their unrealistic growth and investment targets to re-equip heavy industry. "Thus the blame falls upon the General Secretary himself."[39] Tripling the deficit to 6 per cent of the GDP by 1986, Gorbachev preferred to blame Andropov for keeping the fiscal situation secret from his closest associates.[40]

Against this background the Gorbachev government undertook to move toward the NEP model of market socialism, but this proved to be far more difficult in the economy of the 1980s than it had been in the 1920s. In June 1987, under the inspiration particularly of Abel Aganbegian, director of the Institute of Mathematical Economics, the Central Committee and the Supreme Soviet approved what appeared to be a sweeping reform package to relax central controls over prices, wages, allocation of supplies, and enterprise administration, but in their specifics the new laws were vague and inadequate. The authorities still failed to understand the difference between ideological directives to the Party and enforceable statutes governing independent entities. As Washington University law professor Frances Foster-Simons observed,

Most of the post-1985 Soviet legislation . . . contains serious gaps and ambiguities that make practical enforcement of procedural

44

rights difficult . . . . As a result, the radical reforms envisaged for the public sector of the Soviet economy have remained largely unrealised . . . . They relied on the all-too-familiar technique of exhorting local officials not to obstruct cooperatization, rather than stipulating practical legal means to bring such individuals or organs to account for their interference.[41]

In the judgement of the American economist Gertrude Schroeder, the reforms did not achieve

a system of market socialism or of worker self-management as those terms are usually understood . . . . The reforms do not go nearly far enough to create a market environment . . ., a dynamic, self-regulating "economic mechanism" capable of narrowing the technological gap with the West.[42]

The Law on State Enterprises, put into force in January 1988, called for "self-financing," allowed more managerial autonomy, and lifted the lid on wages, while the state eased its exactions from enterprise profits, to the further detriment of the budget. However, according to Schroeder, "Enterprise incentives [were] still oriented toward plans and output targets and biased toward dealing with administrative superiors rather than following signals from markets."[43] Meanwhile, tax yields remained flat or worse, initially on account of the anti-vodka campaign that Gorbachev inherited from Andropov; then when the government cut consumer goods imports (to balance the drop in the price of its oil exports) and lost the markup it could impose; and subsequently as enterprise taxes fell off. The arbitrary price system, in the view of Ed Hewett and Victor Winston, was the rock on which perestroika foundered:

Had the price system been changed, a semblance of a free-market economy might have by now [1990] been in place, functioning well enough to justify added faith in Gorbachev's reforms. But the system did not change, and Gorbachev's half-measures merely accelerated the rise of the budget deficit, the market disequilibrium, and the pervasive stagflation.[44]

The financial picture was further skewed by populist concessions demanded by the new People's Congress and Supreme Soviet in 1989, particularly increases in pensions, the minimum wage, and food subsidies, again covered by printing the money. The deficit, already at 10 per cent of GDP in 1988, went out of control.[45] Currency-fed inflation, part actual and part repressed in an "inflationary overhang" in consumers' pockets, threatened to devastate a none too solid standard of living. Nothing could better vindicate the principles of old-fashioned fiscal conservatism. There was an eery parallel with the fiscal self-destruction of the Tsarist government, beginning with its attempt to suppress the vodka trade as a patriotic gesture in 1914, with the consequent loss of the alcohol monopoly revenues; continuing through resort to the printing press to finance war expenditures; and culminating in the runaway inflation that provoked in turn both the February and October revolutions of 1917.

In the instance of perestroika, both finances in particular and economic performance in general were further undermined by the weakening of central authority over the union republics, as well as by the collapse of Communist rule and economic cooperation in the former East European bloc. Inexplicably, Gorbachev's government responded to the changes in Eastern Europe by suspending its barter trade arrangements with the bloc and insisting that Soviet exports – petroleum above all – be paid for in hard currency. This impossibility immediately disrupted the interdependent connections between the parties, shutting off both supplies and markets each way, and the Council of Mutual Economic Assistance (Comecon – the Communist answer to the European Community) quickly withered away.

Within the Soviet Union itself, the powers accruing democratically to the individual republics by 1990 were immediately turned to the purposes of economic nationalism and autarky, as each republic responded to shortages by restricting or banning exports to other republics, thereby inviting reprisals in kind to the greater detriment of all. Especially damaging to the central government was legislation adopted in 1990 to appease the republics by broadening their tax powers and the revenue items they could retain. The center had to depend on "negotiated upward transfers" to sustain its major responsibilities for the armed forces and the military-oriented industry that went on producing and paying wages reflexively.[46] By 1991, even before the putsch, nothing could compel the republics to contribute their share to the Union government, which had to resort even more to the one powerful economic instrumentality still under its direct control, the printing press. Currency emission skyrocketed, contributing massively to inflationary overhang and assuring that the shelves of the price-controlled state shops would be swept completely clean. After the putsch the Union government became totally dependent on handouts from the republics, and Gorbachev was left financially helpless to resist Yeltsin's determination to liquidate his job.

The economic reforms initiated under perestroika were never fast enough or effective enough to offset the effects of deteriorating labor discipline, regional rivalry, and state-sponsored inflation. Reforms begun in 1987 in agriculture and the service sector, contemplating individual peasant leaseholds and so-called cooperatives, brightened up Moscow and Leningrad but were slow to take effect in the provinces.

Efforts to put state-owned enterprises on a profit-and-loss basis had bizarre effects; often high-priced luxuries were given priority over everyday mass consumption, while state-subsidized culture and publishing gave way to mass tastes. Moreover, though the theory of "market socialism" was supposed to govern perestroika, its operation was severely constricted by the continuing practice of obligatory state orders that commanded major fractions of the output of factory and farm at administratively set prices. "Looking back at Soviet economic policy during the second half of the 1980s," Åslund writes, "it is difficult to avoid the impression that virtually every possible mistake has been made. Perestroika has proved to be an utter economic failure."[47]

By 1989, as the economic crisis deepened and glasnost spread, wide debate commenced about the necessity of quick and radical reform in the direction of a market economy. Radical reformers of the free-market school – Stanislav Shatalin, Grigory Yavlinsky, and others, along with their Western advisors – came into their own, working both with Gorbachev's government and with Yeltsin in the Russian Republic leadership to formulate a total transformation of the economic system. Gorbachev finally made economics a top priority; he created a new "State Committee on Economic Reform" and put the reform economist Leonid Abalkin in charge of it with the rank of deputy prime minister. Abalkin proposed a gradual decontrol of prices and the progressive denationalization and decentralization of industry and agriculture. Yavlinsky, serving as Abalkin's deputy, worked this initiative into the "400 Days Plan" of free market reform and privatization on the Polish model.

In November 1989 the Party broke with "the outdated Party-apparatus style whereby the search for the 'truth' begins with an answer prepared in advance," and held a wide-open conference on the economy. Academician Oleg Bogomolov was the most radical: "selling stocks to the working people" would help the rouble and strengthen society. "The citizen also needs a certain economic independence – his own house or apartment, his own plot of ground, his ownership share or stock certificate." Ideology Secretary Vadim Medvedev cautioned against this "near euphoria" over private property, and advocated leasing as a method to combine socialism and flexibility. An industrial administrator, A. I. Tiziakov, later one of the August conspirators, gave vent to the frustrations at his level, of surpluses and shortages and barter deals uncoordinated by anyone in the ministries; he preferred "if only for a short time, to take a step backward and introduce a command-based system."[48] This is exactly what Prime Minister Ryzhkov undertook to do, rallying the conservative opposition with a prophetic warning: "If . . . we should try to introduce fully-fledged market relations by 1991, it will bring us a serious social-economic upheaval, a new stage of galloping inflation, falling production, mass unemployment, and aggravated social tensions."[49]

Gorbachev himself seemed to invite a radical turn when he told the Central Committee in February 1990 (at the same plenum that voted to give up Communist Party hegemony), "We remain committed to the choice made in October 1917, to the socialist idea, but we are moving away from a dogmatic understanding of that idea, refusing to sacrifice people's real interests to schematic constructs." And he admitted, "The main missing link, which is causing the entire economic reform to spin its wheels, is the system of price formation."[50] Yet in the face of continuing controversy, he temporized, while price increases announced in advance in May 1990 predictably prompted hoarders to clear out the shops. The state distribution system virtually collapsed, while inflation surged in the free peasant markets.

Meanwhile Yeltsin, newly elected as chairman of the Russian Supreme Soviet, embraced the 400 Days Plan (now 500 Days) and made Yavlinsky his deputy prime minister for economic reform. Gorbachev then surprised everyone by turning to Yeltsin to seek an accord on the economy, and the two commissioned a working group of economists under Presidential Council member Shatalin to refine Yavlinsky's plan into a concrete reform program.

The "Shatalin 500 Days Plan," hurriedly worked out in August 1990, envisaged quick implementation of market-oriented reforms including the freeing of controlled prices, rationing and income supplements to protect the poor, further autonomy for enterprises, enhanced opportunities for foreign investment and joint ventures, encouragement of private trade and farming, and acknowledgment of the economic powers of the Union republics, all to accomplish shock therapy and jolt the Soviet economy into recovery. However, the Shatalin plan was challenged by Ryzhkov and even by Abalkin; they preferred to keep a strong centrally planned sector and balked at the private property implications of individual farms and enterprises. Åslund comments,

> In September 1990, President Gorbachev could have possibly opted for a tentative resolution of the national crisis together with an initial cure of the economic crisis. However, he failed on both accounts, because he was not prepared to accept a diminution in his own power, a far-reaching weakening of the Union, and large-scale privatisation. The window of hope was closed by October.[51]

At the moment of truth Gorbachev wavered; the Shatalin plan remained on the shelf; and the Soviet president and the Soviet economy together went into terminal decline.

*

Ever since the Andreyeva letter in the spring of 1988 rumors had been rife in Moscow about the possibility of a *coup de main* by the Communist conservatives. Gorbachev, always remembering the fate of Khrushchev, spoke candidly after the August Coup about this danger:

> At the initial stages, before we had created public opinion and a democratic atmosphere in the country, a coup like this could have been successful . . . . I saw it as my task to preserve the course of perestroika. For the first time in the history of this country I was striving to resolve everything without bloodshed, on the basis of concord.[52]

Unfortunately, to fend off perceived pressure from the Right he kept manoeuvring politically and held back on his reforms, to the growing disgust of his initial admirers. When Foreign Minister Shevardnadze resigned in December 1990 and warned of impending dictatorship, Gorbachev was unmoved. Shevardnadze noted caustically,

> I already knew very well that Mikhail Gorbachev is extremely choosy in his response to things that happen without his knowledge or agreement. With some he may be unusually patient or indulgent. With others, on the contrary, he may be intolerant or irritable. Some destroy his life's achievement virtually before his eyes, and he seems not even to notice. Others attempt to save this achievement, but encounter only lack of understanding . . . . The junta sprang up right under his wing.[53]

For the time being, Gorbachev staved off the coming attack of the conservatives by bringing them directly into the top leadership: Gennady Yanaev, an obscure trade-unionist, elevated from the Party Secretariat to the newly created vice-presidency; Valentin Pavlov, the undistinguished finance minister installed as prime minister after Ryzhkov suffered a heart attack; and Boris Pugo, the Latvian secret police official who was moved from the Party Control Commission to the Ministry of the Interior in place of the liberal Bakatin. At the same time Gorbachev abolished his new Presidential Council with its strong reformist contingent, and practically became the prisoner of his new allies. When the Central Committee met in January 1991, as Shevardnadze described it, "Reactionaries . . . were telling him to his face that perestroika had failed and that his policy was to blame. The seasoned debater, who had persuaded the Party and the country that democracy and innovation were vitally needed, kept silent."[54]

Gorbachev refrained as well from any denunciation of the KGB's attacks on nationalists in Vilnius and Riga in January, though privately he called the actions "a provocation . . . an attempt by reactionary forces to derail the process of reform."[55] When the democratic movement announced a major demonstration in Moscow for late March, Gorbachev ordered it banned and deployed troops, only to hold them back at the last minute. An aide reported, "March 28 was not just a turning point – it was *the* turning point for Mikhail Serge-yevich. He went to the abyss, looked over the edge, was horrified by what he saw, and backed away."[56] Meanwhile, apparently unbeknown to him, Gorbachev's trusted friends, Supreme Soviet Chairman Lukianov and presidential Chief of Staff Boldin, were working hand in glove with the conservatives. KGB chief Kriuchkov, it was later claimed, was busily preparing contingency plans for a forcible change of leadership.[57]

A week before he resigned in December 1991, Gorbachev gave a very revealing interview about these critical months: "I was subjected to colossal attacks and pressures. I had to decide what to do. It would seem normal to go for a decisive battle. But," he claimed,

there was still no support from the people, society was not ready yet, and dissatisfaction was coming to a head in the Party itself. Therefore – and this drew extremely harsh rebukes – we decided first to renew [sic!] the personnel in the strongest structures . . . . Do you think I didn't know that [free elections] would be followed by a blow from the conservative circles of the Party, united with the military-industrial complex? I knew, and I kept them close to me.

The conservatives themselves, Gorbachev thought, had waited too long for popular support: "A year ago or a year and a half ago, if they had made the move then that they made in August, everything would have gone through." But he admitted his own mistake: "At a certain stage, I failed to seize the moment. The threat of a dictatorship was arising. I saw the real danger."[58]

Alarm signals went out among the conservatives after the crisis of March 1991, when Gorbachev suddenly reversed direction, warned against the right-wing menace to his reforms, and sought conciliation with Yeltsin and the virtually independent leaders of the other repub-lics. By summer, negotiations were completed for the new Union Treaty to replace the document of 1922 and recognize the autonomous powers of the republics in a loose confederation.

At the same time, presiding over what was destined to be the last plenum of the Communist Central Committee, Gorbachev once again won great concessions of principle. In the draft of the new program that the meeting approved, Marxist-Leninist dogma and the theory of the proletarian revolution disappeared altogether. Gorbachev announced "a decisive break with obsolete ideological dogmas and stereotypes." No longer should socialism depend on "a forcible coup, the establishment of the dictatorship, and the class struggle," guided by "utopian, hare-brained schemes" and "a vain attempt to build castles in the air." No longer should the Party be "a militarized structure" narrowly preaching Marxism-Leninism; it had to get over its "Communist fundamentalism" and compete for popular support strictly by persuasion.[59] The Mensheviks of 1917 could not have been more completely vindicated. Meanwhile, Yeltsin did what Gorbachev said; enjoying burgeoning popularity, he sought and won direct popular election to the presidency of the Russian Republic, and banned the traditional Communist Party organisations in all workplaces.

All this was too much, at last, for the party conservatives. First they tried to save themselves in a constitutional manner: Prime Minister Pavlov seized one of those dangerous moments when Gorbachev was away from Moscow, to invite the Supreme Soviet to transfer the preponderance of presidential powers to his own office. Gorbachev returned in time to foil the scheme. Alexander Yakovlev tried to warn Gorbachev what was coming next: "I appeal to you – you have terrible people around you. Do something about this dirty circle."[60] Then, with the new Union Treaty about to be signed, which would end the vision of a Russia-centered superpower role for the USSR, the conservatives finally put into play the more forcible measures they had so long contemplated. But now it was too late. The August Coup was a desperate attempt to turn back the flow of history that was already sweeping away everything they represented.

*

The failure of the August Coup, and the steps that Yeltsin's government and the other republics took to assert their own independent powers, signified the formal end of the Communist system. The Communist Party as a dominant, quasi-governmental institution was finally done to death, and its ideology, even in its latest watered-down form, was repudiated, though several Communist-oriented splinter groups managed to stay alive. A little more gradually, but just as inevitably, the governmental institutions of the USSR and Gorbachev's personal office of president of the Union were dismantled and discarded, or appropriated by the Russian Republic.

Gorbachev, recovering from his initial illusion after the putsch that the Party could still reform and survive, attempted to save himself by resigning as general secretary, disbanding the Central Committee, and (in his last act of coercive leadership) prevailing on the Congress of People's Deputies to remake the Supreme Soviet into a council of republic governments and then to dissolve itself. He desperately tried to salvage the concept of the Union by reviving the Union Treaty, though fewer and fewer republics could be induced to agree even to these generous conditions of autonomy. The fate of the Soviet president now lay in the hands of Yeltsin, who emerged finally as the clear victor in their long rivalry. Gorbachev's future depended on maintaining some semblance of the Union over which he could preside; Yeltsin, to finish Gorbachev off politically and crown his own ascendancy, aimed to liquidate the last formal remnants of the Union. In the end, Gorbachev told staffers and journalists at a farewell reception, "I just could not go on. Everything I did in the last few months, Yeltsin was always opposing it. There was just no way. No way."[61]

The changing times were graphically symbolized by the events of 7 November, the traditional revolutionary holiday. There were no military parades and no official celebrations, except for a few thousand die-hard Communists in Red Square, returning to their pre-1917 oppositional role and protesting against "the bourgeois dictatorship." As Lenin statues tumbled everywhere, most non-Russian republics chose to ignore the day; some Russians made it an occasion to commemorate the victims of Communism; and St. Petersburg celebrated the restoration of its historic name, with Patriarch Alexei II and Grand Duke Vladimir Kirillovich Romanov, the grandson of the late Tsar's cousin, prominently in attendance. On the eve of the anniversary Yeltsin finalized his ban on the Communist Party everywhere in Russia.

A month later, meeting in Minsk on 8 December with the presidents of Ukraine and Belorussia, Yeltsin brought off a second and final coup against Gorbachev. Yeltsin had said on 19 August, "On the night of August 18–19, 1991, the legally elected president of the country was removed from power."[62] Though Gorbachev was restored for the time being, one might say that once again "on 8 December 1991 the legally elected president of the country was removed from power." With the agreement of Leonid Kravchuk of Ukraine and Stanislav Shushkevich of Belorussia, seconded soon after by all the other Soviet republics save Georgia and the now independent Baltics, Yeltsin announced the end of the USSR. He took over the last of the Union's ministries in Moscow and proclaimed the "Commonwealth of Independent States," of a form and structure yet to be determined, though inevitably led by the Russians. Gorbachev had no task left except to sign his resignation – on 25 December, with the pen of an American journalist because his Soviet pen didn't work. Two days later, returning to the Kremlin to clean out his office, he found a new name on the door and a new man behind the desk – Yeltsin. The Communist era in the history of the Russian empire had offically come to an end.

*

In the aftermath of the failed coup and the eradication of the institutions associated with Communist dictatorship, Russia and the other ex-Soviet republics completed the transition back through time to the democratic hopes and political pluralism of 1917. Said Gorbachev, "I compare the tasks of the contemporary USSR Supreme Soviet with the mission of the Constituent Assembly in the transition period."[63] As it happened, the destiny of that last Supreme Soviet proved to be as ephemeral as the Constituent Assembly, while the Union was being consumed by the same nationalistic ferments and economic chaos that overwhelmed the democrats of the earlier epoch.

Though writers and leaders of all hues hastened to repudiate the ideology of the Bolshevik Revolution and often any variant of the socialist idea as well, there was surprisingly little re-examination of the alternatives cut off by October. Indeed, more attention focussed on the regime cut off by February, thanks to Solzhenitsyn-style Slavophile conservatives. What emerged as the mainstream post-coup political and economic doctrine was the Western orthodoxy of classical liberalism, or what the ex-Soviets perceived to be that orthodoxy – a matter to which we shall return in the final chapter. But standing out most prominently as almost everyone's operative creed was nationalism, be it Russian in its contractive or expansive modes, or that of the non-Russian minorities in the former Union republics, or, more dangerously, that of minorities within the republics – the many lesser minorities within Russia, those in some of the smaller republics (Georgia and Moldova particularly), and the 25 million Russians who have lived as the dominant minority everywhere else in the USSR. Gorbachev never ceased to warn of the danger inherent in these particularistic feelings. "I support the preservation of the union state and the integrity of this country," he said in his statement of resignation. "Developments took a different course. The policy prevailed of dismembering this country and disuniting the state, which is something I cannot subscribe to."[64]

The August Coup, hailed in the former lands of the Soviets as well as abroad as a magnificent breakthrough into democracy and self-determination, paradoxically introduced new threats to these values. Despite all its zigs and zags, its backing and filling, the reform process under way in the Soviet Union since 1985 had accomplished tremendous and irreversible change. Such a transformation had never before been realized in a major totalitarian state, unless it had been defeated in war and subjected to forcible reconstruction of its political order. Political institutions in the USSR were functioning in a steadily more democratic and decentralist way, though the economy had gone out of control. To be sure, the coup attempt put a swift end to the Communist Party as a state within the state; Yakovlev told American Secretary of State James Baker, "They did for us in three days what would have taken us fifteen years to accomplish."[65] Nevertheless, the effect of the coup and its aftermath was almost as damaging for those elements of the political system – true parliamentary practice, separation of powers, a meaningful federalism on the American model – that represented the most remarkable but delicate achievements of perestroika.

Reacting to the coup and to the opportunities offered by its failure, the Soviet peoples and their leaders plumped for a nationalism that swept much of the political work of perestroika aside, and potentially or actually replaced it with a congeries of feuding ethnic authoritarianisms. Yeltsin assumed personal powers in the Russian Republic that matched everything he had accused Gorbachev of in the months preceding the coup. Most of the other republics found themselves under equally personalistic rule, usually, as in Russia, by ex-Communists. The record of decolonization on other continents offers few examples to encourage optimism about the political future of the Soviet successor-states.

Recalling the course of earlier revolutions, a writer for the new *Independent Gazette* warned,

> For us, too, the impending authoritarianism will be a punishment – for replacing our struggle for the principles of democracy with a struggle against the Union center and the Communist Party; for being ready to choose any passer-by as a deputy if he just declared himself to be a democrat and anti-Communist; for deriding the person who did more than anyone else for Russian democracy – Gorbachev . . . ; for using the collapse of the putsch to destroy the Union once and for all, without thinking in the least about the consequences, including the consequences for the Russian democracy that is just being born; and for much else.[66]

Was the coup and its anti-Communist aftermath a new "revolution," more so than what Gorbachev claimed for perestroika? Full consideration of this question must wait upon analysis of the Russian revolutionary experience going back to 1917. Clearly the August days were one of those historical episodes where a system of rule – already attenuated in this case – dissolves before our eyes when it loses the magical essence of power. Power does not simply come out of the barrel of a gun, notwithstanding Mao Tse-tung's aphorism. Power is not a material force but a psychological one, that rests on a continuous interplay of perceptions between ruler and ruled; like beauty, it exists mostly in the eye of the beholder. Anatoly Sobchak, himself an anti-coup hero as mayor of what was still Leningrad, writes that the coup could well have succeeded "if the people had remained silent." But more particularly, "I want to make a special point of praising . . . those who hesitated . . . those thousands and thousands of waverers – the militia and KGB personnel, soldiers and officers – who sent the coup to its downfall."[67] If the people will not obey and the troops will not shoot, power collapses and falls into the street, waiting, as Lenin said, for someone else to find it and pick it up.

3

SEEDS OF ITS OWN
DESTRUCTION

14 October 1964. The unthinkable has come to pass in Moscow. The Central Committee of the CPSU is assembled in the Kremlin to ratify the Party Presidium's decision to remove Nikita Khrushchev from his posts as first secretary of the Party and chairman of the Council of Ministers. This is the first time in the entire history of Russia that the established leader has been removed, not by death or armed coup, but by a vote, according to the rules.

At the summons of his colleagues, Khrushchev has just flown back to Moscow from a holiday in the Crimea, only to find that the other party leaders – party secretaries Mikhail Suslov, Leonid Brezhnev, and Alexander Shelepin, together with Deputy Prime Minister Alexei Kosygin – have laid plans to get rid of him. In the space of just a few days they have come to agreement that it is time to put a stop to Khrushchev's erratic and destabilizing reforms, and avert their own possible removal from office. The KGB under Vladimir Semichastny and the military under Marshal Rodion Malinovsky are also on board. According to Fyodor Burlatsky,

> A strange symbiosis of political forces was formed. From advocates of consistent progress along the path of the Twentieth Party Congress, to conservatives and crypto-Stalinists, they all rallied against the leader who had helped the majority of them "to the top."[1]

Led by the ascetic-looking ideologist Suslov, the Party Presidium (as the Politburo was called in those years) confronts Khrushchev with its *fait accompli*. Khrushchev remonstrates with his erstwhile lieutenants, then submits with dignity and almost tearfully:

> I'm going, and I'm not going to beat myself. I beg your pardon if I have hurt anyone, if I have shown any rudeness . . . . But all of you present here, you have never spoken to me openly and frankly about my faults, you have approved . . . . History will someday speak its judgement on what is happening today.[2]

Following the Presidium session Suslov takes the floor at the hastily called meeting of the Central Committee to present the indictment that the junta has prepared:

> Khrushchev concentrated all the power in the country in his own hands and began to abuse it . . . . He was surrounded by toadies and flatterers in the press and on the radio as well . . . . Khrushchev got the idea that he was a specialist in all areas – in agriculture, diplomacy, science, art – and lectured about all of them . . . . At the sessions of the Presidium Khrushchev shouted, swore, insulted members of the Presidium and used dirty language . . . .

Forced to sit through this humiliation, Khrushchev turns red and clenches his fists, but he is helpless. Numerous members of the Central Committee, to ingratiate themselves with the plotters, interject their jibes against the fallen chief. "If Stalin destroyed people physically," Suslov concludes, "Khrushchev destroyed them morally. The removal of Khrushchev from power is a sign not of the weakness but of the strength of the Party, and this should be a lesson."[3]

This, of course, is not the whole story. An academician who is close to President Anastas Mikoyan, Khrushchev's only friend in the Party Presidium (and perhaps not a totally reliable one), tells Khrushchev's son Sergei, "The issue now is not Nikita Sergeyevich's mistakes, but the line he personifies and is pursuing. If he goes, the Stalinists may come to power, and who knows what will happen then."[4]

The Central Committee gets no chance to hear Khrushchev or to debate his ouster. Police chief Semichastny, subsequently disgraced, has to wait until the age of glasnost to record his candid recollection: "The old men . . . were afraid for their . . . skins . . . . The Presidium decided everything for the Central Committee, and having decided, prepared, chewed it over . . ., threw it to the CC, saying, 'Vote!' "[5]

Khrushchev bows to the inevitable and plays the game, asking the Central Committee to "release" him from his duties, which it promptly does.[6] Brezhnev assumes the post of first secretary (soon to revert to its old designation of general secretary) and Kosygin becomes prime minister, while Suslov remains the king-maker and *éminence grise*. The reforms so badly needed in this postrevolutionary society are interrupted for almost a generation, as it turns out. Presidium member Gennady Voronov laments long afterwards that with Brezhnev, "Instead of correcting the errors of a brilliant person heading the Party, we gambled on another person far less brilliant."[7] Khrushchev can only console himself that by stepping down without further resistance he has unburdened the country of its fear of another all-powerful leader: "I've done the main thing." Journalist Mark Frankland comments, "Ten years earlier no one would even have imagined that Stalin's successor would be removed by so simple and gentle a process as a vote."[8] The rejected chief lives on in comfortable though obscure retirement for seven more years, the beneficiary of his own precedent of leniency in disposing of fallen rivals.

*

The overthrow of Khrushchev, like the election of Gorbachev in 1985, was one of those unpredictable political events that can redirect the future course of a nation for decades. Khrushchev's fall was a tragic setback, after the brief era of the "thaw" and de-Stalinization that he had courageously initiated. It meant the rejection of fundamental reform, though the country was more than ready for it, and the perpetuation of the Stalinist system of rule, even though that regime had outlived both its effectiveness and its legitimation. To Burlatsky it was worse than stagnation:

> The abandonment of reforms . . ., the freeze of living standards, the general delay of absolutely self-evident decisions and the substitution of trite political verbiage in their place, the corruption and degeneration of power in which whole strata of the people become increasingly involved, the loss of moral values and the universal decline in morality – if that is stagnation, what is a crisis?[9]

To be sure, the Brezhnev–Kosygin regime was Stalinism without the mass terror of the Stalin era. People were not usually arrested unless they actually did oppose the government, and the death penalty was no longer meted out for the crime of falling from power. But the essentials of the system were maintained: rule by a privileged bureaucracy, the *nomenklatura*; the militarized command economy; a monopoly of the media to ensure ideological self-justification of the system and the manipulation of public opinion; police-state controls over everyone; a suspicious and confrontational attitude toward the outside world. The leadership had no real goal except to maintain their own power. For both the Soviet Union and its client governments in Eastern Europe and elsewhere they defined their system as "developed socialism" or "real existing socialism." Western observers were more inclined to call it totalitarianism.

If it was still accurate in the 1960s and 1970s to describe the Soviet system as totalitarian, the question naturally arises of how Gorbachev and Yeltsin could so readily dismantle that system, or how leaders could come up through that system who were even willing to dismantle it. We have already followed the maneuvres by which Gorbachev recast the political face of the country and Yeltsin appropriated the legacy of reform. We have not settled, however, the question of how it was possible for them to mobilize effective political forces for reform and overcome the people who were wedded to the powers and privileges of the past. The answer is not simple – it is the preoccupation of this entire book. The first level of explanation, however, must be sought in the "era of stagnation" that preceded Gorbachev's reforms, and the changes that Soviet society quietly experienced in those years. This will at least help to show how Gorbachev and then Yeltsin could have succeeded where Khrushchev failed.

*

Who were the new men who took over the self-styled land of socialism from Khrushchev and held it back politically for the next twenty years? They were not Joseph Stalin's immediate heirs: those people had been weeded out by Khrushchev (and in the case of the police chief Lavrenty Beria, physically liquidated) during the struggle for power between the time of Stalin's death in 1953 and the disgrace of the "Anti-Party Group" of Viacheslav Molotov, Georgi Malenkov, and Lazar Kaganovich in 1957. Khrushchev's heirs were the second generation of Stalinists, beneficiaries of Stalin's purges of the 1930s who had stepped into the shoes of the slightly older purge victims.

It is not often recognized that when Stalin annihilated the top echelons of his own bureaucracy in the Party, the government, and the military, he set an age limit. Except for the members of the Politburo itself, almost everyone of prominence over the age of 35 in 1937 (i.e., born before 1902, or for the military, before 1898) was executed or died in the camps. Khrushchev himself, born to a south Russian peasant family in 1894 and a veteran of the Civil War and the coal mines, was one of those exceptions, a Communist Party careerist and boss of Moscow by the time of the purges (in which he was undoubtedly implicated), and a Politburo member as of 1939. One theory, suggested by the American historian Robert Slusser, is that Stalin aimed to wipe out everyone not totally under his thumb who had personal recall of 1917 and his own lack of distinction in the Revolution.[10] Whatever the reason, this holocaust, amounting to millions of victims, left gaping opportunities in the bureaucratic structure for Stalin's young "promotees," the *vydvizhentsy*, to move up and fill the void.

The *vydvizhentsy* were a cadre of tough young men brought out of the villages and factories in the late 1920s and early 1930s and given crash courses in engineering and propaganda to prepare them as the future ruling class.[11] Brezhnev, Kosygin, and Suslov were all representatives of this new group. Suslov, the oldest, born in 1902 and trained as an economist, moved up from obscure bureaucratic work to become the first secretary of Stavropol province in 1939. Kosygin, born in 1904, was a foreman in a Leningrad textile mill when the purges began, and a deputy prime minister when they ended. Brezhnev, born in 1906, rose from vocational school principal to deputy party secretary of his home province of Dnepropetrovsk, and thence upward. As a relatively youthful age cohort, the post-purge generation represented by these individuals was able to grow old in office for four decades, supplying most of the top leadership from the 1940s to the early 1980s.[12] Still in their fifties and early sixties in 1964, they succeeded in prolonging the Stalinist system of dictatorial rule and centralized administration in defiance of all the needs and frustrations of the country.

The government of the Brezhnev group showed how little Khrushchev had changed the fundamentals of power in the Soviet Union despite his passionate outbursts against Stalin. Supported by the police and the censorship, the Communist Party (11.5 million strong in 1966) still monopolized political activity in the country, and the hierarchy of the party apparatus – the local, provincial, and central secretaries – monopolized decision-making within the Party. Not only was the constitutional structure of civil government a sham; the nominally democratic rules of party life were equally illusory, and rank-and-file members had little voice except in passing orders on to the general public.

Two important changes, however, had taken place by the 1960s: the indiscriminate terror of Stalin's day, repudiated by Khrushchev, gave way to the selective repression of actual dissent, and the personal power exercised by both Stalin and Khrushchev gave way to a more or less collective bureaucratic leadership in which Brezhnev, despite efforts late in his tenure to build up a cult around him, could never be considered more than first among equals. He was limited by an "implicit compact," a "veritable charter of oligarchy," in the view of the Australian sovietologist T. H. Rigby.[13] The former party secretary P. A. Rodionov thought him "a mediocrity," who "cleaned out anyone smarter and more able" and "surrounded himself, as a rule, with grey people."[14]

Brezhnev did not exercise the circular flow of power to the degree that Stalin and Khrushchev did before him or Andropov and Gorbachev were to do later on. Not only the Brezhnev generation as a whole but many of its individual members as well enjoyed long, undisturbed terms in their party or ministerial offices. Entrenched in power, they could exercise the influence (usually conservative) of what I have termed "participatory bureaucracy."[15] Everyone now had the lesson of Khrushchev in mind, that the top leader was removable by his colleagues if he stepped out of bounds. Brezhnev, in all respects a representative of his bureaucratic circle, "cynical . . ., vain, stupid," in Roy Medvedev's opinion,[16] had no intention of doing that.

*

The remarkable, and now unsung, side of the Brezhnev era was the continuing advance of the Soviet economy despite the political immobilism confirmed in 1964. The old sequence of five-year plans had been broken by Khrushchev's reorganizations of the planners and his experiment in shifting economic authority to the provinces. In 1958 there was no plan in effect at all; then a "seven-year plan" for 1959–1965 got the system back to its five-year cycle. Surprisingly, in the light of current retrospectives on the "era of stagnation," the Soviet economy moved steadily forward throughout the 1960s and on into the 1970s.

The secret of this success was simply the reinvestment of a large fraction of the national product (up to 30 per cent), mainly in heavy industry and defense-oriented enterprises as under Stalin, but also for the first time in agriculture. During the Eighth and Ninth Five-Year Plans (1966–1975), for example, steel output went up from 91 to 141 million tons annually; coal, from 578 to 701 million tons; petroleum, from 243 to 491 million tons.[17] By the mid-1970s the Soviet Union was the world's largest producer of all of these industrial basics (though not the largest exporter). On the agricultural side (subject to varying weather) it became the world's largest wheat producer – though not of all grains combined; it was the need to provide for animal feed that required the massive grain purchases of the 1970s.[18]

Nor was Soviet technology as primitive as it has been represented since perestroika began. Martin Walker warned, "Western smugness about the technological backwardness of Soviet science is dangerously misplaced."[19] In anything related to the military-industrial complex and the space program Soviet research and development work was outstanding, and in metallurgy the Soviets led the world. The problem was not lack of genius in inspiration but unevenness in application, a weakness serious enough to make Gorbachev say in 1987, "We have started lagging behind in scientific-technical development."[20]

A strange lacuna in Soviet priorities was the infrastructure of transportation, storage, and distribution, possibly because the contribution of these sectors was not measurable in discrete units of output. Losses in agricultural produce between the field and the table became an ill-concealed national scandal, but even perestroika seemed able to do little about a source of waste that may have equalled the whole sum of food purchases from abroad. In general, consumer goods were always secondary in the national-power considerations of Soviet planners, and lagged behind heavy industry in quality as well as quantity. Nevertheless, to take one example, the stated output of shoes rose from 486 million pairs in 1965 to 698 million in 1975.[21] While the population was steadily increasing (209 million in 1959, 242 million in 1970, 262 million in 1979), consumer living standards more than kept pace, doubling between the end of the Second World War and 1970, according to the American economist James Millar.[22] But this was not sufficient to satisfy rising popular expectations.

The "era of stagnation" is thus a misnomer. While they were determined to maintain the political character of their system, the bureaucrats around Brezhnev were bent on continuing the quantitative growth of the Soviet Union (and the Soviet empire) in all respects, economically, culturally and educationally, militarily, and in the bloc's international role. Like traditional autocracy, as Zdeněk Mlynář saw it, Stalinism was "capable of concentrating the maximum forces and means in order to achieve a few chosen targets – usually military – regardless of the price (economic, social, or cultural) to be paid." But these powers of the system "become, under different circumstances, its defects and fundamental weaknesses."[23] What the Brezhnevites forgot was the dialectical teachings of their own official theory of Marxism: quantitative change must sooner or later turn into qualitative change, and a political superstructure that fails to adapt to changes in its social and economic base runs a growing risk of disruption and overthrow.

From the inception of glasnost, Soviet and East European reformers consistently rejected the principle of central economic planning. This is not altogether surprising in view of the fact that they were all reacting against the same kind of "command-administrative" system going back to Stalin. In the eyes of the reformers, the Stalinist system of central planning was the "braking mechanism," the main cause of economic retardation and crisis.[24] But they seldom evaluated the Stalinist experience historically and in detail, to ascertain whether the trouble was inherent in the planning system or only in its political context.

The planning system as such was fairly simple. Gosplan calculated the sum of the country's resources and facilities, established priorities for their use, and handed down output targets and supply allocations to the various economic ministries and through them to every branch and enterprise in the entire economy. To be sure, the system had its limitations, including the absence of meaningful price and cost information and the difficulty of extending planning to all the special commodities and enterprises in a modern economy. More serious difficulties stemmed from the attitudes and priorities built into the Stalinist planning system. "From the start," write the Soviet economists Nikolai Shmelev and Vladimir Popov, "the administrative system was distinguished by economic romanticism, profound economic illiteracy, and incredible exaggeration of the real effect that the 'administrative factor' had on economic processes and on the motivations of the public."[25] In other words, the Stalinist economy was not really planned at all, but only commanded. "There are no fortresses which Bolsheviks cannot capture," Stalin proclaimed.[26]

Economic planning had been subjected to political and military imperatives ever since the formulation of the First Five-Year Plan. From Stalin to Brezhnev, planning and management were shot through with corruption, dishonesty, and stupidity, thanks to the political environment of controlled information and repressed disagreement. Waste, along with haste, became endemic to the system. A spirit of gigantomania led to hugely expensive, long unfinished, and environmentally devastating projects. Nevertheless, central allocation of money and materials, always favoring industrial projects and requiring a correspondingly tight belt for consumers when shortages appeared, enabled the Soviet economy to grow at the rate America, Japan, and Tsarist Russia had reached earlier in the century.[27] One wonders, in the light of recent Soviet statements about it, how the Stalinist system ever managed to multiply heavy industrial output in the 1930s and equip an army to defeat the Germans in the Second World War. The answer is that at a certain early level, when development was "extensive," with virtually unlimited labor and natural resources, and for certain purposes, especially military, Stalin's approach was one suitable alternative, though not the most efficient or the most humane. Thus, despite the cost in human suffering and privation, the industrial spurts of the thirties, the immediate postwar years, and the early Brezhnev period established the Soviet Union as a world-class industrial power. This is not to say that the same results could not have been achieved by kinder, gentler methods.

*

A chronic problem under the "command-administrative system," as the Gorbachevians termed it, was incentives for initiative and effort. When the system was put in place under Stalin, bonuses for managers and piece-wages for workers were standard policies in the campaign for plan fulfillment. How did things then come to the point where "They pretend to pay us and we pretend to work"?[28] Yuri Andropov charged when he succeeded Brezhnev,

> Apparently the force of inertia and old habits are still at work. And some people perhaps, simply don't know how to tackle the job. . . . Poor work, sluggishness, and irresponsibility should have an immediate and inescapable effect on the remuneration, job status, and moral prestige of personnel.[29]

Stalin's disciplinarian approach did not survive Khrushchev's era of reform and his attempt to revive the old egalitarian spirit. Under Khrushchev, but continuing under Brezhnev and Kosygin, the working class began to be coddled instead of lashed as it was in Stalin's time. Donald Filtzer of the University of Birmingham notes,

> The draconian labour legislation of 1940–41 was becoming increas-

63

ingly difficult to enforce and was a hindrance to industrial efficiency . . . . Workers have little fear of unemployment while the wage system, combined with the severe shortage of consumer goods, offer insufficient inducement to raise the intensity of labour.[30]

Wages and pensions were leveled upwards, and skilled and manual work began to exceed much mental and professional work in remuneration. The Italian economic historian Rita Di Leo found "a compression of differentials" and a bias for so-called "productive" work (i.e., yielding measurable physical output) over "unproductive" work (services, trade, etc.). "Such a wage policy calls into question the modernization of society, its efficiency, its competitiveness."[31]

Liberalization in the workplace unfortunately ran afoul of deep cultural instincts. As visitors to the Soviet Union have discovered over the years, workers at all levels made the old system function only in a climate of coercion and exhortation. When they were liberated from this pressure the universal response was to slacken the effort and complain about everyone else. Among the Russian masses, for centuries, work was understood as something one was compelled to do for another's benefit, and Communism made no real change in this respect. In other words, there was not enough of a work ethic in the Russian economic culture, not for the masses, not for the nobles and officials who made others do the work, not for the intellectuals who felt they were doing something higher than work.

By the late Brezhnev years, lagging salaries and poor supplies of things that could be bought with them conspired with secrecy and favoritism in the bureaucratic hierarchy to produce a national epidemic of economic crime and corruption. The second economy engulfed a significant fraction of the GDP. Not only individuals but state enterprises as well engaged in these practices, often out of necessity, when extra-legal influence or illegal operations appeared to be the only way to fulfill the demands of the plan. Claims of plan fulfillment that were passed up the hierarchy became as impossible to believe as the targets in the next plan.

For the elite, it was an easy step from the secret enjoyment of legal privileges (apartments, cars, special shops and hospitals) to the illegal enjoyment of secret privileges. For all but the most naive or ascetic among the officialdom, self-seeking supplanted both doctrinal loyalty and personal morality. Shevardnadze wrote of this regime,

You must bear without a murmur all attacks upon yourself and must accept as your due the *diktat* of the political patriarchate . . . . Sit tight, do your work, and take advantage of the privileges and benefits offered to you. Don't try to yank the fishhook out of your mouth, or it will be certain death.[32]

It seemed to Soviet historians looking back from the vantage point of perestroika that the last true believer was Nikita Khrushchev, a lone figure even in his own time. Corruption became especially pervasive among the leadership in certain national-minority regions (where they had to all intents and purposes sold out to Moscow in order to enjoy local power). In Central Asia whole governments of Union republics had to be purged for high-level embezzlement and falsification of economic performance.

A particularly shocking side of the moral collapse of Soviet society was the field of health care. Starved by thoughtless priorities in the state budget, medicine was invaded by unbelievable cynicism. Pharmaceutical supplies and hospital conditions fell to Third World levels. Because salaries were so low in relation to training and expectations, doctors moonlighted illegally and nurses sometimes even had to be bribed to empty bedpans. While patients with money could, in effect, secure the benefits of private health services, not to mention the exclusive facilities for the *nomenklatura*, care for the masses deteriorated – a major factor in declining public health standards.

*

In fairness it must be noted that the Brezhnev regime became aware of some of the self-imposed limitations in the Stalinist economic mechanism. Early on, following the recommendations of the economist Yevsei Liberman, Prime Minister Kosygin undertook to decentralize some business decision-making to the enterprise level, but bureaucratic resistance and fear of unorthodoxy effectively nullified his reforms. Repeatedly he addressed the problems of technological innovation and consumer satisfaction, if only because monetary incentives to work were valueless if there was little to buy. In 1971 he promised that the Ninth Five-Year Plan would increase the supply of food, clothing, and household appliances on the order of 50 per cent, and would double the provisions of "everyday services."[33] Agriculture began to receive substantial state investments for the first time ever, though the new effort ran to grandiose and environmentally detrimental programs for irrigation, fertilizer, and pesticides, and neglected the distribution problem.

Faced with mounting demands for new capital by the industrial, military, consumer, and agricultural sectors, the Brezhnev government made a decision in adopting the Tenth Five-Year Plan (1976–1980) to cut back on industrial investment and rely instead on intensive improvements in productivity and efficiency. (Dissidents called this the "Marshal Plan" because Brezhnev gave himself the rank of marshal at the same time.) Within the confines of the command economy these remedies could hardly make up the difference, and as a result overall economic growth, already slowing down, leveled off.[34] At the same time, the urban population, growing both in numbers and sophistication, posed ever greater consumer demand, while plenty of roubles were in most people's pockets because wages were allowed to rise more than taxes and more than the available supply of consumer goods and services (some of which – bread, housing, transportation – were kept at artificially low prices). The result was the familiar symptoms of suppressed inflation: queues, hoarding, and diversion of supplies, legally by enterprises and illegally by black marketeers.

All these problems were exacerbated by the Brezhnev regime's drive to establish and maintain military parity with the USA. In the old Russian pattern, exemplified by every Tsar from Peter the Great to Nicholas II, the economic prowess and technological sophistication of the West would be offset by numbers, discipline, and sheer effort. Georgi Arbatov, director of the USA Institute and a CP Central Committee member, told the People's Congress in December 1989, "One of the gravest manifestations of the legacy of stagnation is the fact that at that time the military and military industry were given a completely free hand . . . . Military extravagance has made the richest capitalist power – the US – the world's biggest debtor and undermined its competitive position in the world. And it has literally bled our own economy white."[35]

The Soviet Union committed itself in the 1970s to an expensive effort to outflank the American-led alliance in the Third World, by supporting anti-colonial movements and revolutionary governments and building a network of overseas bases. But this was economically costly and politically risky; though victory in war had reinforced the autocratic regimes of Peter the Great in 1721, of Alexander I in 1814, and of Stalin in 1945, defeats – the Crimean War, the Russo-Japanese War, the First World War – had shaken or toppled Russian governments. Soviet assertiveness in the 1970s served only to provoke a threatening US military buildup in the early 1980s. A no-win military involvement, the intervention in Afghanistan, helped convince younger Soviet leaders, already alarmed by the country's high-tech lag, that things could not go on as they had.

The constriction in the Soviet economy in the late Brezhnev years was aptly analyzed by Tatiana Zaslavskaya in her "Novosibirsk Report," the working paper of 1983 that was leaked to the Western press. At bottom Zaslavskaya saw a contradiction between the vast growth of the Soviet economy in scope and complexity, and the preservation of the rigid and simplistic system of decision-making devised for the far less complex economy of the 1930s. The essence of the trouble was "the predominance of administrative over economic methods, of centralisation over decentralisation."[36] In particular, she referred to the practice of setting prices administratively, with little regard to actual production costs or user value, causing the economy to be shot through with irrational hidden taxes and subsidies. Overall, Zaslavskaya observed "the degeneration of the social mechanism of economic development . . ., 'tuned' not to stimulate but to thwart the population's useful economic activity."[37] In her Marxist terminology, "The present system of production relations has substantially fallen behind the level of development of the productive forces," and it was becoming "more and more of a brake on their progressive advancement." This was nothing less than Marx's recipe for revolution.[38] The impasse, for Zaslavskaya, underlay the psychological deterioration of the Soviet labor force:

> Low labor and production discipline, an indifferent attitude to the work performed and its low quality, social passivity, a low value attached to labor as a means of self-realisation, an intense consumer orientation, and a rather low level of moral discipline . . ., a type of worker who is alien to genuinely socialist values.[39]

*

Just as the materialist dialectic would have predicted, the long postwar economic expansion revolutionized the character of Soviet society, not yet in its political structure but profoundly so in the ways of life and thought of the multitude. As Martin Walker has expressed it, "The country went through a social revolution while Brezhnev slept."[40] From a country that was still largely rural at the time of the Second World War, the Soviet Union became, according to the census of 1979, more than half urban. Urbanization, concentrating people to work in the expanding industries, absorbed all of the country's postwar population growth. Thanks to the conditions of life and work and the availability of abortions, the birth rate fell to the bare replacement level among the European nationalities, while the Moslems of Central Asia multiplied at a Third World tempo and altered the whole demographic balance of the country. But the Central Asians preferred to stay on the farm, while the north of European Russia (never a prosperous agricultural region) was seriously depopulated.

Urban living, even under Soviet conditions, meant certain amenities in education, entertainment, and consumer goods, though housing construction never caught up with the influx from the countryside (while abandoned peasant houses were bought up by the urban elite to be used as weekend and holiday dachas). Urbanization meant a population that was more mobilizable but less manipulable. Foreign observers comparing the appearances of Soviet life in the 1950s, 1960s, and

67

1970s could see the steady encroachment of Western mass culture, in dress, music, even language, starting with the youth of the Khrushchev era. "Over the period of the Brezhnev administration," observes Boris Kagarlitsky, "a large section of the population came to enjoy European norms, living standards, and culture . . . . The paradoxical consequence was that, despite an indisputable improvement in life, more and more people began to experience dissatisfaction with their social existence."[41] At the same time, the indicators of social pathology so familiar in other urbanizing societies (crime, divorce, and above all alcoholism) were on the increase, and by the 1970s the indicators of public health (life expectancy, infant mortality) actually worsened. The USSR became a society of rising expectations and rising frustrations.

Stalinist development, artificial and uneven, perversely exaggerated social interdependence and the division of labor without assuring that each element could shoulder the burden placed on it. Simply speaking, it removed half the population from the work of providing everyday subsistence and services to themselves and others, while crippling the ability of the other half to fulfill that role. Thus we now have the paradox of a modern society, with all its technology and research institutes, that cannot function for lack of food and repairmen. People stand in line instead of working to create what they need.

Along with urbanization the greatest force for change in Soviet society was education. The "era of stagnation" witnessed an explosive growth in the Soviet educational system at almost all levels, secondary, vocational, university, and professional. The goal of universal secondary and vocational education was substantially reached, and dozens of new provincial universities were created, some by building on existing professional institutes, others from scratch. According to one official source, the number of annual university and institute graduates grew from 177,000 in 1950 to 343,000 in 1960 and 631,000 in 1970, with a total of graduates employed by the latter date of nearly 7 million.[42] The American sociologist Alexander Vucinich estimates that the number of Soviet scientists doubled between 1947 and 1960, and again in the period 1960–66.[43]

The watchword in this effort was the "scientific-technical revolution" (STR), the Soviet analogue of Western talk about the "information revolution" and "post-industrial society." The STR was supposed to solve the country's economic difficulties by facilitating great leaps in labor productivity and quality. Unfortunately, in the bureaucratic honeycomb of the Soviet economic system, advances in training and in research did not readily pass over to production. In the view of two Soviet sociologists, the result was "a socioprofessional structure adequate to the needs of a scientific-industrial system . . . straitjacketed into a production system that is still stuck in an earlier technical and technological age."[44]

Between the 1960s and the 1980s trained specialists were being turned out faster than the Soviet economy could absorb them, partly in response to the spreading popular ambition to join the intelligentsia. "The desire far exceeds the need," conceded the Brezhnevian ideologist and future *Pravda* editor Viktor Afanasiev in the 1970s. Owing to

the higher prestige that attaches to the intellectual professions, a certain disproportion has appeared in the system of education and professional training of the working people of the USSR. While we have an overabundance (from the standpoint of present needs) of highly trained specialists, there is a shortage of workers, and particularly skilled workers.[45]

The chronic flight from manual work prompted Khrushchev (and much later, Chernenko) to try to force more secondary school students onto the vocational track, to little avail. But the widespread aspiration to join the intelligentsia allowed the authorities to leave the salaries of white-collar workers (notably teachers and physicians, in heavily female occupations) virtually frozen while many categories of skilled workers moved ahead of them. Often engineers in factories found themselves paid less than the workers whom they supervised, and sometimes educated individuals gave up their careers in order to earn more as workers, though the more common aim was to avoid manual work at any price. Zaslavskaya retrospectively blamed declining morale and creativity within the intelligentsia for "the slowing of scientific and technical progress and of the growth of labour productivity."[46] Soviet society was giving birth to an intellectual proletariat, and the intellectual proletariat anywhere becomes a force for revolutionary change.

*

As Gorbachev himself acknowledged, the social force that ultimately propelled and sustained his break with neo-Stalinism was the intelligentsia, broadly construed as the educated class, the consumers as well as the creators of culture and ideas. Hedrick Smith describes the intelligentsia as "a veritable army, awaiting a new political moment, ready to be summoned into battle against the hated apparat."[47] Considered as a social class, the intelligentsia fits neatly into a dialectical model of social change.

This argument, of course, runs against the theoretical Marxian notion that the industrial working class is destined to be the next ruling class after the bourgeois businessmen. It questions whether the proletariat ever became the ruling class in Soviet Russia. As it happens, the theory of classes is one of the least convincing aspects of Marx's philosophical edifice. Classes have never been as sharply distinguished as Marx represented them, nor as neatly linked to particular regimes and revolutions. The role of bourgeois intellectuals in the Marxist movement itself is enough of a qualification to raise a note of caution about the doctrine of class struggle and class governments.

It is true that the class structure of Western societies more nearly approximated Marx's model of exploiters and exploited at the time he wrote, and in Russia his vision was not so wide of the mark in 1917, except that the theory had no well-defined place for Russia's immense majority of peasants. From the moment of victory in 1917 the Communists never ceased to proclaim their government as a "workers' state" exercising the "dictatorship of the proletariat" as per Marx. What actually emerged from the Revolution was something quite different, though it follows logically if the Marxian scheme of history is consistently thought through.

When feudal society was overthrown, as Marx saw it, the new ruling class was not the vast exploited peasantry but the business class that had grown up on the basis of the capitalist market economy. By extension, one should expect that bourgeois society should give way not to the exploited proletariat but to the new class of salaried managers and experts, in Soviet parlance the intelligentsia, required by the high-tech industrial or postindustrial economy. Such an outcome under socialism, a "dictatorship of the intellectuals," was anticipated even before the Russian Revolution by the Polish anarchist Jan Machajski.[48] The Trotskyist Khristian Rakovsky eventually came to see Stalinism as the rule of the bureaucratic class, though Trotsky himself resisted this conclusion to the end.[49] Many writers have observed a similar shift in social dominance going on under the skin of modern capitalist society without benefit of overt revolution,[50] and some of Trotsky's erstwhile followers – the Italian Bruno Rizzi and the American James Burnham – generalized the concept of a bureaucratic takeover proceeding everywhere, whatever the political system.[51] Milovan Djilas popularized the notion of the bureaucratization of Communism in his book *The New Class*, though he confined himself largely to the party elite.[52]

Even though the bourgeoisie was overthrown and expropriated in Soviet Russia and other Communist states, the revolutionary regime was confronted by the same dependence on managers and experts as under contemporary capitalism. If anything, the need under Communism was more naked because the Revolution had liquidated capitalist ownership. In the last analysis, the great revolution of the twentieth century against the social dominance of private wealth has not been the proletarian revolution but the revolution of the meritocracy. This revolution has been going on in disguise, under both capitalism and Communism. Under capitalism the meritocracy has been taking over gradually and peacefully; under Communism it has simultaneously been embraced by one arm of the state and beaten by the other. Perhaps perestroika and the collapse of the Communist Party will eventually be seen as the liberation of the meritocracy in the Soviet successor-states.

If we can accept the proposition that any advanced industrial or "postindustrial" society tends to shift power from individual entrepreneurs to salaried managers and experts, we can see that the intelligentsia in the broad Soviet sense of the term becomes the natural repository of power and influence once the process of modernization is sufficiently advanced. But here the Soviet experience compels us to make another distinction, because the intelligentsia, however necessary its skills, has over the years been more victim than ruler. The Yugoslav philosopher Svetozar Stojanović has suggested a distinction between the "ruling class" and the "dominant class," the one exercising the actual levers of power, the other providing the ideas and expertise needed for national power and progress, somewhat in Antonio Gramsci's sense of class "hegemony."[53]

Possibly a better formulation, since those in power may not constitute a true "class" in the hereditary sense, would be the "dominant class" and the "political elite." The political elite might or might not emanate from the dominant class and reflect its values and interests. If the elite is not so connected with the dominant class, society will find itself in an enhanced state of tension requiring extensive coercion and control to maintain the political status quo. This in fact has been the Soviet situation, in part since 1917 and entirely so from Stalin's purges up to the 1980s. The young activists whom Stalin had recruited from the working class and the peasantry, poorly educated except possibly in some line of technology, brought with them into every branch of the Soviet bureaucratic hierarchy the worst attitudes of the old Russian political culture. They were authoritarian, secretive, anti-intellectual, xenophobic, and usually anti-Semitic, attributes that meshed perfectly with Stalin's own inclinations. This Stalinist elite – we are speaking of 20–30,000 individuals – was by nature profoundly at odds with the experts and the intellectuals whom the elite needed to make their system function. The instincts of the elite were to hide behind Marxist dogma, pile on controls, and stifle any initiative that might threaten their own status. The dominant class of experts and intellectuals, filling the vacuum left by the artificial elimination of the old bourgeoisie, was itself racked by the purges and hamstrung by the web of political controls that the political elite created. Even the professional military were subject to the scrutiny of the apparatus of political officers, not to mention Stalin's disastrous interference in the high command in the Second World War.

Probably the worst time of all in the subjugation of the creative people by the controllers was the postwar years under Stalin, when Soviet society was rudely disappointed in its hope that victory could bring a relaxation in the control system. De-Stalinization under Khrushchev blew in like a wind of freedom, though the intelligentsia quickly learned that the principle of control remained even if its stringency was relaxed. Yet the effect of Khrushchev's "thaw" was so exhilarating to the younger generation of Soviet intellectuals that it inspired them to wait and hope throughout the disheartening years of the Brezhnev reaction.

Meanwhile, growth in the numbers of people educated enough to appreciate the differences between ideology, reality, and potentiality in Soviet life provided a social foundation for ultimate political change much more solid than Khrushchev had enjoyed. More immediately, these changes stimulated the movement of intellectual dissidents, people whose independent minds had gone into high gear during the thaw and could not be completely shut down during the years of neo-Stalinism that followed.

Beginning with the 1966 trial of the writers Andrei Siniavsky and Yuli Daniel for allowing their banned works to be published in the West, the Brezhnev regime did everything it could short of mass executions to put a lid on the expression of dissident thought. Nevertheless, for the next eight or ten years a band of writers of incredible courage repeatedly defied the authorities, despite arrests, beatings, torture in so-called mental hospitals, and commitment to the Gulag. Everything got worse after the shock dealt the regime by the Prague Spring in 1968. Cumulatively the country suffered serious intellectual and cultural losses, in the inhibition of creativity or in the brain drain of expellees and defectors. But the more the "democratic movement" was pressed down, the wider it spread surreptitiously, above all through the medium of samizdat – i.e., "self-publishing" by the dissemination of retyped carbon copies of dissident literature, the only means of written reproduction not controlled by the police. Even though the Democratic Movement was largely silenced by the end of the Brezhnev era, it had accomplished the vital step of de-legitimizing and morally discrediting the regime. Contributions to the same end were made by the victims of persecution of religious independence (almost everyone save the Orthodox, and some of them as well) and of national minority self-assertion. Brezhnev's enemies won in losing.

There was another, more tolerated, area of independent thinking during the Brezhnev era that was not fully appreciated at the time either at home or abroad. The American political scientist Jerry Hough has referred to "institutional pluralism" in the bureaucracy.[54] This also extended to study and research by academic specialists, whose expertise and sophistication were far outrunning the bounds of ideological conformity. A tacit compromise prevailed: keep your independent thinking within your own field, act only through official channels, and avoid overt political criticism, and you will be allowed a measure of freedom within your enclave. Scholars learned the ways of the West by reading foreign works at the special library of the Institute of Scientific Information in the Social Sciences in order to write the required denunciations of them. When the bars finally came down under Gorbachev, an impressive cadre of young intellectuals was ready to support the reforms of perestroika, and at the same time to become a genuine part of international intellectual life in every area.

*

Several points loom large in appraising the Brezhnev era. The country was run by an anachronistic elite, drawn from the peasant culture, that correctly linked its own privileges to the rigid maintenance of the party dictatorship and the command economy. This elite was committed in the name of socialism to the continuing enhancement of national industrial and military power, yet it denied free play to the talents of the intellectual and managerial class on whom these aims depended. Political legitimation came before policy sense. As Tatiana Zaslavskaya reminds us,

> For a long time the party leadership allocated to specialists the role of mere admiring commentators on decisions that had already been taken . . . . Mediocrity prevailed, while talented experts had to stay in the background, doing minor work just to exist.[55]

"What we are up against most of all," Burlatsky wrote, "is the conservative tradition. Russian political culture has not tolerated pluralism of opinions or freedom to criticise governmental activity."[56] Aganbegian commented,

> In the Soviet Union an unjustifiable gap has opened up between industrial power, science, culture, and the educational level of the population on the one hand, and the level of satisfaction of the material and social needs of the population on the other.[57]

Modernization under the Stalinist and neo-Stalinist aegis reached a point of technical complexity and consumer expectations where "command-administrative" methods could not get the best – or even enough – out of either workers or experts. Meanwhile corruption above and cynical disaffection below undermined the basic premises of social solidarity and discipline. James Millar speaks of "acquisitive socialism" and Brezhnev's "Little Deal" that winked at quasi-legal self-seeking as long as the prerogatives of the bureaucracy were not challenged.[58] The émigré sociologist Vladimir Shlapentokh calls the process "the privatization of Soviet society," an "emotional withdrawal" ever since the 1950s:

The state's gradual loss of authority over all strata of the population [means] that everyone – from minister and first regional secretary to the orderly in a hospital or a sales clerk in a rural shop – will exploit their position for their own personal interests against the interests of the state and official policy.[59]

In Mlynář's mind, "The Brezhnevites were only able to postpone the day of reckoning by plundering their last economic reserves" and achieving "stagnation camouflaged as progress."[60] As Giulietto Chiesa put it, shortly before Gorbachev took over, "This country is just as if it were run by the Mafia."[61]

The impasse became visible even in the published economic indicators, let alone the real ones if they could be established. Western analyses of the Soviet economy well before the advent of Gorbachev made it abundantly clear that the system of central planning with its physical output targets, set prices, and allocations of supplies, had reached a dead end. In the judgement offered by Marshall Goldman in 1983, "The Soviet Union is facing a very serious crisis . . . the result of [its] failure to adapt its economic planning model to meet the country's radically changed economic needs."[62] Shevardnadze confided to Gorbachev during a walk on a Black Sea beach in December 1984, "Everything's rotten. It has to be changed." Gorbachev agreed: "It was impossible to live that way."[63] Sensing the depth of the contradictions besetting the country, he committed himself to resolving them in a bloodless revolution.

4

WAS STALINISM COMMUNIST?

26 January 1934. With great fanfare, the Seventeenth Congress of the All-Union Communist Party of Bolsheviks, the "Congress of Victors," has convened in Moscow to celebrate the achievements of the First Five-Year Plan and the first year of the Second in the Building of Socialism. Joseph Stalin opens the proceedings with a three-hour speech in his typical style, at once boastful and pedantic, to review the advances that the Soviet Union has made during the past five years under his leadership:

> The USSR has become radically transformed and has cast off the integument of backwardness and medievalism. From an agrarian country it has become an industrial country. From a country of small individual agriculture it has become a country of collective, large-scale mechanized agriculture. From an ignorant, illiterate and uncultured country it has become – or rather it is becoming – a literate and cultured country . . . . It goes without saying that this enormous progress could take place only on the basis of the successful building of socialism . . . . The present congress is taking place under the flag of the complete victory of Leninism. . . . The Party today is united as it has never been before.[1]

Not a word in all this about the millions of famine victims who have perished in the preceding two years, or about the additional millions banished to ultimate death in the Gulag. Nor is there a hint of the terror that lies in store for his own followers three years hence, though Stalin warns, "We have defeated the enemies of the Party," i.e. the Trotskyist and Bukharinist opposition groups, "but remnants of their ideology still live in the minds of individual members . . ., their counterrevolutionary program of restoring capitalism in the USSR."[2]

Speeches by the congress delegates resound with unctuous praise of the general secretary. Nikita Khrushchev, participating as a congress delegate for the first time, calls him "our genius chief."[3] Stalin takes particular satisfaction as his former Communist opponents, Grigori

Zinoviev, Lev Kamenev, Nikolai Bukharin, Alexei Rykov, and Mikhail Tomsky, eat humble pie. Says Bukharin, "It is the duty of every member of the Party . . . to unite around Comrade Stalin, as the personal embodiment of the mind and will of the Party, its leader, its chief in matters both theoretical and practical."[4]

In fact, trouble is brewing for Stalin among the stalwarts of his own party machine, who have been shaken by the rigors of collectivization and the catastrophic famine of the previous winter, and now fear the signs of their leader's growing megalomania. His own wife, Nadezhda Allilueva, has committed suicide, reportedly in anguish over these events. Clandestine anti-Stalin platforms have been circulating among members of the Party, some even with the endorsement of Central Committee members. A number of regional party secretaries, led by I. M. Vareikis, a Civil War hero and Central Committee member who is now party chief for the Black Earth agricultural region, have been meeting privately to talk about ways of shunting Stalin aside, perhaps to the position of prime minister or figurehead chief of state. Even Politburo member Sergo Ordzhonikidze and candidate member Anastas Mikoyan have taken part in these discussions. (This doesn't deter Mikoyan from hailing Stalin's "steely firmness and genius wisdom" in his speech to the congress.[5]) The idea of demoting Stalin spreads in corridor conversations at the congress, among delegates who recall Lenin's warning in his secret "Testament" of 1923:

> Stalin is too rude, and this fault, entirely supportable in relations among us Communists, becomes insupportable in the office of general secretary. Therefore, I propose to the comrades to find a way to remove Stalin from that position and appoint to it another man who in all respects differs from Stalin only in superiority – namely, more patient, more loyal, more polite and more attentive to comrades, less capricious, etc.[6]

For the superior man the dissidents at the Seventeenth Congress look to the popular Leningrad party secretary Sergei Kirov, who is reputed to be the leader of a more moderate group in the Politburo. Kirov declines to put his name forward, but reportedly warns Stalin to his face that his rough policies are responsible for this opposition. When the time comes to vote on the official list of members proposed for the new Central Committee (including Khrushchev), nearly 300 of the 1,225 voting delegates cross Stalin's name off the slate of candidates printed on their ballots. The chairman of the vote-counting committee, V. P. Zatonsky, upon discovering this ominous development, apprehensively reports it to Stalin's right-hand man, Politburo member Lazar Kaganovich. Kaganovich immediately consults with Stalin and then orders Zatonsky to get rid of the unfavorable ballots. Zatonsky announces to the congress that Stalin has received only three negative votes, the same as Kirov.[7] Stalin nurses his "hostility and a will to revenge against the whole congress, and of course Kirov personally."[8]

Within a year Kirov will be dead of an assassin's bullet. Within five years the old oppositionists who have tried to make their peace with Stalin will get the death penalty for treason. And in the same span of time more than half of the congress delegates – 1,108, to be exact – will be arrested and in the main liquidated for "counterrevolutionary" actions.[9] Such are the penalties for harboring even the potential of resistance to the will of the man who has made himself the personification of the revolutionary legacy.

*

The system of political power and economic management that Stalin had put in place by 1934 survived long after his death. Tempered lightly, as neo-Stalinism, it persisted until Gorbachev initiated perestroika and democratization. As one authoritative journal put it in the age of glasnost, "The Stalinist model of socialism . . . was in its essence preserved up to our own time, when its historically determined collapse was clearly marked."[10] Thus, Stalinism was the system that Soviet reformers of all stripes were rebelling against in 1985: a monopoly of power in the hands of the chief or chiefs of the party apparatus, backed up by the secret police; a totally state-controlled and centrally planned economic system; comprehensive controls over all aspects of cultural life and public communication; and a suspicious and competitive stance toward the non-Communist world. In short, the Stalinist system was the paragon of totalitarianism.

Totalitarianism is a supercharged word, evoking all the loyalties and fears of the Cold War era and associating the crimes of Stalin with the crimes of Adolf Hitler. For twenty years after Hannah Arendt published *The Origins of Totalitarianism* in 1951,[11] the "totalitarian model" of an all-powerful state shackling every interest in society in pursuit of a utopian goal was the conventional wisdom for most Western thinking about the Soviet Union. The guiding premise in the formulation of the totalitarian model was that the Stalinist system was essentially the same as Hitler's system, an equation that early on in the Cold War served to connect all the fear and loathing of the defunct regime of Hitlerism with the persisting though less understood regime of Stalinism.

Critics of Cold War policies in the West have tried to play down or dismiss the totalitarian model as a propaganda theme, at the cost of understating the truth in the model. If anything, Stalinist totalitarianism, with its economy of barracks socialism and its indiscriminate terror, was more nearly total than the Nazi variety, where bourgeois life and private property remained intact. Considering the magnitude of their crimes, an eminent Soviet historian expressed the opinion not long ago that Stalin was "even worse than Hitler."[12]

If the totalitarian model has any fundamental limitation, it is its ahistorical character. Moshe Lewin finds the model "useless as a conceptual category . . . . It did not recognise any mechanism of change in the Soviet Union and had no use for even a shadow of some historical process."[13] Other than perverse utopianism, the totalitarian model offers no adequate explanation of a totalitarian system (Arendt dwelt mainly on the Nazis in this respect), and it allows for no end to the system apart from a national catastrophe in war, like the fate of the Axis powers in the Second World War. But Yugoslavia and Hungary showed well before the East European upheaval of 1989 that totalitarian regimes could evolve internally into systems that might be considered merely "authoritarian," and Czechoslovakia demonstrated briefly in 1968, like Poland in 1980–81, that if confronted by united popular opposition, a totalitarian state could even be turned into a democratic one. Thus there were ample precedents for the decline and fall of Soviet totalitarianism, and there was no outside enemy to nip the new freedom in the bud.

*

Stalinism always couched itself in the terms of Marxism-Leninism as a source of legitimacy and self-justification. Anti-Communists both Soviet and foreign have usually accepted this identification, often wrathfully. Accordingly, some theoretical clarification is in order.

In the old official view, the Russian Revolution and all that followed were supposed to represent the inevitable working out of the laws of history as formulated by Marx and applied to Russia by Lenin. But most of the Marxian corpus, including *Das Kapital* and related works, was devoted to the analysis of capitalism, and stopped short with the anticipated capitalist crisis and the proletarian revolution. Beyond that, Communist futurology has hung tenuously from a single statement by Marx, in his *Critique of the Gotha Program* of 1875. There he distinguished between "the first phase of communist society as it is when it has just emerged after prolonged birth pangs from capitalist society" with "an unequal right for unequal labour," and "a higher phase of communist society, after . . . all the springs of cooperative wealth flow more abundantly." He therefore concluded, in those words that have rung down through the decades, "Only then can the narrow horizon of bourgeois right be fully left behind and society inscribe on its banners: from each according to his abilities, to each according to his needs."[14]

Lenin confused the picture a bit by designating the "first phase" after the revolution as "socialism" and the "higher phase" as "communism,"[15] whence the untutored assumption, notably among American conservatives, that any legislative measure considered "socialistic" would lead inevitably to the horrors of Stalin-style "communism". To Lenin and his successors, the system they had created to implement the Marxian prognosis was the only legitimate kind of socialism, though in fact the term has been subjected to a myriad of interpretations and variations. The eminent French sociologist Emile Durkheim wrote, "We denote as socialism every doctrine which demands the connection of all economic functions, or of certain among them . . ., to the directing and conscious centres of society."[16] Thus construed, "socialism" permits great differences of degree, kind, and political context. In Durkheim's sense, socialism is an analytical category that can measure the kind and degree of public control envisaged or exerted over economic activity, independently of the kind of political system. Both the Leninist understanding of socialism and the Stalinist practice of it fall within the terms of this definition.

Even "communism" in the ideal Marxian sense fits within Durkheim's definition, as an extreme and utopian variant of socialism. Otherwise the term "communism," unlike "socialism," has no analytic value. As usually employed with a capital C, "Communism" simply denotes the governments and parties subscribing to the Leninist example of violent revolution and one-party dictatorship in the name of Marx. It says nothing about the particular policies of the various movements that have borne the Communist label, let alone any correspondence with the theoretical "communist" ideal.

No "Communist" government (with the temporary exception of Mao Tse-tung's China between the "Great Leap Forward" of 1958 and the "Cultural Revolution" of 1966–69) has ever claimed to have gone beyond the stage of "socialism," based on payment to individuals for individual work done. The most that Stalin claimed, when he promulgated the Constitution of 1936, was to have abolished "exploiting classes" and thereby to have achieved "the complete victory of the socialist system," setting the USSR on "the right road to communism."[17] Regimes called "Communist" by the West never designated themselves as more than "socialist countries," though their ruling parties usually bore the name "Communist." Brezhnev's ideologists invented the term "developed socialism" to refer to the indefinite stage of preparing for the "transition to communism."[18] (Incidentally, the term "Stalinism" was a Western coinage never used under that system, though up to 1953 alleged achievements such as the constitution were often labeled "Stalinist" [*stalinskii*].)

So long and so consistently was the Stalinist system officially identified with "socialism" as its only legitimate expression, that the new East European regimes and the Soviet successor republics have accepted this equivalence, and consequently reject the Marxian future completely. More common in the Soviet Union in Gorbachev's time as well as among the Western Left was the contention that Stalinism was not the realization of Marx's socialism but a perversion or betrayal of it. Unfortunately, both of these views are too simplistic to advance understanding of the Stalinist system. Stalin's regime in the economy clearly fit Durkheim's definition of socialism as social direction of economic functions, and yet it assumed a form that horrified other socialists. The problem that needs to be worked out historically, therefore, is how the Stalinist version of socialism actually took shape and how it acquired the characteristics that have turned practically everyone in the formerly Communist world against it. This task requires us, first of all, to dispel the ideological clouds surrounding the notions of "socialism" and "communism" and the place of Stalinism in these formulae. Then we can try to assess more clearly Stalin's climb to power and the use he made of it.

*

The greatest single source of confusion about Stalin is the context of Marxist-Leninist ideology in which he operated. There are two issues here. One is whether there is any reality to the Marxian scheme of history, which has capitalist society inevitably generating socialism and setting up the future transition to ideal communism. The other question is whether Stalin was driven like his revolutionary predecessors by ideological devotion to the mission of making this perhaps fanciful prognosis come true, by whatever means seemed necessary.

Judging the validity of the Marxian scheme of history is complicated by a deep though usually unacknowledged inconsistency within it. This is the contradiction between the deterministic view of society's evolution as driven by the class struggle and the forces of production, and the voluntarist exhortation to organize and struggle for the triumph of socialism and communism that is supposed to be inevitable.[19] Marxism in this messianic reading had a powerful psychological attraction for Russian revolutionaries before 1917, urging the fight to the death against capitalism and at the same time guaranteeing victory.

Now that the Stalinist system has collapsed in the Soviet Union and Eastern Europe, few people would try to maintain this contradictory philosophy. Nevertheless, it was the official line of the Stalinist regime for more than half a century (echoed negatively by the most ardent anti-Communists) to claim that revolutionary struggle had indeed achieved the socialism predicted by Marx and had opened the path to the transition to ideal communism. The Chinese Communist regime still professes to have realized the socialism of the Marxist scheme, but Chinese Marxism has always been more openly voluntaristic about overcoming limiting conditions by revolutionary force.

If we were to try to formulate the real though implicit understanding of Marxism held by Lenin and his followers, as against their explicit but spurious claims, it would be a statement of historical possibility rather than inevitability. The historical dialectic, in this interpretation, laid down the one possible path that a society's development could take, but did not of itself guarantee movement along that path. Conscious revolutionaries would have to take willful action to make the anticipated transition to socialism and communism take place. "If we . . . let the present moment pass, we shall *ruin* the revolution," Lenin wrote in the heat of preparations for revolt in October 1917.[20] "History will not forgive revolutionists for procrastinating when they could be victorious today (and will certainly be victorious today), while they risk losing much tomorrow, in fact risk losing everything."[21] *If and only if* you organize, struggle, and grasp the strategic moment for the violent seizure of power, the implicit theory would say, and *if* your society has achieved the necessary prerequisites, *then* you can move your society along the path to socialism and communism. This shining future would warrant resort to any means of force and deceit to bring it about: the end justifies the means – though the Bolsheviks scarcely foresaw the depths of terror to which events would ultimately bring them. But never mind: revolutionary means, no matter how violent, would assuredly bring about the expected heaven on earth, because the Marxian laws of history allowed no other outcome.

Marxists generally left the details of socialism and communism for history to implement. Other than *ad hoc* and expedient tactics, often for the sake of survival, Lenin and his followers had little sense of deliberately legislating the particulars of either stage. Furthermore, none of the implicit reasoning suggested here about the conditional character of revolutionary victory was explicitly stated and accepted. Official Communist thinking always remained wedded to the contradictory propositions of determinism and voluntarism, of inevitability and struggle.

A path of escape from this quandary for those who still see some merit in the deterministic Marxian analysis is to argue that the Russian Revolution, breaking out before capitalism had established in Russia the material prerequisites for socialism according to Marx, could not have been the revolution that Marx predicted, despite being represented by the Marxist vocabulary. This is more or less the Menshevik view, expressed also by many present-day Russian thinkers who find that the revolutionary attempt at socialism was distorted beyond recognition – i.e., into Stalinism – by the conditions of Russia's backwardness.[22] According to this reasoning, socialism in the prerevolutionary sense of the ideal was not only not inevitable in early twentieth-century Russia, it was not possible under the given circumstances of time and place. In the

81

meantime, in the countries of advanced industrial capitalism, there has been no proletarian revolution at all (except under Soviet occupation), but at most only trade-unionist and welfare-state reformism.

Oddly enough, Lenin was quite right about the West when he wrote in 1902 (contrary to Marx), "The history of all countries shows that the working class, exclusively by its own effort, is able to develop only trade union consciousness."[23] The only native revolutionary movements to succeed in industrially advanced societies have been those of the radical Right. One can indeed observe a weakening of the classical entrepreneurial class, but the successor to its dominant role is not the working class; under both Western-style capitalism and Soviet-style socialism the ultimate winner is the meritocracy of managers and experts. Marxism was simply wrong about a workers' revolution, and even if Marxism were right, Stalinism would not have fit it. Consequently, there can be no real substance to Stalinist (or anti-Stalinist) claims that the Soviet regime was the expression of the Marxian laws of history, and that the working class had come to power to build "socialism" and prepare for the transition to "communism." This particular aspect of Marxism, a utopian dream in any case, was doubly misplaced in the Russia of 1917.

*

Did the Communists, believing that their revolution was Marx's, proceed to do what they did because of their beliefs? Did they really think that they were carrying out the mission of achieving socialism despite Russia's backwardness, and moving on to communism according to Marx? There was indeed a powerful core of faith among the Communists in the early years of the Soviet regime, a conviction that they were creating a new society with new communitarian values to replace the rotten old bourgeois ethic. But victory or the settling of old scores may become ends in themselves. One cannot simply assume that actions are motivated by stated beliefs, and overlook the possibility that people, especially fanatics, may choose their beliefs to justify the motives that already impel them to behave as they do.

The Bolsheviks' simultaneous adherence to Marxism and to their own revolutionary role in a country unprepared for the Marxian scenario was not logical but it was psychological: theory supported impulse. However, their psychological commitment to Marxism, with its promise of world revolutionary victory, set up an unresolvable conflict between Marxist belief and Russian circumstances. In such a situation people may go to great lengths to avoid the cognitive dissonance between legitimizing beliefs and actual outcomes. This is one of the keys to Stalin's behavior.

For Stalin, the relationship between ideology and power eventually came to be completely reversed. Instead of a source of guidance, ideology was reduced to a mere instrument, bent to the achievement, preservation, and extension of power. "The doctrine . . . distinguishing itself in both versatility and cruelty," assert the émigré historians Mikhail Heller and Alexander Nekrich, "could change instantaneously, switching to its antitheses, but in the interval between the changes it remained immobile . . ., expressed only in the exact words of the Leader."[24] The famous Hungarian Marxist György Lukács, who finally came to his senses after the Twentieth Party Congress, wrote,

> Stalin's unscrupulousness in this matter reached the point of altering the theory itself if necessary . . . . Principles were simplified and vulgarized according to the exigencies . . . of practice . . . . Because Stalin wanted to maintain at any cost a continuity "in quotation marks" with Lenin's work, not only facts but Leninist texts were distorted. For him, in the name of *partiinost*, agitation is primary. Its needs determine . . . what science must say and how it must say it.[25]

Eventually Mikhail Gorbachev made this point explicit himself:

> In the past, the Party recognized only Marxism-Leninism as the source of its inspiration, and that teaching itself was distorted to the utmost to suit the pragmatic purposes of the day and became a collection of canonical texts.[26]

Corresponding to the formula that Marx and Engels proposed for the role of free-enterprise doctrine under capitalism, Marxism-Leninism thus became the ideological "false consciousness" of the Stalinist system.[27]

Did Stalin therefore become self-consciously cynical about the ideology? Or was he so consumed by his own righteousness that he had to persuade himself of the ideological correctness of his every move? The record as we know it cannot answer this question, but psychological theory suggests that Stalin's fury toward his ideological critics reflected his own need to believe, even as he was gutting the basic elements of that belief.

The inevitable discrepancy between the Marxist ideal and Soviet reality does not mean that the ultimate Stalinist system was not socialist. But it was not the product of the laws of history as Marx propounded them, and it was not the kind of socialism that Marx and his immediate followers had in mind. This is why critics from Trotsky to Khrushchev who have tried to hold onto their Marxism have had such a difficult time accounting for Stalin and Stalinism, except as the usurpation of the Revolution and the whole dialectic of history by a criminal adventurer.

Stalinist socialism was a hierarchical, centralized, bureaucratic system of militarized, barracks socialism. It resulted from a combination of revolutionary zeal, Russian tradition and backwardness, and choices by the leader at a vulnerable point (the late 1920s) in the postrevolutionary development of the country. The primary purposes to which this form of socialism was devoted under Stalin and his immediate successors were system maintenance and the enhancement of national power. In no real sense was this kind of socialism moving toward "communism" as the old theoretical ideal of a classless, stateless, moneyless society. With the partial exception of Khrushchev, Stalin and his successors had no intention of trying to move in that direction. Throughout the Brezhnev era, the "transition to communism" remained an empty slogan whose realization was constantly put off into the future – like the horizon, an imaginary line that recedes as you approach it.

*

The Stalin phenomenon is necessarily at the center of any effort to understand the decline and fall of communism since 1985. While there are wide differences in interpreting Stalin, there is no disagreement that his will decisively shaped the system that prevailed in the Soviet Union over most of its history. Beyond this there are fundamental disputes over the reasons for Stalin's rise, over his connection with his revolutionary forebears, and over the steps needed to wash away the residue of his influence in Soviet society.

Joseph Stalin had to work long and hard to reach the exalted position in which he was confirmed by the Seventeenth Party Congress. He was a most improbable candidate for the role that history had in store for him. A revolutionary from age 17, even before he dropped out of the Orthodox seminary in Tiflis (now Tbilisi), and a Bolshevik from the time of the Russian Marxist split in 1903, this native of Georgia in Transcaucasia (who always spoke Russian with a foreign accent) appears to have been driven by ambition and vindictiveness as much as by ideology. His biographer Robert Tucker notes the early evidence of his "urge for personal power" and "intolerance of dissenting opinions," and quotes a disciplinary report in the seminary, "Djugashvili is rude and disrespectful toward persons in authority."[28]

Dzhugashvili-Stalin would never have got into the position to bid for supreme power had it not been for Lenin's patronage. Lenin recognized his talent for underground conspiracy and his skill as a propagandist, and co-opted him into the Bolshevik Party leadership in 1912. In 1917 he was recognized as one of the top leaders of the Party. He served as co-editor of the party newspaper, and chaired the Bolshevik party congress held in August 1917 while Lenin was in hiding. Though his role in the

October Revolution was modest, he became a key organizer and trouble-shooter for the new Soviet government, unwaveringly serving Lenin and accumulating grudges against the other leading Bolsheviks. He was commissar of nationalities, commissar of the Workers' and Peasants' Inspection, an army group commissar in the Civil War, and a member of the Politburo from its beginning as a permanent body in 1919. He led the intra-party struggle on behalf of Lenin against the Trotskyists and the Workers' Opposition in 1920–21, and won control of the party organiz-ation in 1921 when the Trotskyist party secretaries (Nikolai Krestinsky, Yevgeny Preobrazhensky, and Leonid Serebriakov) were replaced by his own allies (Molotov, Yemelian Yaroslavsky, and V. M. Mikhailov). At Lenin's behest, he took direct charge of the party apparatus as general secretary in 1922.

Thenceforth Stalin worked assiduously to fashion the machinery of personal dominance over the Party by means of the circular flow of power, down through the hierarchy of party secretaries whose appoint-ments he controlled, and up through the layers of party committees and conferences managed by those same secretaries. Power flowed rapidly around the circle during the months of Lenin's final illness, in spite of the crippled leader's belated reconsiderations about Stalin in his "Testa-ment." These reservations unfortunately remained unknown to most party leaders until too late, and meanwhile Stalin had lent his strength to the Politburo majority – Zinoviev, Kamenev, Rykov, Tomsky – to crush the challenge raised by Trotsky and his supporters late in 1923.

After Lenin died in January 1924, Stalin maneuvered shrewdly to displace all the rest of Lenin's original lieutenants and make himself the unchallenged leader of the Party and the country. In 1925 he isolated Zinoviev and Kamenev, and in 1926–27, in alliance with Bukharin, Rykov, and Tomsky, he defeated the combined opposition of Trotsky, Zinoviev, and Kamenev, and had them expelled from the Party. Then, in 1928–29 he turned against the Bukharin group, denounced them as a "right deviation," packed the Central Committee and the Politburo with his own appointees, and thereby consummated the circular flow of power.

Thus did the rude and rebellious Georgian youth become dictator over one-sixth of the world's land area, and put every revolutionary and every revolutionary idea at his mercy. For Stalin, issues and doctrines were secondary to the pursuit of power and the destruction of his former colleagues. As Bukharin confided to Kamenev in 1928 when Stalin was closing in on the Right Opposition, "He is an unprincipled intriguer, who subordinates everything to the preservation of his own power. He changes his theory according to whom he needs to get rid of."[29]

Bukharin recognized here a crucial feature of Stalinism that has been misunderstood by the majority of Western commentators and even by many Soviet writers in the age of glasnost – namely, the peculiar relationship of Stalinism to Marxist-Leninist doctrine. The official line from the 1920s to the 1980s was, of course, that Soviet Russia was the true embodiment of the Marxian futurology, and that the self-styled dictatorship of the proletariat was the realization of the laws of history brought about by the heroic struggles of the Communist Party. Lenin, to his credit, tried in the last two years of his life to rethink Russian reality and adapt his objectives to the country's backwardness. This was the essence of the New Economic Policy, a long-term approach to prepare gradually the cultural and economic prerequisites of socialism.

Stalin, pursuing his personal obsessions, was never capable of such reflection. When he reached the highest level of leadership responsibility after Lenin's death, at a time of struggle against the more brilliant and supple Marxist minds of the Left Opposition, he felt compelled to find security in doctrinal authority, appropriately adapted to his own political needs. This was the function of his famous "theory of socialism in one country," which he contrived in order to disarm the Opposition's embarrassing suggestion that the NEP regime could not be properly socialist in the absence of international revolution. On the basis of one old quotation from Lenin, taken out of context, Stalin insisted that socialism could nevertheless be "built" in Russia alone. Lenin had written in 1915, "Unevenness of economic and political development is an unconditional law of capitalism. From here it follows that the victory of socialism is possible at first in a few capitalist countries or even in one taken separately."[30] Though Lenin had in mind only the most advanced capitalist countries,[31] Stalin calmly added his own words to the Lenin quote: "the victory of socialism in one country, even if that country is less developed in the capitalist sense."[32]

The significance of this theological hair-splitting had nothing really to do with the stability of the Soviet government or a less revolutionary foreign policy, as conventional history has assumed. Instead, the real importance of "socialism in one country" was to establish the method and machinery of doctrinal reinterpretation. It shows how Stalin went about arranging a semblance of ideological legitimation for the politics of the moment, imposing convenient reinterpretations by party authority as though they were the sole, original meaning of the doctrine. Then any critic's appeal to an earlier sense of Marxism could be crushed by party authority on the grounds, early on, of "petty-bourgeois deviation" or, ultimately, of "counterrevolutionary wrecking." Marxism became the least free of all subjects for thought. With his ideological flanks thus guarded, Stalin liberated himself from all doctrinal constraints in fashioning his future policies, while he retained the useful smokescreen of Marxist language for propaganda purposes both at home and abroad.

No longer did doctrine set the direction of policy; the immediate needs of policy determined the meaning that would be imputed to doctrine.

*

Until 1927 Stalin worked with the Bukharin group to defend the NEP and the gradualist approach to socialism, against the complaints of the Trotskyists that the government was too lenient towards the "petty-bourgeois" peasantry and neglectful of the industrial workers. At the same time he condemned the Opposition's call for "workers' democracy" as a manifestation of "factionalism" and a threat to the Leninist unity of the Party, and used the struggle against them to tighten the hold of the party apparatus over the membership as a whole. Then, in 1928, he shamelessly adopted the slogans of the Left Opposition, without attribution, and carried them to an extreme never envisaged by their authors as he implemented the First Five-Year Plan of forced industrialization along with the violent collectivization of the peasants.

In all probability the NEP could not have gone on indefinitely. The Czech historian Michal Reiman has analyzed in depth the social and economic crisis confronting the Communist regime as it tried to move ahead economically while facing the great peasant majority.[33] Alec Nove of the University of Glasgow has argued persuasively of the political impossibility, for anyone who subscribed minimally to the Communist program and wanted to keep the Party in power, of continuing the NEP very long.[34] These conclusions reflect the "Preobrazhensky dilemma" defined by the late Alexander Erlich in his ground-breaking book on the industrialization debate of the 1920s – the Communist regime appeared to have the choice of "mortal illness" if it continued the gradualist Bukharin line, or "sudden death on the operating table" if it adopted the Left Opposition position of rapid, state-financed industrialization.[35]

At bottom the impasse of the NEP stemmed from the original anomaly of the Communist regime: the lack of a sufficient economic foundation for socialism as it had been conceived up to 1917. Industralization and modernization were prerequisites for the affluent egalitarianism of the Marxist ideal. But they could only be accomplished (a) by a favored class of trained experts and managers together with material incentives for the work force; and (b) with a massive infusion of capital that could only come from squeezing surplus value out of the Soviet Union's own people as long as ideology excluded foreign investment.

If the demise of the NEP was a near certainty, the manner of its termination was not. The Bukharinists offered a programme of gradually stepping up the tempo of industrialization and drawing the peasants voluntarily into a more socialized form of economy through cooperatives. This was the basis of the resolutions on the Five-Year Plan and on the peasantry that they put through the Fifteenth Party Congress in December 1927. But they were afraid to go faster. This fear Stalin cleverly prepared to take advantage of.

The circumstances of personal ambition and internecine struggle among the Communist leaders in the 1920s are extremely important in understanding the formation of the Stalinist system in the "revolution from above" of 1928 to 1934. The point of departure was the last phase of Stalin's struggle to oust Lenin's old lieutenants from power, when, after crushing the Left Opposition of Trotsky and Zinoviev, he turned against his former colleagues of the NEP leadership, Bukharin, Rykov, and Tomsky. It was in the fight with these rivals that Stalin became committed to the policies of forced collectivization, intensive industrialization, and totalitarian political and cultural controls that define the Stalin Revolution.

Stalin's immediate purpose in 1928 was to drive Bukharin's group into a stance of open protest where they could then be denounced as a "right deviation." These people, Stalin's allies throughout the struggle with the Left from 1923 to 1927, were a much more formidable adversary, well entrenched in the party organization and identified with a popular policy. Stalin undertook to provoke them into open disagreement so that, like the Left Opposition, they could be condemned for factionalism. One can track these manoeuvres, month by month, as Bukharin's group tried to compromise with Stalin in order not to look like deviators, and as Stalin raised his sights for industrialization and collectivization to a tempo that the Bukharinists, fearing a peasant uprising, would be compelled to oppose. By early 1929 the Bukharinists were calling Stalin's new course a policy of "military-feudal exploitation" and "promoting bureaucracy."[36] Events were to show that the Bukharinists overestimated the peasants' political threat to the regime, while Stalin underestimated their potential resistance to forced collectivization.

Late in 1928, to hasten things along, Stalin had the Supreme Economic Council (i.e., the industrial commissariat, headed by his man Valerian Kuibyshev) short-circuit the more cautious and scientific Gosplan by drawing up exceedingly ambitious, high-tempo versions of the plan, which Bukharin was forced to oppose openly as unattainable.[37] Such warnings were beside the point. Stalin was committed, and Bukharin and his friends had exposed themselves sufficiently to be labeled a "right deviation." They were removed one by one from all their high offices, while Stalin went ahead with the program he had initially adopted to flush his opponents out into the open. Thus his new policies became a permanent commitment, whether they were workable or not.

In April 1929, after purging the cautious economists of Gosplan, Stalin had the Party give its stamp of approval to the most ambitious version of the Five-Year Plan (actually backdated to October 1928!) and to massive collectivization of the peasants. He conjured up a new wave of class-war emotion by staging a series of show trials of alleged wreckers and saboteurs among the "bourgeois specialists" – ironically, just when they were most needed for the industrialization drive. First came the Shakhty trial in 1928 of mining engineers from the coal town of that name in the Donets Basin. This was followed by the "Industrial Party" trial of 1930, the trial of Menshevik economists in 1931, and the "Metro-Vickers" trial of British engineers in 1933.

Simultaneously with this harassment of engineering talent, the Party launched an offensive on the cultural front, to root the genuine professionals out of all positions of influence on the ground of sympathy with the "right deviation," and to replace them with party hacks who mouthed the correct phrases about class war in their respective sectors. "It is essential to develop to a significantly broader degree work in instilling the methodology of Marx, Engels, and Lenin in the various fields of specialized knowledge," resolved an academic conference called for this purpose. "The proletarian revolution, after shaking up old notions and prejudices among the broad masses, puts forth the task of working out a new world view among the broadest strata of the working class."[38] "Partiinost" – party spirit – became the ultimate criterion of truth and value in any intellectual endeavor.

The policies that Stalin thus set in motion in the late 1920s and early 1930s appeared in many contemporary eyes to be a genuine revival of the revolutionary Bolshevik spirit of 1917 and the Civil War. Robert Tucker has written of the "culture of War Communism" that lived on in the minds of Stalin's party workers in the 1920s and blossomed forth again in the Stalin Revolution.[39] Many of Trotsky's supporters perceived Stalin's new line as more or less a vindication of their own polemics with the NEP leadership. Sooner or later they "capitulated," as the expression went, and received new jobs for the time being in the Stalin administration. Stalin made a point of their conversion in his address to the Seventeenth Party Congress. But Trotsky himself, after taking some initial satisfaction at the discomfiture of the Bukharinists, rejected Stalin's methods. He called the Stalin regime a "bureaucratic deformation" of the workers' state and "a dress rehersal for Bonapartism."[40]

*

Stalinist economic planning such as was practiced in the Soviet Union beginning in the late 1920s, and in Eastern Europe since the late 1940s, was far from being the only possible form of central planning activity. Its political origins gave it a very peculiar form. First of all, it was implemented not under conditions of careful scientific judgement, but in the course of an emotional political struggle against Stalin's Trotskyist and

Bukharinist opponents. As the radical reformer Alexander Tsipko has asserted, "Stalin's general policy was not backed by calculations of any sort."[41] It was not worked out in an atmosphere of open inquiry and rational experiment, an atmosphere of glasnost, but under conditions of conspiratorial secrecy and anti-sabotage propaganda. Finally, it did not take shape as a rational assessment and allocation of the country's human and material resources, but as a system of commands and targets, decreed in a military manner, with sanctions of treason, not just bankruptcy, for economic failure anywhere along the line. Yuri Andropov made the revealing comment during his brief tenure as general secretary,

> We have not yet properly studied the society in which we live and work and have not fully disclosed its inherent laws, especially its economic laws. Therefore, we sometimes are compelled to act empirically, so to speak, using the highly irrational trial-and-error method.[42]

During the 1920s there was a serious effort in the Soviet Union to develop a scientific system of economic planning, particularly by former Menshevik economists working for Gosplan. This work was the initial basis of the five-year plan concept adopted by the Communist Party in 1927. But during the next two years, in the course of his struggle against the moderate Bukharin group, Stalin tore up the scientific plan and ordered his own wild targets. Western retrospective analysis has shown that Stalin's version of planning was not only unattainable but positively detrimental, because of the haste, waste, bottlenecks, and shortages that it entailed.[43] Since Stalin's plans were always formulated in terms of the physical quantity of output, both quality and efficiency suffered. Bureaucracy impeded the transfer of technological innovation from the research laboratory (or from abroad) to the factory floor. Because of the refusal to figure interest on capital in the plan allocations, capital was wastefully committed to huge construction projects that tied up the money for years.

The priorities as well as the methods of the Soviet planning system reflect an implicit set of values embedded in the Stalinist dictatorship. This was, in a word, militarization: the imperatives of maintaining national military power; the mentality of struggle against both external and internal enemies; the military mode of enforced discipline and command from the center; and a broad disdain for the everyday areas of consumer goods, services, and entertainment (except as these were to be enjoyed in secret by the privileged elite, or used to impress foreigners). Equating "socialism" and the transition to "communism" with industrial progress and national power, Stalin and his successors used state control of the economy to push the development of heavy industry and the extraction of natural resources at all cost. Steel was virtually deified (not without a psychic connection to the dictator's revolutionary pseudonym); excess steel plants became the Soviet equivalent of pyramid-building. Whenever things got tight, resources would be shunted to the favored heavy industrial enterprises, in effect modifying the plan in midstream, to the greater detriment of the consumer sector (and often the physical purging of its managers for "sabotage"). Throughout, the Stalinist economy was permeated with military models of thought – in its organization, in its goals, in the language and psychology of the many campaigns to boost production, and in the spirit of warfare against both class enemies and potential foreign foes.

At the same time, those sectors of the economy addressing the direct needs of consumers – agriculture, consumer goods and handicrafts, consumer services, retail trade – were systematically starved when the party command allocated resources. If these sectors, largely in the hands of private farmers and independent proprietors until the Stalin Revolution, had been left alone by the command economy, they could have gone on more or less meeting the needs of consumers even if not in a very modern or efficient way. Such enterprises were not "capitalist" in any meaningful sense of the word, but precapitalist, or "petty-bourgeois" in the Marxian terminology. In Poland and Yugoslavia the postwar Communist regimes allowed the precapitalist sectors to survive, though hobbled by restrictive laws. In the Soviet Union and elsewhere in Eastern Europe they were forcibly nationalized or collectivized, even though the natural process of capitalist concentration foreseen by Marx had not yet taken place. Consequently, the inappropriate nationalization or collectivization of the individualist, consumer-serving sectors had an absolutely negative, retrogressive effect on each country's ability to sustain its consumer standard of living. This effect was only worsened by the fact that the central command system into which the consumer-oriented sectors were incorporated was guided by military and heavy industry priorities, and never gave the consumer sectors an opportunity to meet the human needs of the population.

The overall result of the Stalinist style of planning was to achieve certain priority goals, but at great cost, with chronic shortages throughout the consumer sector and even in some industrial commodities. The planners could not think of everything, and managers at the enterprise level had little scope for initiative. Nevertheless, with the limited exception of the peasant markets, the central authorities would not relinquish control of any sector of the economy, however mundane, to allow individual enterprise to respond to everyday needs. Paraphrasing the Marxists ironically, the economist Michael Ellman calls the system "production for plan rather than use."[44] Whatever the logic of socialized administration of large-scale enterprise, the Communist assault on individual proprietors in trade, services, handicrafts, and agriculture was deeply and enduringly counterproductive. The whole economic effort was enshrouded in secrecy and propaganda, while consumers and industrial managers alike turned to the black market, barter deals, and outright bribery to secure their essential needs. Thus the phenomenon of the second economy, "*na levo*" (literally, "on the left"), was built into the Stalinist version of the planned economy, while measures of plan fulfillment were inflated by false reporting or faulty methodology at every level from the enterprise to the Central Statistical Administration.

In sum, the Stalinist "planned" economy was overcentralized, too far-reaching, neglectful of consumers, political and military rather than economic in its inspiration, and undermined by secrecy, falsification, and corruption. Soviet Russia moved on into the second half of the twentieth century with an economic system devised by Stalin more to win his political wars than to rationally advance the country's well-being. Even so, total industrial output, according to Western corrections of Soviet figures, expanded perhaps twenty times from 1917 to the 1980s.[45]

*

The Stalin Revolution falls fairly clearly into two periods, each of which contributed essential features to the subsequent Stalinist system. In its first phase, from 1928 to 1931 or 1932, Stalin laid down the economic foundations of his system – collectivization of the peasants, abandonment of the NEP in favor of military-style command over the economy, re-nationalization of small enterprise (the "Nepmen"), and the shackling of the trade unions. These policies were paralleled by the imposition of comprehensive party authority in cultural and intellectual life through the dictates of extreme Marxists in each field.

It soon became clear that revolutionary commands and exhortation would not suffice to get the work done. In consequence, acting between 1931 and 1936 through the expanded machinery of party control, Stalin authorized drastic changes in policy in one area after another. Industrial policy shifted to wage and salary incentives, which Stalin justified by amending the meaning of equality under socialism: "Equalization . . . has nothing in common with Marxism, with Leninism . . . . Every Leninist knows (that is, if he is a real Leninist) that equalization in the sphere of requirements and individual life is a piece of reactionary petty-bourgeois absurdity."[46] In the same speech Stalin dismissed the doctrine of the "withering away of the state," and soon afterwards the school of revolutionary law associated with Yevgeny Pashukanis was purged and replaced with Andrei Vyshinsky's ostensibly conventional legal doctrine. The peasants, decimated by forcible collectivization, dekulak-ization, and the artificial famine of 1932–33, were conceded the right to cultivate private garden plots, though they were denied the internal passports required for free movement. For all practical purposes they became serfs of the state, as many had literally been before 1861.

Stalin's changes in the cultural line after 1931 were very clear and often quite abrupt, though they have been neglected or misunderstood in most subsequent retrospectives on Stalinism.[47] Beginning with education in 1931 and literature in 1932, he purged the party figures who had been in charge during the first phase of his revolution. He denounced experimental ideas as un-Marxist, and caused the most conservative and conventional standards to be instituted under the Marxist label. This was the pattern in all artistic fields, according to the formula of Socialist Realism, "national in form, socialist in content," but more accurately, petty-bourgeois kitsch in form, nationalist-propagandist in content. The change is still directly visible in architecture: compare the clean modernist lines of the Gosplan building in Moscow, built in the 1920s, and the wedding-cake style of Moscow University, built in the 1940s. Comparable twists and turns were imposed in the natural sciences, though less consistently and usually later. Along with taboos on Einstein's theory of relativity and Freud's theory of the unconscious, the best-known case of political interference in science was the imposition of pseudo-Marxist nonsense by the quack Trofim Lysenko in the field of genetics, not relieved until 1950. (Lysenko enjoyed a temporary but less authoritative revival under Khrushchev.) Stalin turned history writing around to glorify the national past of the Russian empire, in consonance with his new patriotic propaganda line (coinciding with his attempt to form alliances with the democracies against the Fascist powers), and he resumed the Tsarist programme of Russifying the cultures of the non-Russian minorities. One recalls Lenin's comment about the "Great-Russian chauvinism of russified non-Russians," and the advent of other super-nationalistic dictators from peripheral places, Corsica or Austria.

Taken as a whole, Stalin's steps of 1931–36 added up to a veritable counterrevolution in Soviet cultural life, undoing everything of substance that the cultural revolution of 1928–1931 had attempted. What remained of the first phase in Stalin's cultural policy was the new party controls and the principle of the Party's last word. Only the anti-religious line remained unchanged, and this was toned down as regards the Orthodox Church to get its patriotic support during the Second World War.

Social theory and policy tracked with the turn to traditionalism in culture. The whole modern philosophy of environmental explanation of human behavior and misbehavior gave way to doctrines of individual responsibility and individual evil. Hence the whole range of policy shifts in this spirit, from incentives in the factory and grading in the school to vindictive penology and the wholesale purge of "enemies of the people," all in the name of Marxism-Leninism. To strengthen the family as the basic unit of responsibility, divorce was made difficult and abortion illegal, even though urbanization driven by the five-year plans far outpaced the volume of housing construction needed to meet the essential physical needs of family life. The "New Soviet Man" of Stalin's propaganda was not the raging revolutionary automaton often imagined on the outside, but only dutiful, disciplined, and diligent, a Communist embodiment of the Boy Scout Oath and the Protestant Ethic that was rarely achieved in any case.

The kind of social system fashioned by Stalin in the 1930s, far from being a realization of the Marxist future, had more in common with pre-Emancipation Russia. It was politically autocratic, centralized, and bureaucratic; socially stratified and rank-conscious; economically enserfed; and culturally conservative. Along with his claim to have realized the classless society Stalin abolished the "party maximum" limiting the earnings of party members. He abandoned the preference for proletarians in education and party membership, thereby helping the new privileged officialdom to pass their status on to their children. Symbolic steps taken just before or during the Second World War, such as the revival of military ranks and insignia, the new national anthem, the recognition of "heroine mothers of the Soviet Union" who bore more than ten children, and renaming commissariats as ministries, garnished the new social pyramid. Ideological formulas aside, one can observe a progressive convergence of Stalin's totalitarianism with that of his contemporaries among the Fascist dictators.

Stalin's turn to the traditional in cultural and social policy helps set the context for the most horrible and inexplicable event of the entire Stalin era, the Great Purge or Yezhovshchina of 1937–38. Beginning with roundups of the alleged culprits in the murder of Kirov, Stalin set in motion the ever-widening circle of denunciations, arrests, trials, and executions that established his regime as a new pinnacle in the history of terroristic despotism. Not confining himself to the humiliation and liquidation of his opponents of the 1920s, Stalin even turned against the people who had staffed his apparatus and implemented his own policies. These individuals were not publicly tried, but instead were unceremoniously shot or consigned to near-certain death in the Gulag. Estimates vary, but somewhere between one and four million people were arrested, the majority perishing. The higher the rank, the more intensive the purging, sparing only Stalin's cronies in the Politburo. In this manner Stalin swept away almost everyone who had contributed to the Revolution of 1917 or to his own revolution from above. Having redesigned the system, he now restaffed it with his own creatures, almost all under the age of 35.

Seen in the context of Stalin's social and cultural policy reversals, the Great Purge was a true counterrevolution, albeit under revolutionary colors. Stalin killed more Communists than all the world's Fascist dictators put together. The *nomenklatura*, renovated and restaffed, became the new privileged ruling class, and Marxism-Leninism as interpreted by Stalin became the ideological "false consciousness" to legitimize the new social order.

*

Could Stalin, then, have been the natural successor to Lenin, realizing the full implications of Leninism, for better or for worse (and despite Lenin's personal reservations)? Or was he a traitor to the cause who merely covered himself with the outer garments of Leninism? Among most writers today, Western, émigré, or ex-Soviet, the first proposition is the answer: Stalinism was the horrible end product, the "utopia in power," resulting from an attempt, conceived by Marx and launched by Lenin, to create the New Man and the perfect society by force and violence.[48] In the hypothesis that "Stalinism was the natural and logical outcome of the Revolution and the socialist idea," Alexander Yakovlev found "the main watershed in the political, ideological, and overall intellectual struggle – the struggle between faith in the ability of man and society to organize their life on a worthy and just basis, and the denial of that faith."[49]

One of the hardest-hitting of such denials came from Alexander Tsipko:

Stalin and his works . . . were the progeny of a revolutionary movement that began long before Stalin assumed power . . . . Socialism is precisely that historically unique society that is consciously built, on the basis of a theoretical plan. And it is already clear that the defects in the structure are not just due to Stalin's departure from the original blueprint . . . but they also represent departures of theoretical thinking from life.[50]

The whole tragic story is thus carried back to the original sin of utopian thinking about the rational perfectibility of man, a sort of heresy that antedates Marx. Some writers trace this alleged wrong-headedness all the way back to the philosophers of the eighteenth-century Enlightenment, who are thought to have laid the intellectual foundations for "totalitarian democracy."[51]

Apart from its negative view of the outcome, this line of argument squares fully with the old Stalinist party line: Lenin and Stalin were simply realizing the dictatorship of the proletariat and the transition to the ultimate communist society that Marx's theory of history held to be matters of scientific inevitability. In both the negative and positive versions of this determinism of ideas, Marxists who disagreed with Lenin are dismissed as incomplete Marxists, and Leninists who resisted Stalin are impure Leninists. Stalin is thus credited with being the direct, logical, and exclusive consequence of the aspiration to a revolutionary transformation of society. Otto Latsis, one of the more reflective of recent Soviet writers, comments on these views: "Just one sign distinguishes them from the orthodox Stalinists – a minus instead of a plus. They identify Stalinism with Marxism-Leninism not to praise Stalin but to condemn Marxism-Leninism."[52]

Was Stalinism, then, Communist? The question is not as simple as doctrinal polemics or abstract semantics would make it. Yet it is the key to understanding the Soviet historical experience and the all-too-present background against which the former Soviet peoples are rebelling. Stalinism was obviously "Communist" with a capital C in the sense that it professed a philosophy and controlled a movement identified by that name. It was not "communist" with a small c in any sense that could honestly be derived from or explained by that philosophy. It was linked to the Revolution and to the leadership of Lenin and could not have come into existence apart from these circumstances; but it was not the direct intention of those who made the Revolution, any more than the Revolution was intended by the rulers of the system that brought it on.

Stalinism was shaped by diverse forces that Stalin did not create but only steered and used: the authoritarian tradition, high and low in Russian society; the utopian dreams of Russians who set themselves against that tradition; the elemental violence and inhumanity of the revolutionary experience; the drag of backwardness on a state that wanted to be a great power and in any case had to defend itself. In the precise form it took, in its unbelievable cruelty, mendacity, and power-corrupted stupidity, Stalinism was very much the expression of its creator's personality. None of its particulars were inevitable, though some of its features – the bureaucracy, the industrialization effort, the embrace of Russian nationalism and cultural conservatism – were logical responses under the circumstances. Stalinism was a unique synthesis of past, present, and future, of the actual, the possible, and the utterly improbable, following the prerevolutionary "thesis" and the revolutionary "antithesis."

To see how all these elements came together, one has to re-examine the whole experience of the Russian Revolution. Stalinism was a horror, but it cannot be dismissed as an alien nightmare that sprang upon the Russian nation and its satellites, as it were, from outer space or the nether regions. The critic Viktor Yerefeyev, observing the 1991 end of the Soviet system with some skepticism, commented,

This Euroasian essence, this unique interplay of Europe and Asia

. . . will continue to amaze the world . . . . What was imported in Western Marxism will vanish. But Communism will not disappear, inasmuch as the spirit of collectivism is at the heart of this nation. The nation will always say "we" rather than the Anglo-Saxon "I."[53]

5

THE LONG AGONY OF
THE RUSSIAN REVOLUTION

Late evening, 24 October 1917 (6 November, New Style). Vladimir Ilyich Ulyanov-Lenin is fuming in the Petrograd apartment where he has been hiding from the police of the Provisional Government. His Bolshevik lieutenants in the Smolny Institute, the former school for aristocratic girls commandeered by the Petrograd Soviet of Workers' and Soldiers' Deputies to serve as its headquarters, have been dragging their feet in the face of the stream of messages he has been sending them urging them to seize power. They have preferred to wait for the impending Congress of Soviets, representing local soviets all over the country, to vote itself into power in place of Alexander Kerensky's shaky regime.

Although the delegates elected to the Congress are mostly Bolsheviks or members of the sympathetic Left Socialist Revolutionary Party, Lenin does not trust them. He is obsessed with the idea of mobilizing pro-Bolshevik soldiers and sailors to overthrow Kerensky before the Congress can meet, so that he can present it with the *fait accompli* of power that has been forcibly seized in its name. In his letters he has been railing against "constitutional illusions" and "a childish game of formality" that would allow the unique revolutionary opportunity to slip by. "To hesitate is a crime. The success of both the Russian and the world revolution depends on two or three days of struggle. Delay means death."[1] So much for Marxian laws of historical inevitability.

Now, the day before the Congress of Soviets is to convene, a feeble government attempt to close the Bolsheviks' printing shop jolts the people at Smolny into action. Fearing a pre-emptive coup by Kerensky, the Bolshevik leaders call on all the sympathetic units they can muster of soldiers, sailors, and "Red Guards" from the factories to defend Smolny and the Congress. To their surprise, most of Petrograd falls into their hands in a matter of hours, with scarcely a shot being fired. The officer cadets and Cossacks on whom Kerensky must rely think he is too radical, and decline to fight for him.

Unsure whether his orders to attack are actually being carried out, Lenin sets out in the dark with his bodyguard and makes his way to the

Smolny Institute to find out what is really going on. Wearing a wig and shorn of his characteristic beard, he escapes recognition by a patrol of Kerensky's officer cadets who accost him along the way, but neither is he recognized by the guards at the gate to Smolny. They momentarily deny him admittance because he doesn't have one of the new red passes.

Once inside with the Bolshevik leadership, Lenin takes firm charge. In the chaotic excitement at Smolny, it certainly looks as though his insurrectionary orders are being carried out, and none of his subordinates cares to tell him that this had not really been their intention. Thus the myth is established of the most carefully planned revolution in history. Nevertheless, Lenin's presence at Smolny after midnight clearly turns the defensive moves of the pro-Bolshevik forces into a systematic insurrection against Kerensky. By daybreak the Provisional Government is virtually isolated in the old Winter Palace of the Tsars. Only Kerensky escapes, driving off to the front past Bolshevik sentries to try to find loyal troops to put down the revolt.[2]

Meanwhile the Bolshevik leaders snatch a couple of hours' sleep in the bare rooms at Smolny. In the morning they gather to decide how to complete their revolution, and then what to do with it. One of the participants, meeting Lenin for the first time, recalls later,

I was stunned and shocked: "Ilyich! So here he is, the sovereign of our souls . . . . What a plain ordinary person he is," was the first thought that entered my head. It was hard to believe, and hard to square this real Ilyich with the Lenin I had created in my imagination, who had to be of powerful stature, with a loud voice, etc. Under this powerful impact of such an unexpected meeting, I was practically stupefied, and froze against the wall.[3]

Lenin sits down at the table that is almost the only piece of furniture in the meeting room, and writes out a proclamation:

To the Citizens of Russia!

The Provisional Government has been deposed. State power has passed into the hands of the organ of the Petrograd Soviet of Workers' and Peasants' Deputies, the Military Revolutionary Committee, which heads the Petrograd proletariat and the garrison.

The cause for which the people have fought, namely, the immediate offer of a democratic peace, the abolition of landed proprietorship, workers' control over production, and the establishment of soviet power – this cause has been secured.

Long live the revolution of workers, soldiers, and peasants![4]

By 10 a.m. these words have been set in type and broadcast around the city as a leaflet, the fastest form of mass media of that day. The die is cast. Lenin and his Bolsheviks must now rule as a revolutionary dictatorship if they are to survive at all.

Early in the afternoon Trotsky calls the Petrograd Soviet into session to celebrate the revolutionary victory: "In the name of the Military Revolutionary Committee I declare that the Provisional Government has ceased to exist."[5] One of the deputies recalls later, "Another such speech I never managed to hear. It was like molten metal, every word burned the soul, it awakened thought and roused adventure, as he spoke of the victory of the proletariat."[6] Then, to tumultuous applause, Lenin makes his first public appearance in nearly four months: "Comrades! The workers' and peasants' revolution . . . has been accomplished . . . . The oppressed masses will themselves create the power. . . . Long live the world socialist revolution!"[7]

The beginning seems easy. Late in the evening of the 25th the poorly defended Winter Palace finally falls to a mob of soldiers and workers. The ministers of the Provisional Government are incarcerated in the same dungeons of the Peter and Paul Fortress where the Tsarist government imprisoned former generations of revolutionaries.

Simultaneously, 600 delegates to the Congress of Soviets convene in the school assembly hall at the Smolny Institute. Protesting against the Bolsheviks' armed uprising, the small minority of Mensheviks and Right Socialist Revolutionaries walk out of the Congress and into "the dustbin of history," to quote Trotsky's famous parting shot.[8] Then, untroubled by any opposition, the Bolshevik leaders get the Congress to adopt a series of revolutionary decrees. First is a decree establishing a provisional workers' and peasants' government, to be called the "Council of People's Commissars" and chaired by Lenin.[9] (That "provisional" decree, with minor modifications, remained in effect until 1991.) Other decrees, all drafted by Lenin, follow in quick succession. The "Decree on the Land" abolishes private ownership and turns landlords' estates over to the peasants (who have been seizing them anyway).[10] The "Decree on Peace" calls for an end to the hostilities of the First World War and invites world revolution.[11] The "Decree on Suppression of Hostile Newspapers" is supposed to be of a "temporary nature," but it proves to be the first step toward totalitarianism.[12] It is not undone until Gorbachev's time of glasnost. Then the Congress of Soviets adjourns, and the great experiment in creating socialism under the dictatorship of the proletariat begins.

*

The events of October 1917, the "Ten Days that Shook the World," dramatic as they were, do not by any means tell the whole story of revolution in Russia. The Revolution, or its consequences, continued to unfold for decades. The ordeal of civil war and then of Stalinism was its direct outcome. Even Gorbachev's era of reform and the final collapse of the Soviet system have to be seen in the context of the Revolution, to appreciate both their seriousness and their limits.

To put this point more generally, a phenomenon such as the Russian Revolution is not a momentary event but a long process. This means simply that one event or set of circumstances leads to another in a recognizable, in part even predictable, chain of cause and effect. True revolutions like the upheaval in Russia cannot be explained merely as the deliberate work of revolutionaries, for good or for ill; they are the violent expression of a deep crisis in the historical development of the society in question. Napoleon Bonaparte, looking back from his last years of exile at St. Helena, wrote, "A revolution can be neither made nor stopped."[13] If the times are not ready, revolutionary behavior is at best a nuisance and at worst a provocation that may cause a society to recoil into right-wing authoritarianism. If a society is in fact experiencing a true crisis, revolutionaries may ride the crest of the wave, but where it casts them they cannot control. "What has happened to us?" exclaimed Alexander Yakovlev at the 1990 party congress, "to the party that once roused the people to revolution in the name of justice and brotherhood? A disaster has occurred, for the party of an idea, a revolutionary idea, has turned into a party of power."[14] He could have been warned by Friedrich Engels, who wrote in 1885 to his Russian friends,

> People who boasted that they had *made* a revolution have always seen the next day that they had no idea what they were doing, that the revolution *made* did not in the least resemble the one they would have liked to make.[15]

The revolutionary process has a characteristic shape, manifested one way or another in all the great revolutions of history. They break out when the tension between a changing, modernizing society and a rigid traditional government can no longer be contained. Shaken by some triggering event such as defeat in war or a financial crisis, the Old Regime yields to liberal reformers, who hope to cure the country's ills by legal and non-violent means. But radicalism grows, with the political mobilization of the masses and the howl of popular demands that have long gone unmet. At the same time the liberals are challenged by counterrevolutionaries trying to preserve the old authoritarian order, even at the price of bloody conflict. By civil war or by *coup d'état*, radical leadership takes over and sets a course of violent utopianism, often accompanied by terror. There is discord, however, between those radicals whose inspiration is more the utopia, and those more excited about the conquest and exercise of power; typically the first become victims of the second. Finally, of its own volition or by force of another coup, the revolutionary government adjusts to the need to retreat from its extreme goals, and experiences the "Thermidorean Reaction," made famous in the annals of revolution by the downfall of Robespierre in that summer month of the French revolutionary calendar.

This model of upward and downward curves in the revolutionary process has been noted by many writers, best known of whom was the American historian Crane Brinton, author of *The Anatomy of Revolution*.[16] Brinton used a medical image of the process, likening the revolutionary society to a patient suffering from a fever that rises up to a point of crisis, and then subsides. This is an instructive metaphor as far as it goes, but it understates both the driving forces at work in revolutionary societies, and the degree of social change registered by revolutions. Moreover, Brinton had little to say about the path a country might follow after the Thermidorean Reaction had moderated the revolution's excesses. Generally this period witnesses the reassertion of authority by an individual – sometimes the radical leader, more often someone else – who accomplishes a synthesis of old methods and new rhetoric, and launches revolutionary war against foreign powers or against his own people. This characteristic stage I call "postrevolutionary dictatorship." The term is designedly broad, so as not to limit its applicability by naming it after one particular practitioner such as Bonaparte or Stalin, or by connecting it exclusively either to the revolutionaries or the counter-revolutionaries.

*

The course of the Russian Revolution tracks almost perfectly with the model I have outlined. This is not surprising, since it was the Russian Revolution and the obvious correspondence of its stages with the French Revolution that prompted the formulation of the process model of revolution in the first place. To begin with, we have a classic revolution of the moderate liberals, when they grasped power in the February Revolution of 1917 and set up the Provisional Government. This was actually a second try, by the same kind of people who won a toehold in quasi-representative government after the abortive Revolution of 1905 and the creation of a limited parliament, the Duma.

Both in 1905 and in 1917 the liberals quickly had to share the stage with more radical representatives of the workers and peasants. In 1917 they also had to reckon with the millions of peasants in uniform. The fall of the Tsar in February 1917 and the evaporation of all coercive authority released a variety of spontaneous revolutionary mass movements: the peasants were seizing the land; the workers were striking or taking control over industry through their factory committees; the soldiers were organizing committees to defy the military chain of command; and the national minorities, then as now, were electing their own leaders and pressing demands for autonomy or independence. The local soviets that sprang up all over the country replaced the old bureaucratic administration with a decentralized direct democracy.

As these swift responses to the new freedom showed, the notion that the Russians did not understand or appreciate democracy is false. Their problem was carrying democracy to excess, including areas of public life such as industry and the military where traditional bourgeois democracy had never entered. The year 1917 saw an orgy of democracy and mass action, which ironically swept the Bolsheviks to the verge of revolutionary dictatorship through the Congress of Soviets. The stage was thereby set for the armed uprising that Lenin hungered for and, by a fortuitous chain of circumstances, secured.

The October Revolution initiated the extremist phase of the revolutionary process in Russia, but was not yet its climax. Direct-action movements of workers and peasants continued into 1918. One-party dictatorship, though never an acknowledged Bolshevik goal before October, became a reality as Lenin responded to each crisis by clamping down further on the opposition – banning the conservative parties and press, reviving the secret police in the form of the Cheka ("Extraordinary Commission to Fight Counterrevolution"), dispersing the democratically elected Constituent Assembly, dispensing with his allies of the Left Socialist Revolutionary Party, and by mid-1918, as civil war was engulfing the country, banning all non-Communist parties from the soviets.

As revolutions become more serious, the extremist revolutionaries split, between the idealists and the power-oriented. In the English Revolution the ultra-Left were the Levellers (democrats) and the Fifth-Monarchy Men (religious millenarians), used and then discarded by the pragmatic Cromwell. In the French Revolution the corresponding people were the Enragés and the Hébertistes, patrons of the proletarian sans-culottes, purged and guillotined by Robespierre before he himself fell. In Russia the utopian Left were the Communists who tried to stay on the course of the anarchistic, decentralist egalitarianism that they thought was the meaning of the October Revolution, while Lenin shifted his ground to become the successful dictator. Rooted in a considerable tradition of ultra-Left romanticism before 1917, people of this persuasion emerged as the "Left Communists" of 1918, and under the banners of the "Group of Democratic Centralists" and the "Workers' Opposition" fought the trend towards authoritarian rule and bureaucratic administration until Lenin finally suppressed them in 1921. With the demise of these opposition groups ended the last true effort to make the Communist system an "experiment."

The Civil War that raged from 1918 to 1920 was a critical experience in hardening the Communist dictatorship, undercutting the idealists, and steering the regime in the direction of authoritarian and centralist forms of rule – precisely the opposite of the spirit of 1917. The Communists reversed their stance towards all the popular movements so decisive in 1917: abolition of workers' control in industry in favor of individual management by appointees of the center; rebuilding a new Red Army on conventional lines of rank and discipline; "requisitioning" of food from the peasants; and forcible incorporation of independence-seeking minorities into the Soviet Union. All of these steps, vainly resisted by the ultra-Left, contributed to Russia's distinctive form of revolutionary extremism, namely War Communism, an attempt simultaneously to mobilize Communist-held territory for civil war and to impose a utopia of collectivist egalitarianism by military-style command.

Revolutionary fanaticism continued to drive the Communists until the counterrevolutionary "White" armies were defeated and the Soviet government was confronted by growing and sometimes armed opposition within its worker and peasant base. At this point, events in Russia took an unusual turn: Lenin opted for a strategic retreat from the Party's revolutionary goals, and in effect carried out his own Thermidorean Reaction, before popular hostility might cause the downfall of the Communists altogether. It was as though Robespierre, recognizing that he had outrun his popular base, declared an end to the Terror before his enemies could act against him – or to refine the parallel more exactly, as though the pragmatist Danton-Lenin had the power to stop the Terror and push the fanatic Robespierre-Trotsky aside. This simile indeed represents Lenin's role better, when he decided in the winter of 1920–21 to abandon the frontal attack of War Communism and fall back on a long-term, gradualist approach to educate the Russian peasant masses into socialism, while Trotsky was left momentarily advocating even more centralism and coercion to address the crisis brought on by revolutionary extremism. The actual parallel with Lenin's self-executed Thermidor was closer in the English Revolution, when Cromwell decided in 1653 to put an end to his brief experiment in religious utopianism and dissolved the short-lived "Parliament of the Saints."

Thanks to Lenin's timely concessions in introducing the New Economic Policy and in accepting a lengthy semi-socialist purgatory in preparation for Russia's entry into the communist heaven, the Communists were able to cling to power while the country passed from one stage of the revolutionary process to the next, from extremism to Thermidor. (To be sure, no Communist acknowledged the Thermidorean nature of the NEP until long afterwards.) The superficial preservation of Communist Party rule and Marxist ideology from the time of the NEP onwards has made it difficult to appreciate the depth of change that Soviet society went through as the revolutionary process unfolded

104

further. Nevertheless, some Russian writers now see the transformation very clearly. Maria Chegodayeva exclaimed in *Moscow News*,

> The Russian Revolution perished: it choked itself to death with its own blood and was burned out in the conflagration of the civil war. Russia made an effort to reach out for the sun but her wings were heavily burdened by slavery, hatred, and war. The counterrevolution triumphed very soon, though we do not know the exact date, a Russian Thermidor 9, which could be a holiday for the members of the present-day Communist Party of Russia to celebrate.[17]

With the NEP came all the social and psychological signs of Thermidorean relaxation. The country enjoyed a successful economic recovery and a return to something like "normalcy" in the non-political side of life. "Many people still believe that the NEP was only a manoeuvre, only a temporary retreat," Nikolai Shmelyov wrote in 1987. "But the basic, lasting significance of the NEP was something else. For the first time the basic principles were formulated for a scientific, realistic approach to the tasks of socialist economic construction."[18] Yet as Michal Reiman points out, the Revolution plus war and civil war had "destroyed not only Russia's old social order, but also the not yet sufficiently developed and stabilized forms of existence and functioning mechanisms of the rising industrial civilization," so that Russia's developmental needs could not be met without a drastic new change in the system.[19] Against this background, the persistence of the one-party dictatorship and the centralist legacy of the War Communism period, along with "the disintegration of societal life . . . cynicism, dual morality, and loss of faith," to cite Alexander Yakovlev,[20] paved the way for an aspiring postrevolutionary dictator.

Joseph Stalin, anointed as party organizational chief by Lenin, who then fell ill too soon to correct his mistake, was the man to seize this opportunity. The apparatus of personal power that he built up within the Party was the functional analogue of Bonaparte's command of the revolutionary army, enabling him to bid successfully for the role of postrevolutionary dictator. Humbling all his Communist rivals, Stalin soon found himself in a position to put an end to the era of relaxation and initiate a new revolutionary storm with the Five-Year Plan and collectivization.

With the advent of Stalin's "revolution from above" the familiar theories of revolution no longer applied, and Stalinism remains subject to widely different interpretations. Naturally Stalin claimed full continuity with Lenin, and in mood and method he seemed at first to be reviving the era of War Communism. Yet he subjected the masses to a more oppressive and exploitative regime than anything they had suffered under Tsarism, and with the aid of the Communist Party hierarchy he amassed total power in his own hands. Thus, in the terms of the process model of revolution proposed here, Stalin brought the Soviet Union into the phase of postrevolutionary dictatorship, where an opportunistic egomaniac, mastering the main levers of power, proceeds to combine old autocratic methods of rule with the revolutionary mythology, and declares war on the nation's alleged enemies. In Stalin's case, up to the Second World War, these were internal foes – the bourgeois specialists, the "petty-bourgeois" peasants, former Communist rivals, and finally the men of his own political apparatus.

The USSR did not, of course, move on from the "Bonapartist" phase of postrevolutionary dictatorship to an outright monarchical restoration. One can imagine something on this order if Hitler had waged political warfare more astutely in 1941, and had successfully sponsored a counterrevolutionary government to get Russia out of the war. But even though this outcome did not materialize, the real character of the Soviet political and social system, including the new nationalistic symbolism introduced during and after the war, could be described as the functional equivalent of a monarchical restoration.

Postrevolutionary dictatorship under Stalin was uniquely deceitful and despotic. It entailed the death, by starvation or firing squad or the rigors of the Gulag, of millions of people in the categories that Stalin had marked as enemies of the regime, extending even to the major part of his own Communist officialdom. It proceeded under the labels of Marxist-Leninist orthodoxy, to the confusion of friend and foe alike. It included the sweeping reversal of most of the libertarian and egalitarian social policies and cultural standards that had been introduced or encouraged by the Revolution. All of these features, together with a totally centralized, arbitrary, and deceitful use of power and violence, are aspects of the phenomenon of totalitarianism.

Stalin's totalitarianism now falls into place historically in a way that enables us to understand its origin, its persistence, and its decay. The revolutionary process led characteristically to postrevolutionary dictatorship, and postrevolutionary dictatorship with twentieth-century techniques of organization, communication, coercion, and surveillance characteristically takes the form of totalitarianism. It makes little difference to the outcome whether a country follows the classic process of revolution, as Russia and China did, or whether the revolution is usurped by a postrevolutionary dictatorship of the Right, as the German Revolution that began in 1918 was eventually taken over by the Nazis. Apart from small countries in the shadow of a large postrevolutionary totalitarian power, a revolutionary process in motion is the necessary condition for the establishment of any totalitarian regime.

The identification of totalitarianism with modern postrevolutionary dictatorship explains a number of things. It clarifies, first of all, how

Communism under Stalin and right-wing dictatorship under Hitler could turn out so much alike, approaching the same outcome by different routes and under antithetical ideologies. One needs only to realize that right-wing totalitarianism could be ideologically more consistent, whereas, in the words of German Diligensky, editor of *World Economy and International Relations*, "The ideology that became established in our country was contradictory in the highest degree," trying to maintain a bridge between "the personality cult and authoritarian state power" and "the basic democratic and humanistic principles contained in the original socialist ideal."[21] Secondly, if totalitarianism is recognized as a manifestation of postrevolutionary dictatorship, then it no longer looms as an immutable amd inexplicable tyranny. Postrevolutionary dictatorship, whether brief or lengthy, eventually is sloughed off by a society that it can no longer hold in thrall.

*

If the stages and consequences of revolutions conform so closely to a common pattern, there must be some sort of sociological law at work in all cases. The movements of the revolutionary process are clearly visible in the Russian Revolution, and to a point readily explainable. Does this mean that the outcome was inevitable, that the Communist leaders from Lenin to Stalin were only carrying out the commands of History, and that there is no scope for moral judgement of their actions?

There are two fallacies in such a conclusion. First, the details of the revolutionary experience are specific to the particular case, and may substantially color its impact and outcome. For example, if the October Revolution had not been incited by Lenin and triggered by Kerensky's provocation, the radical phase might have been much less severe. If the Communists had not beaten a retreat in 1921, they would probably have been overthrown, leaving the Russian Thermidor and the postrevolutionary dictatorship to proceed under counterrevolutionary rather than pseudo-revolutionary auspices. If Stalin had not prevailed over the Party in 1928–29, the trend to postrevolutionary authoritarianism and New Class rule could have been guided much more pragmatically and much less murderously. What we can still say from the observed regularities of the revolutionary process, however, is that it is difficult for well-meaning leaders to avoid a revolutionary breakdown when rapid modernization brings a country to a point of crisis; or to stop an extremist movement that surges up following a moderate revolution; or to keep a revolution's ideals intact in the face of postrevolutionary pragmatism and cynicism.

Secondly, recognizing unfortunate tendencies in a given historical situation does not mean that the actual choices of individual historical actors are predetermined, any more than the predictable murder rate, say, determines whether a particular individual will pull the trigger. Political leaders are answerable for their choice of allegiances and their selection of means, even if some other scoundrel is awaiting nomination by History for the villain's role. It is hard to overlook the spirit of fanaticism and moral relativism that Lenin institutionalized in the Bolshevik Party and then injected into the extremist phase of the Russian Revolution, even if he was capable of serious reconsiderations later on. He clearly bears some of the responsibility for Stalinism, even if the latter ran far afield from his own revolutionary goals. But then so do Tsar Nicholas and Prime Minister Stolypin's assassin and everyone else who by resisting reform helped bring Russia to the point of a revolutionary explosion.

*

Thanks to accidents of leadership, timing, and circumstances, the Russian Revolution naturally differed from its predecessors in the political details of each phase. But there was a greater difference of a programmatic and ideological nature, a difference of basic social values, that distinguished the revolution in Russia. By and large the revolutions that the Western world experienced from the seventeenth century to the nineteenth were movements driven by commitments to freedom and equality in religion, politics, and the law. They were indeed, as Marxists style them, "bourgeois" revolutions, devoted to the set of individualist values that was most closely associated with the rising middle class. Aside from their ultra-left offshoots, these revolutions distinctly did not extend to the equalization of individuals in the economic realm. A transformation of this nature in the economic order was the new mission addressed by all the various currents of socialism, including Marxism, that arose in Europe in the mid- and late nineteenth century. The Russian Revolution was the first successful revolution to be animated by a set of values turning on economic equality and community.

It was also the first revolution to be prepared by a long and self-conscious tradition of revolutionary conspiracy, sustained by a faith in socialism antedating the influence of Marxism. Lenin, the school superintendent's son radicalized by the execution of his revolutionary brother, typified this movement of disaffected aristocratic and bourgeois intellectuals, trying to carry the revolutionary idea to the masses. He did not invent either the conspiracy or the socialism, though his distinctly Russian conviction that socialism could be achieved only by means of conspiracy indelibly colored the regime that he succeeded in establishing.

The emotional force of socialism in the Russian Revolution cannot be overestimated, either in the politics of the revolutionary country or in the responses of the champions and enemies of socialism abroad. In 1917 some kind of attachment to socialism was professed across a broad band of the Russian political spectrum, embracing Bolsheviks, Mensheviks, Menshevik-Internationalists, Socialist Revolutionaries of the Left, Right, and Center, Anarchists, People's Socialists, and socialists in the various minority nationalist movements. To be sure, many of these *soi-disant* socialists, faced with the tumult of a real revolution, lost the courage of their convictions and hid behind the version of Marxism that held Russia to be unprepared for their ideal. The Menshevik leader Irakly Tsereteli apologetically told an audience of workers the very day he got back to Petrograd from Siberian exile in March 1917, "The time has not yet come for achieving the ultimate aims of the proletariat, the class aims which have nowhere as yet been achieved . . ., the bright ideas of socialism."[22] Still, the words of socialism gave everyone in its orbit a warm feeling of political virtue, much as "democracy" still does in the lands of earlier revolutions. The vacuum in socialist action among the democratic parties helped the Bolsheviks become a party of mass appeal. Socialism was central to the self-righteous militancy of the Bolsheviks, and to the compulsive self-justification of every succeeding form of Communist rule whether in Russia or anywhere else. It was not lightly to be given up even when perestroika dawned in the 1980s; the limiting condition in Gorbachev's reformist mindset was the retention of some form of economic framework that he could continue to call socialist.

Despite the popularity of the socialist faith in Russia, it was taken for granted up to 1917 by Marxists (including the Bolsheviks) and by many others that Russia was unready for socialism. The country had not completed the capitalist passage to modern industrialism, and the vast majority of the population were distinctly premodern peasants, often still illiterate. How to explain and legitimize a socialist revolution in a country such as Russia, which until 1917 had not had its "bourgeois" revolution, agitated the Bolsheviks more than any other ideological issue. Trotsky had argued in his often misunderstoood "theory of permanent revolution" that mass mobilization stirred up by the bourgeois revolution could sweep a workers' government into power, but that the support of international revolution would be required to sustain such a regime in Russia. Lenin made this reasoning the centerpiece of his argument for the seizure of power in October 1917; failure to act, he insisted, would be a "betrayal" of the international workers' movement. Only when Stalin invented the "theory of socialism in one country" in the 1920s were worries about the viability of socialism isolated in Russia officially dismissed.

Democratic Marxists, exemplified by Karl Kautsky, turned the proposition of Russia's unreadiness for socialism against the Bolsheviks, to explain their excesses.[23] Soviet historians in the years of perestroika have used the same reasoning to explain the perversion of socialism under Stalinism. But the comparative perspective suggests that the Russian Revolution was not unique in advancing goals that were premature with respect to the country's level of development. In fact, relative to the ability of a country to realize the promises of its revolution, all revolutions are more or less premature. Unattainable hopes drive them into extremism, and then harsh realities drive them back to Thermidor and postrevolutionary dictatorship.

This law of revolutionary disappointment creates a highly ironic prospect for socialism. Where the need for socialism is most strongly felt to achieve elementary social justice, it seems, the country is not ready for it. By the time a country is ready for socialism, it may no longer need it.

*

Socialism has, of course, been proposed by a host of particular theorists and movements, differing on such fundamentals as centralism vs. decentralism, statism vs. communitarianism, and bullets vs. ballots. All schools of socialism, however, have held in common the conviction that ending the economic domination exercised by some people over others by virtue of private property would usher in a new moral order. (The Russian Revolution soon showed that socialism could accommodate far worse forms of domination.) Marxism, despite its claims to exclusive virtue, was only the most popular and most successful of socialist movements. Even within Marxism there has been no single conception of socialism, and competing orthodoxies have been asserted by feuding Communist governments.

The Russian Revolution embraced socialism more as feeling than as thought. It is difficult to reduce this socialism to a particular set of policies, especially since a series of different models of socialism actually prevailed in Russia in different phases of the revolutionary process. Each model in its time was represented by the Communist leadership as the one true and proper way to implement Marx.

In the early, liberating phase of the Revolution, from the fall of the Tsar to the serious consolidation of the Communist dictatorship in mid-1918, the specifics of socialism were determined more by direct popular action under the banner of "revolutionary democracy" than by considered acts of government: peasant land seizures, workers' control in industry through the factory committee movement, outright seizure of bourgeois homes to use as workers' apartments. During their first few months in power the Bolsheviks did little more than stamp their seal of approval on what the populace was doing anyway. In 1917, socialism and democracy seemed like Siamese twins, neither viable without the other, and both took the direction of maximum decentralization and spontaneous popular action through the soviets and the myriads of other councils and committees that sprang up all over the country and at every level. Under these conditions, Russian socialism of the first phase was close to the anarcho-syndicalist model of autonomous work collectives.

Before he acquired the responsibilities of governing, Lenin hailed these elemental movements and enlisted them to support the Bolshevik bid for power. He made them the basis of his theory of government in his treatise *State and Revolution*, which he composed while still in hiding in 1917. The revolutionaries would "smash" the bourgeois state and turn everything from the administration of justice to the management of banks over to "the armed people." This was the approach to socialism legislated in the decrees that Lenin submitted to the Congress of Soviets in October 1917.

Lenin's new angle of vision as chief of the revolutionary government quickly led him to see the problems of political control and economic organization in a very different light, much to the disgust of the utopian purists among his following, who saw him embracing "bureaucratic centralization" and "state capitalism."[24] But this was the direction the Communists were compelled to take, both by the technological requirements of modern society, and by the life-and-death struggle of the Civil War. The result was the War Communism model of socialism, corresponding to the extremist phase of revolution: total centralization and military command methods everywhere except in agriculture (which was subject to the forced requisitioning of produce), and a spirit of militant egalitarianism and class war.

The future of this model of socialism was the main issue when the Communist Party became embroiled in 1920–21 in the so-called Trade-Union Controversy. Trotsky proposed to continue the War Communism model, with "labor armies" and the "governmentalizing" of the trade unions. The idealists of the Workers' Opposition and Democratic Centralist groups wanted to return to the 1917 model and turn the whole economy over to democratic administration by the unions. Lenin, realizing that no extremist or utopian solution would work, opted for the retreat to a semi-capitalist economy that became the NEP, with the unions consigned to the traditional role of guarding the interests of the workers *vis-à-vis* management. For the next seven years the "Thermidorean" model of socialism remained in force. It was restricted in scope (to the "commanding heights" of banks, large-scale industry, and the transportation and communication infrastructure), in method (with the resurrection of money and the market), and in outlook (a long, gradual evolution rather than a system suddenly and forcibly imposed).

When Stalin broke with the NEP in 1928–29 in the course of disposing of his rivals within the party leadership, he committed the country to yet another model of socialism. This was the system of totally nationalized or collectivized economy, centrally planned and bureaucratically administered, corresponding to the phase of postrevolutionary dictatorship. It differed from the War Communism model in its broader scope (including the peasantry), in its rejection of egalitarianism in favor of a frank inequality of authority and rewards, and in its embrace of cultural conservationism. If this was "barracks socialism," it was barracks socialism complete with the hierarchy of military rank and privilege, and complemented with huge disciplinary battalions for the misfits.

The durability of the Stalinist model of socialism and the intensity of propaganda identifying it with the revolutionary goal led much of the outside world to take the identity of Stalinism and socialism for granted. This was equally true for adherents of the socialist ideal for whom Stalinism was thereby prettified, and for enemies of socialism for whom Stalinism became proof of its iniquity. The international Left was divided and confused, while up to the Second World War the international Right thrived on the Communist menace. For most of the people affected, the collapse of the Stalinist model in the 1980s carried the socialist ideal down with it. "We ourselves," says Yakovlev, "did a great deal to deform the image and values of socialism."[25] It can well be said that its identification with the Russian Revolution and the tragic burden of that experience was the worst thing that could have happened to socialism.

*

How do events in the Soviet Union in the 1980s and 1990s relate to the revolutionary process in general and to the postrevolutionary dictatorship in particular? Time does not stand still, and the revolutionary process does not end with the postrevolutionary dictatorship or even with monarchical restoration. Typically there comes a point – it was the Glorious Revolution of 1688 in Restoration England, and the Revolution of 1830 in postrevolutionary France – when restorationist authoritarianism is thrown off. A similar purgation can be observed in countries – in West Germany after 1945, in Spain after the death of Franco in 1975 – where the revolution had come to grief in avowedly counterrevolutionary dictatorships. Seeking a new beginning at this point, the nation turns back to the principles of the earliest, liberal stage of its revolution, with emphasis on personal liberty and representative government.

This final stage of the revolutionary process I therefore term the "moderate revolutionary revival." It takes place when a country manages to start its revolution over again, so to speak, without so much of the fanaticism and polarization that undermined the original attempt at liberal reform and drove the process on to dictatorship and civil war. Gorbachev had the point when he said of perestroika in 1989, "It is a revolution within a revolution, not a negation of the values, slogans, and ideals of October. It is the unfolding of these ideals in a new situation, on the basis of what has already been achieved."[26]

This return to beginnings, of course, does not fully determine the choices that a society may make, or guarantee its future stability. In 1848 France went into a new cycle of revolution and dictatorship, capped by a bloody contest for the nation's political soul at the time of the Paris Commune of 1871. But the general tendency is still to work out some kind of alternative based on the early revolutionary experience.

In the trajectory of the Russian Revolution the point of moderate revolutionary revival was finally reached in the 1980s with Gorbachev's perestroika and democratization. All that Russia had gone through from 1917 to 1985 – the phases of the revolutionary experience, the successive models of socialism, the black night of totalitarianism – went into the agenda of reform that the country undertook under perestroika. We have already followed Gorbachev as he retraced step by step the path by which the Soviet state had arrived in the sad conditon of Stalinism. And we have seen Yeltsin seizing the initiative to go back all the way to revolutionary beginnings when his rival hesitated.

Gorbachev took Khrushchev's exposé of Stalinist terrorism as a point of departure, but went far beyond. Khrushchev never questioned the record of Stalin's dictatorship before 1934, including collectivization, the famine, and the five-year plans. In contrast, Gorbachev began his journey back in time by challenging the whole organization and performance of the Stalinist economic system, and rejecting the model of central planning and bureaucratic administration. Probing much more deeply than Khrushchev did into the fundamentals of Stalin's regime, Gorbachev took issue with the premises and methods of the whole system of five-year plans and collectivization from 1929 on. The rehabilitation of Bukharin in 1988, recognizing a historic alternative to the Stalinist path, fitted in very logically here, as the Gorbachev team tried to devise a sort of market socialism on the lines that had facilitated the country's economic recovery in the 1920s. Pushing even further back, Gorbachev took issue with the primal Leninist bias against petty-bourgeois enterprise, especially in services and in agriculture, the nationalization of which has been universally inappropriate and counterproductive. He held out for the ideal of socialism and the sanctity of Lenin, but he allowed socialism to be redefined very loosely and extolled the very un-Leninist Lenin of the last, deathbed writings of 1923.

Going beyond economics, Gorbachev's reforms challenged the power of the Stalinist party apparatus and even called into question the essence of Lenin's political system, the monolithic discipline of the Communist Party and its controls over all other institutions in Soviet society. To do battle with the apparatus conservatives, Gorbachev had to abandon the principle of unity that Lenin had imposed on the Party with the 1921 ban on organized factions. He attacked the rule of the apparatus over the rank and file in almost the same terms that Trotsky had used against Stalin in the mid-1920s. In rejecting the Party's direct domination over the civil government of the soviets, and in inviting non-party organizations to engage in pluralistic dialogue with the Party instead of serving as mere "transmission belts" of the Party's will, he went against the power arrangements that had prevailed ever since the Russian Civil War.[27]

Other steps that Gorbachev took in 1989 and 1990 ran counter to the Bolshevik Revolution itself. Toleration of organized opposition groups in the 1989 elections, and the abdication of the Communist Party's constitutional leading role in 1990, carried Soviet politics all the way back to 1917 and the democratic election of the ill-fated Constituent Assembly, before the infant Soviet regime became a strictly one-party affair. The dethronement of Marxist-Leninist orthodoxy eliminated the basis of the Communists' claim to exclusive political virtue (and in many minds, to any virtue at all). Yakovlev took the occasion of the 200th anniversary of the French Revolution to compare the Bolsheviks with the Jacobins: "It must be said that the idealization of terror made itself sharply apparent in the October Revolution." The great mistake was

> to use the means of terror not only to put an end to counterrevolutionary activities, but also to stimulate the processes involved in building a new society. A cruel price had to be paid for these mistakes, for the immorality of pseudorevolutionary behaviour.[28]

One obvious objection to the concept of the moderate revolutionary revival as applied to the Gorbachev era is the great span of time that elapsed under the postrevolutionary dictatorship. But this is not such a puzzle if we consider the Khrushchev years as an attempt to bring about the moderate revolutionary revival thirty years earlier. Khrushchev's reforms were incomplete and abortive, but if he had remained in power longer without the challenge of the party apparatus hanging over his head, it is possible to imagine the irreversible breakup of the postrevolutionary dictatorship even then. Khrushchev's failure and the ensuing delay in fundamental reform can be explained partly as a failure of leadership, partly by the sheer immobility of the Stalinist bureaucratic system, and partly with reference to the deep roots that the Stalinist and neo-Stalinist regimes were able to put down in the authoritarian soil of Russian political culture. Then, recognizing the inordinately long sway of postrevolutionary dictatorship in the Soviet Union, we can better

114

appreciate the growing contradictions of modernized society and rigid government that undermined the Brezhnev regime and then swept the old system away.

*

By the time of the August Coup little remained of the postrevolutionary dictatorship either in theory or in practice, except for some inertia in provincial administration. Psychologically vaporizing the last vestiges of Communist rule, the August Coup finally undid the power grab of the October Coup. It thereby returned the Soviet realm to the joyous political chaos of the 1917 interregnum, when even Lenin called Russia "the freest country in the world."

Is the moderate revolutionary revival irreversible? History does not give us any reason to think that it will be "the end of history," writing finis to all political change or uncertainty. As the Soviet Union under Gorbachev and the Russian successor state under Yeltsin have shown all too clearly, the moderate revolutionary revival does not immediately guarantee a stable outcome of freedom and democracy. It has reopened all the viewpoints and options that flowered in the earliest months of the Revolution, letting the entire political spectrum from monarchism through the dictatorship of the proletariat spread out again across the Russian firmament. This is not quite the same as the original explosion of political passions when the monarchy collapsed in 1917; now, after all, the country is experiencing the end of a revolutionary process and not the beginning of a new one. Nevertheless, we still cannot say what mix of goals and values from the early phase of the revolution may prevail – whether, for example, the future synthesis might incorporate the more socialistic norms of late 1917 or approximate the classical liberalism heard more loudly at the beginning of the revolutionary year.

Post-coup politics in Russia have swung further to the right than might have been expected. This is a reaction to the unusual prolongation of the postrevolutionary dictatorship under the Communists and their perpetuation of the revolutionary vocabulary for appearances of legitimacy. The ideology of socialism and the workers' state was denied the opportunity to recover its honesty and live down its excesses that would have been afforded if the Communists had been overthrown by avowed counterrevolutionaries in the 1920s or 1930s instead of being purged in the name of Communism by Stalin's surreptitious counterrevolution. For the same reason, rightist and restorationist sentiments never had a chance to work themselves out openly under Stalin's camouflaged restoration, and now they have finally burst forth angrily but anachronistically. Still, the post-coup signs of convergence between Communist conservatives and nationalist-religious conservatives testify to the underlying affinity of these traditions in their Russian nationalism, authoritarianism, anti-Westernism, and antipathy to modern mass culture and economic individualism. They even concur in their suspicion of Masonic-Zionist plots.

Notwithstanding such manifestations of nostalgia, the moderate revolutionary revival shatters the authority and credibility of the postrevolutionary dictatorship as much as the original revolution broke up the psychological foundations of the Old Regime. But now the conditions of revolutionary turmoil and cultural backwardness under which the postrevolutionary dictatorship was established in the USSR no longer hold. The international empire and the global confrontation that the revolutionaries initiated, and their postrevolutionary heirs clung to, have dissipated. It would not be an easy matter to reconstruct the old coercive system in a society that has changed so much in the meantime. No one would respond to the old lies and excuses, and probably not many would respond even to new lies and excuses. The experience of other countries with the postrevolutionary endgame indicates that whatever perturbations and pendulum swings post-Soviet society may still undergo, the revolutionary process is finally coming to a close.

6

THE END OF
REVOLUTIONARY EMPIRE

7 October 1989. Mikhail Gorbachev is in East Berlin to celebrate the fortieth anniversary of the "German Democratic Republic" (a historical misnomer, neither German nor democratic nor a republic, but really just what the West Germans have always called it, the "Soviet Occupation Zone"). He has flown in from Moscow with a message that the East German Communists, challenged by the increasing number of their subjects fleeing to the West, prefer not to hear. East Germany has, as he puts it to the assemblage of Western journalists, "the capacity to learn from life and when it is necessary, to make the corrections that it requires . . . and base their policy on the realities."[1]

In his formal speech at the modern Palace of the Republic (built on the site of the bombed-out imperial residence) Gorbachev advises the East German leaders, "Issues concerning the GDR are decided not in Moscow but in Berlin."[2] This means that Moscow will not support East Berlin in its current anti-reform stand; simultaneously with Gorbachev's visit, the nearly half-million Soviet troops in East Germany get orders to stay at their bases, and this news is appropriately leaked to the East German media.

After Gorbachev, the unrepentant old Stalinist Erich Honecker takes the podium. Honecker has run East Germany and the "Socialist Unity" (i.e. Communist) Party on behalf of the Soviets for eighteen years, and now he even censors the news of Soviet reforms. He can only repeat the tired old clichés of Stalinism: we are still moving forward, and we reject "policies leading back to capitalism."[3] Privately Gorbachev warns him, "Those who are late will be punished by life itself."[4]

At a meeting with the Politburo of the Socialist Unity Party, according to one East German official, Gorbachev makes it very clear that neither the spectacle of thousands of people fleeing the country, nor the prospect of violence to keep them in, are helping him in his own difficult situation at home.[5] "Look at the situation in the world," he warns them.

Everything changes, and we cannot act as before. For many years

117

we used to say the West was stagnating and would collapse. But they've overtaken us in terms of technology, and socially they have done much more than we have. You live close to them and must feel this.[6]

Gorbachev's appearance is greeted by thousands of East Berliners who pack the vast space of Alexanderplatz surrounded by East German government buildings, shouting for their champion of reform, "Gorby, Gorby!" and "Freiheit, Freiheit!" Polish Foreign Minister Mieczysław Rakowski, standing next to Gorbachev, is heard to say, "It looks as if they want you to liberate them again!"[7] According to Timothy Garton Ash, Gorbachev gives "direct encouragement" to the younger East German leaders to get rid of Honecker.[8]

As soon as Gorbachev leaves for the airport, the police are ordered in to break up the Alexanderplatz crowd, in defiance of all the Soviet leader's reform talk. They try especially to nail the television cameramen, but West German television nonetheless gets good footage to broadcast back to the East Germans. Honecker issues orders to Security Chief Egon Krenz that any more such demonstrations will be put down with tanks and live ammunition. He is particularly worried about the situation in the famous old Saxon city of Leipzig, which has been a center of dissent organized around the Lutheran Church and the unofficial reform organization "New Forum," founded just a month before for "the restructuring of the German Democratic Republic" on lines of democratic socialism.[9] To the Chinese representative at the anniversary celebration Honecker explains the trouble as "aggressive anti-socialist action by imperialist class opponents," and he invokes the Tiananmen Square massacre of the previous June (a crisis also precipitated by a Gorbachev visit): "There is a fundamental lesson to be learned from the counterrevolutionary unrest in Beijing and the present campaign."[10]

Two days later, on 9 October, the Leipzig protesters gather outside the Nikolai Church in the city center, where they have been holding weekly peace vigils. They now plan a massive demonstration in the name of New Forum, which West German television has made a household word. In response, the police and security troops are mobilized and issued live ammunition. According to the former East German intelligence chief Markus Wolf, "There was a written order from Honecker for a Chinese solution. It could have been worse than Beijing."[11] Some of the troops anxiously apologize to the inquiring writer Christof Hein, "We're just regular draftees. We had our orders." But Hein writes, "They sense the contempt of the populace and feel that they themselves are victims."[12]

Meanwhile a group of Leipzig intellectuals and churchmen persuade the local Communist leaders to meet with them at the apartment of the well-known orchestra conductor Kurt Masur, to try to find a way to avoid violence. One of the Leipzig party officials then and there phones Security Chief Krenz in East Berlin for last-minute instructions. Krenz, as it turns out, understands Gorbachev's message better than Honecker and the Old Guard: no more violence, and no support if you try it. He fears, according to associates, that "hundreds of dead and wounded would be a fatal blow to the East German party's standing at home and abroad."[13] Accordingly, Krenz takes the crucial step: he flies to Leipzig to countermand Honecker's orders in person and let the demonstration proceed. The local Communists broadcast a statement that they are ready to talk reform with the dissidents, and 70,000 people march, unimpeded, shouting demands for freedom and democracy.

This is the true revolutionary moment for East Germany, the point where the Old Regime hesitates to use force against its opponents and the populace shed their fear of being shot at. "People are not afraid any more to stand up and rally in masses, and proclaim their desires," observes a Western diplomat on the scene.[14] It is like the fall of the Tsar in Russia in 1917, or even the fall of the Bastille in revolutionary Paris. From this time on, East Germany is ruled from the streets, until the Communists are driven out of power altogether.

After Leipzig, demonstrations roll on with impunity while the effective authority of the East Berlin regime steadily unravels. Within the next fortnight the Socialist Unity Party will depose Honecker and install Krenz as leader in an unavailing series of concessions to the multitude. Honecker will put the blame on Gorbachev-inspired "intrigues that were aimed at destroying our party . . . . It was the same scenario in all the former socialist countries."[15] No matter. Exactly one month after the turning point in Leipzig, pressed by the continuing hemorrhage of East German citizens to West Germany through Hungary and Czechoslovakia, Krenz will get Gorbachev's OK to order the Berlin Wall opened,[16] and East Germany as a political entity and a Soviet strategic bastion will be finished.

*

In Eastern Europe in 1989 one of the most extraordinary revolutionary events of all time took place with scarcely a drop of blood being shed, outside of Romania. Six different countries – the so-called Soviet satellites – who had suffered for decades under the yoke of Stalinist or near-Stalinist political and economic systems, responded that year to the surge of change in the Soviet Union in a chain reaction of reform and revolt that threw off both the internal Communist regimes and submission to Soviet great-power interests. Equally surprising, in the light of its long record of forcibly curbing East European independence,

Moscow acquiesced completely in the loss of its East European security zone. At the same time the Soviet reformers allowed the national minorities who made up nearly half of the population of the USSR to express their long-pent-up aspirations in free elections. Never before in history had a great power retreated so precipitously from its sphere of dominion without having been crushed in war.

Such overwhelming events as the Soviet surrender of Eastern Europe and the easing of constraints on the Soviet minorities require an explanation going much deeper than the politics of the moment. The explanation is at hand, however, in the same historical circumstances that have underlain the transformation in Soviet internal political life since the mid-1980s. The end of the Soviet empire and the end or at least abeyance of Russian imperial interests are direct consequences of the playing out of the revolutionary process in the Soviet Union and the repudiation of the Stalinist postrevolutionary dictatorship. In the foreign relations of a revolutionary country, as in its domestic affairs, the moderate revolutionary revival means an end to the long and feverish attempt to maintain a center of imperial power by confrontational force and oppression of the helpless. When Eduard Shevardnadze was challenged at the party congress in 1990 about "the collapse of socialism in Eastern Europe," he responded,

> Soviet diplomacy did not and could not set itself the goal of opposing the elimination of administrative-command systems and regimes in other countries, systems and regimes that were imposed on them and alien to them. That would be at variance with our own actions and the principles of the new political thinking . . . . Any other position would be a reversion to complete chauvinism and an imperial great-power attitude . . . . We couldn't interfere . . . in the affairs of other states. I think we acted correctly.[17]

*

Revolutions, though they break out in particular countries, are international phenomena with powerful international effects. The issues and tensions that prompt a revolutionary breakdown and drive the revolutionary process are not unique to the country in which the revolution actually occurs. In varying degrees the same strivings are felt in neighboring countries that have reached a level of modernization presenting the issues of the given epoch, but that have not yet satisfactorily resolved those issues. The European democratic revolution, for instance, was centered in France, but that was only because, among

Europe's absolute monarchies, France had the strongest unsatisfied middle class. The socialist revolution broke out in Russia because rapid development without commensurate political reform had generated the world's strongest working class that still lacked basic political and economic rights. In this respect Lenin was correct in calling Russia "the weakest link in the chain of imperialism."[18]

Since the issues in a revolution are international, the event automatically evokes both sympathy and hostility in the outside world. There is sympathy among those social elements who feel aggrieved in their own countries, and hostility among the adherents of the status quo who feel threatened by the potential or actual response in their own countries to the revolutionary example. These reactions can quickly lead to overt international conflict, as the revolutionary country finds itself tempted to provide active support to its sympathizers in neighboring countries, and as foreign governments fearing such infectious politics intervene militarily to crush the revolutionary regime. "As long as any portion of this nest of vipers is left intact," said Winston Churchill of the Bolsheviks, "it will continue to breed and swarm."[19] Such alarmist threats in turn heighten the revolutionary country's sense of mission and give it the ferocity of a struggle for survival.

The pattern of international impact and foreign intervention was strikingly similar in the French and Russian revolutions. Revolutionary France roused believers in democratic reform all over Europe, and revolutionary Russia captured the allegiance of a large segment of the international socialist movement, to form the Communist International. France faced Prussian and Austrian intervention as early as 1792, even before the Terror; fear of intervention on behalf of the counterrevolutionaries helped push the revolution into its most extreme phase. Revolutionary Russia inherited the ongoing war with the Central Powers, and then, after the peace of Brest-Litovsk, had to contend with intervention by the Allied powers, Britain, France, the USA, and Japan. The Allies initially excused this step by the hope of getting Russia back into the war with Germany, but after November 1918 their only purpose (aside from restraining Japan's territorial ambitions) was to help the Russian counterrevolutionaries stamp out the source of potential revolutionary example for the masses in their own countries.

Intervention has rarely succeeded in stopping a revolution, though naturally the ability of a revolution to withstand intervention and to export its example depends on the relative power of the revolutionary country. Spain in the 1930s is one case where a revolution did succumb to foreign intervention. On the other hand, France – immediately – and Russia – eventually – found themselves in a position to move outward, link up with their foreign sympathizers, and impose satellite revolutionary governments in neighboring regions. Nazi Germany, as the base of a revolution of the Right, did the same throughout continental Europe before and during the Second World War.

Some of Russia's circumstances as a revolutionary power were unique. To begin with, Russia was a multinational empire where most minorities took a view of the Revolution quite different from that of the Russian majority. Maintenance or restoration of the integrity of the Empire was a priority for many revolutionaries, both moderate and Communist, while for the minorities the Revolution was the long-awaited opportunity to declare their own independence.

Secondly, the Russian Revolution ran through its phases against the background of wide changes in the international correlation of forces. During the extremist and Thermidorean stages, i.e. up to the 1930s, Russia remained relatively weak and was unable to act decisively on behalf of foreign revolutionary sympathizers. At the same time, exploiting those sympathizers, Moscow was able to develop in the Communist International a unique political instrument in support of its own security and foreign policy interests. The rise of the German and Japanese threat after 1931 coincided more or less with the consolidation of Stalin's postrevolutionary dictatorship, and drove him to seek alliances with foreign governments – the democracies to 1939 and then the Fascist powers themselves in 1939–1941 – instead of relying on foreign revolutionaries. Finally, the aftermath of the Second World War found the Soviet Union one of the two superpowers, at least on the surface, and gave urgency as well as opportunity at long last to expand the area of Soviet-style revolution. By this time, however, the export model was the Stalinist postrevolutionary dictatorship, accompanied by the requirement of complete subservience to the Soviet Union.

The Revolution of 1917, the terms of the Brest-Litovsk peace with the Central Powers, and the circumstances of civil war dealt a severe blow to the territorial integrity of the Russian empire. First, the Soviet government recognised the independence of Finland, in the vain hope that it would swing into line with the Bolshevik Revolution. The Ukraine and the three states of Transcaucasia were detached by the Treaty of Brest-Litovsk, but went on trying to assert their independence after the collapse of the Central Powers. Poland and the Baltic provinces, occupied by Germany until the Armistice, declared their independence. Except for Central Asia, Russia was temporarily reduced to its boundaries before the reign of Peter the Great.

Lenin had made a great point of promising self-determination to any nationality that wanted independence. Once in power, he showed himself determined to hold or recover the minority areas. They would be compensated only with cultural autonomy plus the elaborate fiction of a federal state. Using the Red Army, Lenin was successful in the Ukraine and Transcaucasia, but he failed in Poland and the Baltic states, leaving *irredenta* that later became prime targets of Stalin's reborn Russian nationalism.

*

The Second World War altered the whole picture. The collapse of the Nazi revolutionary empire throughout Europe offered Stalin the opportunity of revolutionary expansion that Lenin never had. He was able immediately to incorporate into the Soviet Union most of the lost imperial territories – the Baltic states, Bessarabia (Moldavia), and western Belorussia – plus the western Ukraine that had never been part of the Muscovite empire. Then, by tactics of intrigue and repression that are all too well known, he installed throughout the region of the Red Army's maximum advance in Eastern Europe a series of one-party governments in the Soviet image.

A problem remained to bring these pseudo-revolutionary regimes fully into line with the Soviet standard. Like the French under Bonaparte, by the time Stalin's army moved into neighboring countries, it represented not the spirit of pristine revolutionary idealism but the cynical and twisted aims of the postrevolutionary dictatorship. The opportunity for expansion was to be exploited for the enhancement of imperial power – and for sheer plunder – rather than to genuinely share the original ideals of the Revolution. Nevertheless, in the countries they moved into, the Russians were greeted by revolutionary enthusiasts who lacked the popular support to take power on their own (except in Yugoslavia), and happily made themselves tools of the "liberators."

Unfortunately for themselves, Communism's foreign sympathizers were out of phase with the revolutionary process in the Soviet Union. They still thought of the Revolution in the terms of its extremist-utopian phase, not as the postrevolutionary dictatorship that the USSR had by this time become. Installed in power by Soviet manipulation and pressure between 1945 and 1948, the satellite Communists remained dependent on Stalin's patronage, and were helpless to resist when he moved to impose his own postrevolutionary norms and imperial ambitions. The result was a quick falling out between the revolutionary power and its clients. "National Communist" leaders in the East European satellites tried to resist the Soviet diktat, but were brutally purged in favor of pure lackeys of the CPSU. Between 1948 and 1952, show trials like those of Moscow in the 1930s pronounced death sentences on top Communists in Bulgaria, Hungary, and Czechoslovakia. Tito's Yugoslavia was the exception that proved the rule, successfully breaking away at this point from the Soviet bloc and asserting its own brand of Communism.

The underlying political culture in Moscow's East European sphere was far from uniform. Deeply embedded national distinctions, above all the long-standing division between the realm of Western-Catholic civilization and that of Eastern-Byzantine-Orthodox Christendom, governed the firmness with which local Communist regimes could be implanted. Not counting the special, complex case of Yugoslavia, every country in the western group, i.e., "East-Central Europe," attempted mass defiance of Soviet control at least once prior to the eruption of 1989: East Germany in 1953, Hungary in 1956, Czechoslovakia in 1968, Poland tentatively in 1956 and then massively with the Solidarity movement of 1980–81. No such thing happened in the eastern part of the bloc comprising Romania and Bulgaria, though Romania's government did assert its diplomatic independence of the Soviet Union in the 1960s (while internally the country slid deeper into Stalin-type dictatorship). There are both recent and long-term explanations of the difference between the two regions. At the time of the Communist takeovers, East-Central Europe was further along than the Balkans in modernization and industrialization, thanks in part to the benefits of prior Austrian rule as compared with Turkish. The religious tradition in East-Central Europe was one of internationalism and equality with the state (Catholic), or of religious pluralism (Protestant), as against the Orthodox experience of subservience to foreign rule.

The efforts in each country of East-Central Europe to throw off Stalinist oppression underscore the limits of totalitarianism. Where totalitarianism has been unnaturally established, so to speak, as a foreign export of a revolution already in its postrevolutionary phase, it is vulnerable to popular resistance from below unless it can count on being shored up by the outside power that sponsored it. It is even vulnerable to reform from within the regime, as Poland showed briefly when the erstwhile National Communist Wladislaw Gomulka was restored to power in 1956, as Hungary showed gradually beginning in the early 1960s, and as Czechoslovakia showed absolutely in the Prague Spring of 1968. Differences of political culture and the absence of a natural, internal revolutionary process to sift out the idealists led even the most genuine Communists in this region to resist the real principles of the Stalinist model once they showed through the ideological veil. After Khrushchev exposed Stalin's criminal record the veil concealed practically nothing, and the various Communist governments and parties, Stalinized though they had been, eased away from automatic obedience to Moscow.

*

The moderate revolutionary revival entails the abandonment of everything that has gone into revolutionary imperialism – the illusions, the methods, and the conception of irreconcilable conflict with the non-revolutionary world. Embodied in Gorbachev's perestroika and democratization, this ultimate phase in the revolutionary process abruptly changed Moscow's relationship both to its inner empire of the Soviet minorities and to its outer empire of the satellite countries. Almost at one stroke, the Soviet Union abjured both the motive and the means for maintaining postrevolutionary oppression in either zone.

Perestroika and glasnost were felt first in the inner empire of the Soviet minorities. Here, taking advantage of the new freedom for political activity in 1988 and early 1989, avowedly nationalist movements were able to organize, express their hopes, and win control of local governments. By contrast, in the outer empire Stalinist governments that had been sponsored and shored up by the Soviet Union showed some temporary staying power against the current of reform. Ultimately, however, the retreat from revolutionary empire was somewhat longer and more difficult in the inner zone than in the outer.

The national minority problem was the Achilles' heel of democratization in the Soviet Union. If the Soviet peoples were granted democratic rights of self-expression, the immediate desire would be to get out of the Union. Conversely, the deepest concern that many if not most Russians would feel, certainly the concern of Russian officials, would be to hold the Union together and prevent minority succession movements. This proved to be one of the compelling motives of the August Coup.

These contradictions are a legacy of the distinctive history of the Russian empire, as it expanded during the three centuries before the Revolution to annex non-Russian lands that represented almost half the population, a quarter of the area, and much of the key resources of the USSR. Without the regions added to the Empire in the course of its long expansion, Russia would never have become a first-rate power. Anyone, in the leadership or in the rank and file, who identified with the international status of the USSR could not look sanguinely upon the dismemberment of the Union in the spirit of minority self-determination.

Despite this potential concern, the Gorbachev regime was not deterred in the early stages of democratization by fears of centrifugal tendencies among the minorities. The minorities took part in the elections of 1989 and the formation of the new constitutional government as enthusiastic partisans of all-Union reform. Potential divisiveness could be seen, however, in the newly organized popular fronts who defeated the candidates of the Communist Party in most minority areas in the European part of the USSR. Interestingly, the pro-forma federalism embodied in the structure of the USSR took on a new reality, and the union republics created by the Communists became the vehicles for this liberated nationalist sentiment.

National self-confidence crystallized rapidly in the atmosphere of glasnost and free political debate. The republic-by-republic elections in the early months of 1990 brought avowed separatists to the lead in the Baltic republics, Moldavia, Georgia, and Armenia, as well as in the western Ukraine. These new governments immediately challenged Moscow with declarations of "sovereignty" and, in the case of the Baltics, claims of total independence (while they rejected the long-drawn-out secession process that Gorbachev offered them). Such manifestations of separatism threw the USSR into a state of constitutional chaos, the "war of laws," as republics asserted their right to override actions of the central government. This stance recalled the "nullification" doctrine proclaimed by several Southern states in the USA just before their attempted secession and the American Civil War.

The surge of minority separatism and defiance in 1989–1990 was an acute embarrassment to the Gorbachev government, as it fought the Communist conservatives and tried to find a formula for dealing with the country's deepening economic crisis. Episodes of fatal violence, as when the central authorities attacked nationalist demonstrators in Tbilisi in April 1989 and intervened in Baku in January 1990 to stop anti-Armenian riots, turned separatist enthusiasm into anti-Moscow bitterness. Lithuania's declaration of independence in March 1990, followed by Moscow's futile effort to cow the Lithuanians with a two-month trade blockade, was only the most publicized instance in a nationwide ferment. Even the smaller nationalities organized in "autonomous republics" within the Russian Republic tried to claim "sovereignty" and control over their local natural resources. By November 1990 Gorbachev was warning frantically about Fascistic tendencies, "a struggle for power," "furious attempts to discredit the institutions of state power which embody the idea of a federal union state," and "superfragmentation and chaos."[20]

A paradoxical role in this upsurge of nationalism was played by the government of the Russian Republic, after reformers carried the election of March 1990 by a narrow margin and made Boris Yeltsin chairman of the Russian Supreme Soviet. Yeltsin immediately spoke out as if he headed one of the aggrieved minorities, denouncing the vacillations of Gorbachev's Union government toward the aspirations of the nationalists, asserting Russia's own "sovereignty," and even entering into commercial treaties with other republics. The anomaly here is that Russia with its overwhelming size and position is not just one among many; it is itself *the* center, whether of an empire, a Soviet Union, or a Commonwealth of Independent States. Russia cannot be independent from itself. The practical questions were, which government would prevail in Russia, and how much autonomy from Moscow it would allow the peripheral areas.

Yeltsin's broad-mindedness about the minorities reflected the extra year of political maturation and the democratization of the electoral rules that had taken place between the election of the Union government in March 1989 and the election of the Russian government in March 1990. To assert Russian sovereignty *vis-à-vis* the Union government implicitly meant to support the other republics' claims to sovereignty. It also reflected the personal animosity between Yeltsin and Gorbachev, as the Russian chief seized upon every available issue to repair his own fortunes and embarrass the Union president.

The political base in the Russian Republic for Yeltsin's autonomist position was not solid. When the distinct organization of the Communist Party for the RSFSR was formed in June 1990, the conservative Unionists took firm control of it. Likewise, the influential Union of Writers in the Russian Republic turned out to be a bastion of conservative and nationalistic sentiment. Russian backlash against minority separatism and the Soviet Union's potential loss of great-power status welled up particularly in the armed forces. Pressure from the military to save the Union probably contributed to Gorbachev's retreat from reform in the fall of 1990. The nationalism of the minorities and reactive imperial nationalism among Russians, especially in the organs of armed force, put the process of democratization in a unbearable squeeze. "All of my convictions are based on preservation of the Union," Gorbachev told the country on TV in February 1991. "Huge efforts were made to make it so powerful, and we could lose it very quickly."[21] With so much at stake, clashing nationalisms along with the economic crisis put further prospects of the moderate revolutionary revival in the Soviet Union in a parlous situation indeed.

*

While the reforms of perestroika and the self-assertion of the Soviet minorities were still gathering momentum, the Communist satraps in the outer empire split over whether to follow Moscow's example. Honecker in East Berlin and Gustav Husak in Prague (followed there by Miloš Jakeš in 1987) dug in their heels to resist reform, in the knowledge that they could not survive in office unless the Soviet conservatives came back to power. János Kádár in Hungary and Wojciech Jaruzelski in Poland, presiding over less obdurate regimes, pointedly endorsed the Gorbachev approach. Nicolae Ceauşescu's Romania, consistently anti-Moscow, condemned perestroika, while Todor Zhivkov's Bulgaria, as always, swung into line behind the Soviet lead. Dissidents and reformers everywhere in the East European bloc saw Gorbachev as the symbol of long-awaited liberation well before his decisive appearance in East Berlin in October 1989.

Gorbachev carefully avoided any overt hint of Soviet action to export perestroika, but he gave no encouragement to Old Guard Communist

127

leaders that he would indefinitely support their hold on power. "In the past," he remarked in 1987, "it used to be said that the orchestra was conducted by Moscow and that everybody else listened. That is no longer the case."[22] First implicitly and then explicitly Gorbachev abandoned the "Brezhnev Doctrine" of 1968 – that the Soviet regime could legitimately intervene in the territory of any of its "allies" to support the cause of "socialism" against "counterrevolutionaries."[23]

Thus left to their own devices, the East European regimes moved in different ways and at different paces. Of the six satellites, if we count Romania, the one that had proceeded furthest with its own internal reconstruction was Hungary, where Kádár, the Quisling of 1956, had embraced reform in the 1960s with the slogan, "He who is not against us is with us." Hungarians had regained considerable intellectual freedom and enjoyed their long experiment in gradually marketizing and decentralizing the Stalinist command economy, until it ran up against limits to its growth in the 1980s. Swayed by the currents of change coming out of the Soviet Union, the Hungarian Communists ousted Kádár from the party and governmental leadership in 1988 and replaced him with a reform-oriented team led by Károly Grósz. The new leadership relaxed restraints on private enterprise and foreign investment, and legalized political opposition, but the spirit of reform outran it. Grosz was dropped in turn, and at its congress of 6–9 October 1989 the Hungarian Communist Party (officially the "Hungarian Socialist Workers' Party") split into a reformist majority (the "Hungarian Socialist Party") and a hard-line minority. Then free elections held in March 1990 swept all brands of Communists out of the government and put power in the hands of the Democratic Forum, more or less the equivalent of the Christian Democrats in the West. The new government set about vigorously dismantling the socialized economy and integrating Hungary into the international capitalist system, while negotiating the withdrawal of Soviet troops and aiming at a neutral foreign policy. Hungary represented the most gradual, orderly, and far-reaching instance of dismantling the heritage of the Communist regime.

Poland was another instance of step-by-step escape from the Communist past. Some reforms had survived from 1956, including the cessation of efforts to collectivize the peasants, a modest arena for small-scale private enterprise, and freedom for the Catholic Church. Poland remained the least totalitarian of the satellites, a country that Soviet theoreticians hesitated to classify as "socialist." The hold of the Communist regime was deeply shaken by the rise of the Solidarity labor movement, based on the class whom the Communists claimed especially to represent. Only the turn to the military, the installation of General Jaruzelski as president, and the imposition of martial law in December 1981 averted the collapse of the regime and probable intervention by the Soviet Army. Under Lech Walesa's leadership Solidarity remained a potent force underground, and by 1988 it was able to challenge the Jaruzelski government with a wave of crippling strikes and thereby force negotiations on political reform. In the spring of 1989 Jaruzelski agreed to allow competitive elections to one-third of the seats in the hitherto rubber-stamp parliament, plus the creation of a new senate to be completely chosen in free elections. Solidarity won almost all of the legislative seats it was allowed to contest in the June ballot, and in August, at Gorbachev's prodding, Jaruzelski accepted a coalition cabinet with Tadeusz Mazowiecki from Solidarity as prime minister.[24] Thus the combination of popular opposition, the messages of reform from Moscow, and the local Communists' loss of confidence in their own legitimacy allowed Poland, like Hungary, to move through a series of small steps from dictatorship to democracy.

It was quite another matter for the hard-line governments of East Germany and Czechoslovakia, both directly dependent for their existence on the armed Soviet presence. Both regimes resisted the example of perestroika, and East Germany even banned liberal Soviet publications from its territory. Then came the crisis for the East German Communists, posed by the flight of thousands of their subjects to West Germany, and precipitated by Gorbachev's appearance in East Berlin for the fortieth anniversary of the GDR. East Germany experienced what often happens during revolutions, the sudden evaporation of the nation's fear and consequently of the government's effective authority. In the absence of any assurance of Soviet backing, no concessions in reforming the leadership or even in opening the Berlin Wall sufficed to save the regime. Between mid-November and early December 1989 the Communists simply surrendered. They accepted a coalition cabinet, deposed the Krenz leadership, abandoned the party's "leading role" in the state, scheduled free elections, and put their fallen leader Honecker under house arrest (before he was spirited off to Moscow for medical treatment). Soviet acquiescence cleared the way for the unification of Germany and the extirpation of the entire heritage of the Communist regime in the eastern zone.

With East Germany gone, the days of the Communist government of Czechoslovakia were numbered. From the time of the initial triggering event – a police assault on a student demonstration in Prague in mid-November 1989 – less than three weeks elapsed before the Czechoslovak Communists, like their East German counterparts, surrendered, accepted a coalition cabinet, and let the old rubber-stamp National Assembly elect Václav Havel, the playwright-hero of the dissident movement, as president of the republic. To affirm connections with the Prague Spring of 1968, Alexander Dubček was made president of the National Assembly.

There remained of the old bloc only Bulgaria and Romania. These two Balkan states took diametrically opposite courses to dispose of the old regime. In Bulgaria the Communists simply dumped the aging Zhivkov, proclaimed their democratic intentions, renamed themselves the Bulgarian Socialist Party, and went on to win the reasonably honest election of June 1990. Only some months afterward did popular pressure and a general strike lead to the installation of a coalition cabinet under non-Communist leadership, leaving the "Socialists" as a strong opposition. Romania was the only one of the former Soviet satellites to experience the end of the Communist regime as a classic revolution. It began with police atrocities committed against demonstrators in mid-December 1989, and culminated in the defection of the army; the flight, capture, and execution of dictator Ceauşescu and his wife; and the establishment of a provisional government under the "Council of National Salvation," dominated by dissident Communists.

Yugoslavia, first of the original Communist bloc to begin reform when it broke with Stalin in 1948, was the last to complete the process (if we do not count the ultimate Stalinist die-hards in Albania). In the 1950s Marshall Tito's government had carried out its own Thermidorean Reaction like Lenin did in 1921. It rejected the worst features of Stalinist totalitarianism and accepted individual farming, small-scale private business, cultural and religious freedom, and the right to travel abroad. It remained a one-party state, authoritarian if not totalitarian, tempered over the years by major grants of power to its six constituent republics. This federal system reflected the country's complex ethnic makeup straddling the West–East cultural boundary. But in the wake of the revolutions elsewhere in Eastern Europe, even the Yugoslav compromise had become an anachronism. In 1990, one by one, the Communist governments of the Yugoslav republics conceded free elections, only to see rearing up again the forces of nationalism that had threatened to tear the country apart prior to the Communist era. The western, Catholic republics voted secessionist governments in; Bosnia-Herzegovina in the center split on religious lines, Catholic, Orthodox, and Moslem; and the Orthodox Serbs kept their Communists in power with the hope of preserving the Serbian-dominated federal union. The upshot in less than a year was open civil war, with no solution in sight.

A number of common themes emerged in the East European revolutions of 1989 despite wide differences among them in the actual course of events. All took place under the stimulus of reform in the USSR and in the assurance that the Soviets would not intervene against them. All testify to the fragility of totalitarianism when it is not the product of a natural, native revolutionary process but a system imposed by a larger revolutionary neighbor. In every case, economic frustrations had built up as the planned economies bumped into a ceiling and ceased to grow.

In all but Romania (under a deranged dictator) the old Communist leadership, overwhelmed by adverse circumstances and popular hatred, essentially abdicated. Last-minute attempts of the respective Communist parties to save themselves by installing new chiefs and promising reform and democracy availed them naught. Like the federal structure within the USSR, the rubber-stamp parliaments and dummy non-Communist parties that the Communists had maintained in Eastern Europe for the sake of appearances suddenly came to life and provided useful channels for shifting power out of the hands of the Communists with minimal disruption to public life.

*

Nothing demonstrates the artificiality of the postrevolutionary imperialism imposed by the Soviet Union in Eastern Europe as much as the immediate revival of pre-Communist political life. Democratic forms complete with the standard European institutions of cabinet government and proportional representation were embraced everywhere. On the Central European side of the great cultural divide – in East Germany, Poland, Czechoslovakia, and Hungary, plus the Yugoslav republics of Croatia and Slovenia – the Communist legacy was spurned like a bad dream. Reformist Communists won little more appreciation than the Old Guard, and anything that smacked of "socialism" was rejected on principle. Economic salvation was sought in the free market and privatization – in other words, in the restoration of capitalism, against which the Communists had fulminated throughout their tenure of power. For a comparable situation, we have to imagine the survival of Bonaparte's empire down to the 1850s, with all it would have meant in French domination and imposed social change in Central Europe. It would not have been altogether surprising if the nations concerned, having thrown off the French yoke, would want to restore the privileges of the Church and the aristocracy and abolish such discredited experiments as equality before the law and the right to vote.

Even more striking than the return to pre-Communist politics and economics in Eastern Europe was the upsurge of nationalist and separatist passions in all their old intensity. Apart from the special case of Yugoslavia, Czechoslovakia was the most affected, in the form of Slovak separatism. Slovaks actually rioted for the insertion of a hyphen in "Česko-slovensko"; the solution was a new official name of the country – "Czech and Slovak Federated Republic." The formula did not allow any rights for the substantial Hungarian minority in Slovakia, who found themselves in a position similar to the sub-minorities in the USSR. Poland virtually restored the Catholic Church, the traditional vehicle of national consciousness, to the status of a state religion. East Germany

131

was carried away by sentiment for unification with the Federal Republic, despite the grave risks in a sudden economic merger that became all too apparent soon after unity was consummated in 1990. East of the cultural divide, by contrast, revolution brought a measure of relief to ethnic relations, as the systematic persecution of Hungarians in Romania and of Turks in Bulgaria was called off by the new governments.

Everywhere in the Eastern bloc, once the Communist straitjacket was removed, old pre-Communist ideologies and political cultures came back to life. It was as if they had just been dormant for half a century, without any chance really to mature or progress in the meantime. Whether the former Soviet satellites might salvage anything of value from their Communist experience is a question we will turn to in the concluding chapter.

In defense of their intense responses to the new freedom, it must be remembered that since the Middle Ages (for Poland, since the eighteenth century) none of the nations of East-Central Europe or the Balkans had enjoyed the luxury of independent statehood until the mid- or late nineteenth century (Serbia, Romania, and Bulgaria) or the end of the First World War (Poland and the former Austrian dominions, as well as the Baltic States). The immediate post-Communist response throughout the region recalled the democratic honeymoon of 1919, before right-wing dictatorships took over everywhere except in Czechoslovakia ("the only democracy east of the Rhine"). Now again there are clouds on the horizon in the direction of the populist Right. Following the "struggle for freedom," writes the number-one anti-Communist intellectual in Poland, Adam Michnik, comes the "struggle for power and revenge."

> Every revolution has its logic and every one has the tendency to devour its own children. If the logic of compromise between the main political actors prevails, a democratic order will prevail. If the logic of revenge wins, we will face the hell of dictatorship. We can choose a normal European order, a world of normal conflicts and normal human compromises, a varied world that is, because of its variety, also dangerous. Or we can choose an authoritarian state, a nationalism that rejects a pluralist culture, an order that gives up on religious tolerance, a strong quasi-dictatorial power that offers, as a solution to the common poverty, a populist envy and a chauvinism that distorts the human face with hatred.[25]

*

A revolutionary empire cannot survive the end of the postrevolutionary dictatorship that held it together. What was exceptional in the case of the Soviet empire was the voluntary dismantling of the postrevolutionary dictatorship, and with it renunciation of the coercion or threat of coercion that had kept both the inner – Soviet – and outer – satellite – zones of Communist domination under Moscow's control. Thus the inescapable price of perestroika, of leading the Soviet realm into the era of the moderate revolutionary revival, was to let the subjects of the revolutionary empire go their own way. No change in the Gorbachev years could testify so convincingly to the genuineness of perestroika as Soviet acceptance of the vast losses in strategic power and position entailed by the independence of Eastern Europe and the tolerance of national independence movements within the USSR.

The challenge to Moscow's authority took different forms not only in Eastern Europe but in the various Soviet republics, reflecting their differences in culture and circumstances. Beginning with the elections in the spring of 1990, the separatist drive was most pronounced in those republics where the basic cultural heritage is European but the language is non-Slavic: the three Baltic states, the Moldavian Republic (or Moldova, as it now calls itself in Romanian), and Georgia and Armenia. In these areas anti-Communist leaders won electoral power democratically, forthwith claimed sovereignty, declined to participate in Gorbachev's referendum of March 1991 on saving the Union, and refused to sign the new Union Treaty. Defiance of the Union by the Slavic republics – Ukraine and Belorussia – and the Moslem republics – Azerbaidzhan and the five republics of Central Asia – came only after the August Coup and in most cases was led by Communists-turned-nationalist whose opposition to the coup was belated and opportunistic.

By the time of the coup Russia's revolutionary empire had all but dissipated. The East European satellites were completely gone, and the Baltic states were only awaiting international recognition. The other non-Russian Soviet republics had taken control of their own destinies, to determine for themselves how tight or how loose their relations with the Russian center would remain. The coup itself did nothing more than remove the last inhibitions on absolute self-determination among the Soviet republics. In most cases it was their Communist leaders – some reformed, some not so reformed, especially in Central Asia – who led the assertion of *de facto* and *de jure* independence. In this they were powerfully encouraged by Yeltsin, against the instincts of some of his more moderate supporters such as St. Petersburg mayor Sobchak. For his own Russian state, Yeltsin seized the opportunity of the coup to appropriate the institutions and properties of the old central government and to claim the status of legal successor to the USSR in all international matters.

The ultimate abolition of the USSR was no more legal than the August Coup, or for that matter, the coup of 1917 that created the Soviet regime. Yeltsin, having rendered Gorbachev's government impotent just as the

Bolsheviks had Kerensky's in 1917, administered the *coup de grâce* by proclaiming at Minsk on 8 December 1991 together with his colleagues from Ukraine and Belorussia (now "Belarus") that the Soviet Union no longer existed. This was, as Gorbachev pointed out, a pre-emption of the rights of the nine other remaining members of the Union, though in fact none of their leaders cared to see the Union preserved. All were happy to affiliate with the newly announced "Commonwealth of Independent States," an ill-defined association with no powers from above and no obligations from below.

The breakup of the Union was much more wrenching in its consequences than the abandonment of Communist control over the satellites. The latter, after all, had always remained juridically sovereign entities with their own laws, money, and diplomats, however their lives had been skewed by Soviet influence. The former Soviet republics had all been part of a Russia-centered polity for at least a century (Central Asia) and in some cases (part of the Ukraine) more than three centuries. (The only exceptions were the western Ukraine and the brief interwar independence of the Baltic states.) Thus, release of the subject minorities meant not only the retrenchment of revolutionary power but the sacrifice of old annexations to the Empire that long antedated the Russian Revolution.

In addition to the trauma that secession of the Soviet minorities dealt to Russian pride and to Moscow's international status, there were practical difficulties impeding their independence. Within the confines of the Soviet state, economic integration was far advanced, and considerable demographic integration had taken place as well, in comparison with the much more modest degree of economic reciprocity with the satellites and the absence of population-mixing in that zone. Major investments carried out during the Soviet five-year plans were concentrated in particular places without reference to the boundaries of the union republics. This made all parts of the country highly interdependent, and prone to economic disruption by the ethnic tensions uncovered during perestroika. Thus, for example, the largest enterprises for the production of detergents and pharmaceuticals happened to be located in the Armenian SSR, leaving supplies to the whole country vulnerable to such non-economic circumstances as Armenian environmental protests and Azerbaidzhan's blockage of rail traffic to and from Armenia.

Demographically the various Soviet nationalities had mixed, migrated, and intermarried to a significant degree since Tsarist days. Boundaries could not and cannot be neatly drawn between the areas of settlement of different nationalities. All minority republics as well as the Russian part of the country have members of other nationalities living within them as sub-minorities, whom the dominant nationality of a

134

given republic are as much inclined to suppress as they themselves were suppressed in the past by Moscow. Further, Russians have been settling for centuries in the minority areas, making many of the larger cities in those regions more Russian than native, while significant numbers of the minority nationalities have lived for generations in Moscow, St. Petersburg/Leningrad, and other Russian centers. In these circumstances there has been a high rate of marriage between members of different nationalities.

Though now nominally independent, the former Soviet republics have not yet sorted out the different principles of nationality, whether it should be purely territorial or based on subjective national identity. In the extreme case, to protect their ethnic identity, the Baltic republics have tried to deny equal rights of citizenship to Russians and others who may actually have been born there and lived there all their lives. Conversely, Russians in the Baltic states have vociferously resisted secession.

Disposition of the revolutionary empire, outer as well as inner, was the highest hurdle that the moderate revolutionary revival had to surmount. Following the vote for the Union Treaty in the spring of 1991 in the nine republics who considered it, Gorbachev called secession "impossible, madness," even if the die-hards had to be given the option to "decide for themselves what they need and what kind of society they want to have."[26] Independence in fact meant the rupture of social ties at every level from the governmental to the personal (exacerbating the economic crisis of perestroika), and the creation *ex nihilo* of the attributes of independent statehood (with worrisome implications for the control of a superpower military force and its nuclear stockpile). Overshadowing the whole process is the power of Russia, the heart of the former empire, which began almost reflexively to reclaim that status as soon as the formal existence of the old Communist center had been terminated.

With the proclamation of the Commonwealth of Independent States, the Communist revolution in the Russian empire formally came to an end. Whether the Empire was altogether finished, in substance as well as form, remained to be seen. For the moment, the most successful accomplishment of the Commonwealth was scored by its Unified Team in Olympic sports.

7

THE END OF
THE COMMUNIST MENACE

18 November 1985. An Aeroflot jet touches down at the world's peace-making capital of last resort, Geneva, bringing General Secretary Gorbachev – accompanied, Western style, by his wife Raisa – for the first meeting of the Soviet and American leaders since Jimmy Carter got a bear hug from Leonid Brezhnev in Vienna six years before. Already waiting for him is President Ronald Reagan, who has been relaxing for a day and a half after arriving all smiles together with the First Lady. Nancy Reagan is flushed with success for her part in making this event come to pass in order to assure her husband's "place in history,"[1] while the arch-hawk, Defense Secretary Caspar Weinberger, has been left back home vainly writing out warnings about Soviet cheating and leaking them to the press. The Evil Empire and the citadel of capitalist imperialism have come together to attempt a "fresh start" in Soviet–American relations, in Reagan's words, and, as Gorbachev said on his arrival, "to halt the unprecedented arms race" and "avert the threat of nuclear war."[2] They are beginning a process of diplomacy that will revolutionize the configuration of world politics.

Both Reagan and Gorbachev have been constrained by domestic political pressures to do something about the relations between their two countries, which have steadily worsened since the time when the two men reached the top policy-making level, Reagan when he was elected over incumbent president Carter in 1980 and Gorbachev when he joined the Politburo in Moscow in 1978. The low point came in September 1983, when a Soviet fighter plane shot down Korean Airlines flight 007 as it strayed inexplicably over Sakhalin Island – a deliberate atrocity, the Reagan Administration charged; defense against a hostile intelligence incursion, retorted Moscow.

Ever since the mid-1970s, under cover of the nuclear parity acknowledged by the Nixon Administration, the Soviet Union has been engaging in political adventures to win influence in the Third World, notably through armed intervention in Afghanistan. This behavior has revived for Americans their old fear of Communist world revolution. Under

136

Reagan the USA has deferred ratification of the SALT II nuclear arms treaty negotiated by Carter, and has launched an arms buildup to force an end to the Soviets' expansionism by making them overstrain their economy in the effort to keep up. But this program has provoked Americans into cries of domestic economic woe and demands for a nuclear freeze. Simultaneously, a new leadership generation has come to power in the USSR, aware of the country's underlying weaknesses and anxious to relieve it of the burden of the arms race. So for both Reagan and Gorbachev the Geneva summit meeting has become politically unavoidable.

The two leaders meet personally for the first time on Tuesday morning, 19 November, at the American conference headquarters in a lakeside villa called Château Fleur d'Eau. American officials are worried that preparations are incomplete and that Reagan has not absorbed enough of their briefings. The plan is for fifteen minutes of get-acquainted chit-chat with only the interpreters present, followed by formal negotiations with full staffs. Instead, in front of a fire on the hearth, Gorbachev and Reagan get into a serious discussion and do not move on to the plenary negotiating session for over an hour.

Gorbachev's negotiating position in this "Fireside Summit" is simple – cut all long-range nuclear weapons by 50 per cent, as Foreign Minister Shevardnadze has already proposed. Reagan has the same idea, but his stance is more complex: during the past two years, in lieu of his "evil empire" language, he has become wedded to the "Strategic Defense Initiative," popularly known as "Star Wars" – the multi-billion-dollar program to guarantee American security by means of anti-missile weapons orbiting in space. The Soviets, less convinced than many American critics that SDI would never work, balk at a program that might give the US and its Western partners an even greater advantage in high-tech weaponry.

Neither Reagan nor Gorbachev gives ground in the course of five more hours of private talks and nine hours of full-scale negotiations held during the next two days. Reagan gets so excited about SDI that at one point he goes on for ten minutes without realizing that he has to stop for the interpreter. Each leader avers his own good intentions and complains of the offensive potential of the other. "Why should we trust you more than you trust us?" Gorbachev asks.[3] Reagan pulls out index cards to read dubious quotations from Lenin and Stalin against Gorbachev.[4] The verbal sparring goes on to human rights and Third World conflicts, with no more progress toward any solution. Apart from endorsing the arms control talks that have already been going on, the two sides eventually come to agreement on only three concrete matters – to extend the cultural exchange treaty, to make a joint statement at the end of the summit, and to have more summits soon, both in Washington and in

Moscow. But a vast intangible has been accomplished, "a new psychological climate," in the view of *Pravda*'s correspondents at the meeting.[5] The leaders agree in their joint statement, "A nuclear war cannot be won and must never be fought."[6] Reagan reveals how far he has moved when he says to Gorbachev at one point, "I bet the hard-liners in both our countries are bleeding when we shake hands."[7] Gorbachev tells the press at the end, "I will be so bold . . . as to say that the world has become a more secure place."[8]

*

The Geneva Summit of 1985 was soon overshadowed by the succession of startling changes in Soviet–Western relations that followed it. But it was the turning point. It headed the superpowers away from a ten-year escalation of their old hostility and toward the total transformation of their relationship. Even before the formal collapse of Communist rule this turnabout was recognized as the end of the Cold War.

Central to such a momentous change was the Soviet Union's decision to abandon the role of a revolutionary superpower. This did not happen all of a sudden on 21 August or 8 December 1991. Like the internal dictatorship, Cold War rivalry with the West had been softening steadily under Gorbachev. From the start, retreat from international confrontation had been an integral aspect of his reform program, to rescue the Soviet Union from the impasse of isolation, stagnation, and exhaustion into which Stalinist and neo-Stalinist rule had led the country.

The end of the Cold War and the taming of Soviet international behavior, followed by the formal dissolution of the USSR, raise as many questions for history as they have settled for diplomacy. How was such a vast transformation possible? How could the confrontation of revolutionary and anti-revolutionary forces that had set the context of Soviet–Western relations since 1917 so quickly give way to cooperation for the good of humanity, and then to negotiations for emergency Western aid to the former Soviet republics? How could the Communist superpower change so abruptly? How could it have mustered such seemingly formidable power on the world scene, only to implode, in the words of two Soviet conservatives, into "a second-class country"? "The catastrophe that befell the USSR in international relations was equal to the consequences of a defeat in World War III."[9]

The seeming ease of the Soviet Union's retreat from superpower status, even before its collapse, raises further questions. Was it really just a tactical maneuver, as many Westerners initially thought, a ruse to buy time and wheedle aid from the capitalists while the citadel of proletarian dictatorship rectified some of its economic errors and readied itself for a new revolutionary drive? Or had it just been an illusion that the Soviet Union ranked as a superpower, an expensive pretense easily abandoned by a reforming government? If so, how could Western leaders have thought the Soviet Union so dangerous, for so long? What really had been the role of Marxist ideology in impelling the Soviets to threaten the peace or to keep up the appearance of doing so? What happened to the presumed imperial urges in Russian political culture? How much of Soviet intractability was inherent in the Communist regime, how much in old Russian habit, how much only in fears and assumptions on the part of outsiders?

Clearly, a great source of international tension embedded in the Soviet regime disappeared in the period from 1985 to 1991. The reasons for this exhaustion of belligerence take us back to the broad question of the revolutionary process in Russia and the kind of social and political order it had introduced. How did the character of the postrevolutionary dictatorship govern the Soviet Union's international behavior prior to Gorbachev? What new attitudes toward the revolutionary legacy permitted the moderate revolutionary revival to take hold in Soviet foreign policy?

Revolutionary governments always have abnormal relations with the outside world. As we have noted in the previous chapter, the revolution inevitably arouses passionate reactions abroad, pro and con, over the same issues that bring about the upheaval in the revolutionary center. The revolutionaries expect their own principles to spread everywhere else, and if their country is strong enough they may be tempted to use its power to advance the revolutionary cause – or to advance other interests of their country in the name of the revolutionary cause. Equally, anti-revolutionary powers may be tempted to intervene and crush the new challenge to the old order. Severe tension is inevitable between the revolutionary country and its adversaries, and war at some point is very likely.

Since revolution is so intimately bound up with a country's foreign relations, it is not surprising that the actual character of those relations should change as the revolutionary process unfolds through its characteristic stages and alters the nature of the revolutionary regime. Terminology may not keep up with changing leadership and new aims, and outside perceptions even less so; thus, foreigners may continue to react for and against the revolution long after revolutionary principles have yielded to more down-to-earth considerations in guiding the regime that arose in the name of those principles. This is exactly what happened in revolutionary Russia's relations with the outside world.

Long before the events of the 1980s and 1990s, during the successive phases of the revolutionary process, Soviet international behavior, goals, and methods changed as much as the internal system. As in internal affairs, the Stalinist and neo-Stalinist regime maintained a deceptive ideological continuity to justify its postrevolutionary and counterrevolutionary behavior in revolutionary terms. In the West, both sympathizers and enemies of the Revolution continued for decades to see the Soviet Union in the revolutionary garb in which it enshrouded itself.

After the Second World War, Western leaders credited the Soviet state with far more underlying strength than it really enjoyed. They were overly impressed by the success of the militarized Stalinist dictatorship in channeling its resources into the support of national power, and its solid propaganda facade. Judging the Soviet Union to be both revolutionary and powerful, Westerners took it to be a profound threat to the bourgeois social order, and blew the appearance of Soviet power up into a terrifing menace. Then, after 1985, overwrought assumptions about the Soviet threat evaporated as quickly as the Soviet Union's own pretenses in the sunnier light of glasnost.

*

Russia's revolutionary foreign relations, like the revolutionary government itself, took shape in the fiery crucible of the First World War. Just as it helped drive the revolutionary process from moderate to extreme, the war embittered relations between the new Soviet state and all the other major powers, enemy or allied, and left its mark for many years to come. The February Revolution was naturally welcome to Russia's democratic allies in the war with Germany, and it removed the last impediment to America's entry into the war. What consternation among the Allies, then, when revolutionary fanatics believed to be in the pay of the Germans overthrew the Provisional Government, denounced Russia's treaties, and took their country out of the war. Not that the Bolsheviks were simply German agents, as alleged at the time, though it is clear that Germany welcomed the fall of the Tsar as an opportunity to destabilize an enemy government, and spread money liberally among many radical factions in Russia. The worst thing about the Bolshevik Revolution, in Allied eyes, was German support, and this prompted their earliest attempts at intervention in 1918 in the quixotic hope of installing a government that would bring Russia back into the war.

No sooner were they in power than the Bolsheviks defiantly repudiated the traditional pursuit of national interest. Lenin wrote in his Decree on Peace of 26 October [8 November] 1917,

The government abolishes secret diplomacy, and . . . proclaims the absolute and immediate annulment of everything contained in these secret treaties in so far as it is aimed . . . at securing advantages and privileges for the Russian landlords and capitalists and at the retention, or extension, of the annexations made by the Great Russians.[10]

In this spirit the Bolsheviks erected a barrier of assumptions and rhetoric that walled the Soviet Union off from normal international life for the next seventy years.

Seeing themselves as the vanguard of a ripening international revolution against the capitalist order, the Soviet leaders launched the Communist International to upstage the "revisionist" Socialist International and coordinate revolutionary efforts around the world. "Bourgeois order has been sufficiently castigated by socialist critics. The object of the international communist party is to overthrow that organization and to replace it by the socialist state," wrote Trotsky in the manifesto of the First Comintern Congress.[11] Thus threatening the bourgeois way of life with the specter of a vast conspiracy run from Moscow, the Communist challenge had an indelible impact on the consciousness of the West, particularly among the Center and the Right. As for the Left, it was tragically divided, half paralyzed by the spectacle of revolutionary dictatorship in Russia and half mesmerized by it. Until comparatively recent times, the latter half continued to see the Soviet Union as the beacon light guiding their own unfulfilled revolutionary aspirations.

World revolution held a central spot in the thinking of Lenin and his followers, because it was part of their justification for attempting to seize power in Russia in 1917. Although all Marxists conceded that Russia was still too backward industrially to support a program of socialism, Lenin believed that revolution in Russia would provide the "spark" to set off the brewing international upheaval. In 1917, the Bolsheviks implicitly embraced the argument earlier worked out by Trotsky in his "theory of permanent revolution," according to which the Russian workers could temporarily seize power, but could not sustain a socialist regime unless they were supported by a proletarian revolution in the advanced countries – which their revolutionary example in Russia would supposedly trigger.

Once in power, Lenin quickly changed his priorities, as his position on the Brest-Litovsk peace showed: survival of the new regime in Russia came before taking risks to encourage the revolution abroad. One may even wonder, as the Italian historian Piero Melograni has argued, whether Lenin really wanted any foreign revolution at all, fearing to provoke truly serious anti-Communist intervention.[12] In any case, all that Moscow managed to accomplish internationally in the revolutionary era of 1918–1923 was to split the old Socialist parties and bring the left-wing schismatics under Soviet control in the name of proletarian internationalism. Without any support from victorious revolution abroad, Russian socialism was left hanging in mid-air, theoretically speaking, without a proper foundation in its own society, until Stalin came along with his "theory of socialism in one country" to say that the international revolution did not matter that much for socialist virtue in Russia.

*

From the beginning, Western responses to the Communist revolution were far more intense than any material challenge by the new Soviet state could account for. This reaction, transcending subsequent phases of Soviet belligerence and accommodationism, points to stresses and conflicts already disturbing the major Western societies that merely found in the Communist menace a focus of articulation. At least four such issues can be distinguished in the anti-Communism aroused in other countries by the Russian Revolution.

The first of these reactions, expressed from the outset in 1917, was the fear of revolutionary example, above all of "anarchy," social degeneracy, and the threat to private property. Robert Lansing, the American secretary of state under Woodrow Wilson, warned early on against recognizing a regime "wanting in international virtue" and

> striving to bring about . . . the "Social Revolution," which will sweep away national boundaries, racial distinctions, and modern political, religious, and social institutions, and make the ignorant and incapable mass of humanity dominant in the earth.[13]

Winston Churchill railed at Communism as

> a war against civilized society which can never end . . . . They too aim at a world-wide and international league, but a league of the failures, the criminals, the unfit, the mutinous, the morbid, the deranged, the distraught in every land.[14]

A little later he advised his Scottish constituents, "Civilization is being completely extinguished over gigantic areas, while the Bolsheviks hop and caper like troops of ferocious baboons amid the ruins of cities and corpses of their victims."[15]

"Communism" was socially anathema in the West as well as an economic fright. For many the word already implied the notion of communal living in place of the family, and the bourgeois mind was well prepared to receive reports that the Communists in Russia had outlawed the family and "nationalized women."[16] "They have utterly destroyed marriage, the home, the fireside, the family, the cornerstones of all civilization, all society," declaimed a US Senator.[17] This horrible revelation, coupled with a postwar strike wave and a scattering of unexplained bombings, set off the Great Red Scare, a national panic in the United States over the putative menace of Soviet-inspired revolution. The new American Communist Party, temporarily driven underground, never recovered from the conspiratorial mentality implanted by this experience.

A second element in anti-Communism, more prominent in the democratic Center and among the moderate Left, was revulsion against the violence, dictatorship, and ultimately the totalitarianism of the Soviet regime. The extreme Right was more inclined to copy these themes than to condemn them. Following the defeat of Fascism, the defense of democracy against Communist despotism was an effective unifying theme almost everywhere in the West.

Thirdly came the religious issue. This was present in the earliest form of anti-Communism, but it assumed major proportions in the 1930s after the Spanish Civil War counterposed Communism and the Catholic Church (even though it was the Anarchists who were guilty of most of the anti-religious atrocities in Spain). Hatred of the atheist Reds surged in the US after the Second World War. FBI director J. Edgar Hoover warned,

> Communism . . . is a materialistic religion, inflaming in its adherents a destructive fanaticism. Communism is secularism on the march . . . . Communism means godlessness. Godlessness means slavery. Slavery means spiritual and physical death. The definition of Communism is as simple as that.[18]

All these earlier sources of antagonism toward the Soviets were capped after 1945 by the perception of Soviet military power as the engine of Communist revolution. Subsuming the first three elements of anti-Communism, fear of Soviet revolutionary expansionism governed Western policy toward the USSR throughout the era of the Cold War and the nuclear arms race. Yet the world revolution theory of Soviet behavior is wrong, on two counts. In the first place, the theory rested on a misreading of Marx and Lenin. Marxism was not a simple set of commandments to commit revolution; it was more predictive than prescriptive, envisaging a worldwide sequence of revolutions stemming from the anticipated crisis of mature capitalism. Marxist doctrine did not require military action by a revolutionary state to extend the proletarian revolution to other countries, though Lenin conceived of that possibility. In the second place, in assuming that the Soviets were obliged to do what the doctrine was thought to say, the world revolution theory ignored the whole evolution of the Soviet regime and the purely instrumental function to which Communist ideology was relegated by Stalin.

*

Despite the ferocious polarization that it set up between revolutionaries and counterrevolutionaries, the Russian Revolution did not long dictate the concrete aims and methods of Soviet international action. Russia's retreat from revolutionary extremism in 1921 automatically brought about the first major reversal in attitudes toward the outside world – "the NEP in foreign policy," as E. H. Carr termed it,[19] accepting a long-term relationship with the capitalist world and restoring normal commercial and diplomatic relations. Despite the "capitalist encirclement" and its own revolutionary odor, the Soviet state found that it could survive as one power among many – peaceful coexistence, in effect. The last direct effort by the Comintern to promote revolution abroad was its half-hearted attempt at a coup in Germany in 1923, called off at the last minute, while the Soviet Foreign Office had already concluded an alliance of convenience – the Treaty of Rapallo – with the Weimar Republic.

From the mid-1920s until 1939 the USSR did not seriously threaten anyone else, either as a military power or as a center of revolutionary plotting. Unlike the world of Napoleon, the international constellation of forces gave the postrevolutionary dictatorship in Russia no other choice. After 1924 only the USA among the major powers held off from diplomatic recognition of the USSR, though it was not so fastidious as to abstain from business dealings with the Communists. Generally speaking, Americans manifested a deeper and more emotional anti-Communism than anyone else except countries that openly opted for dictatorships of the Right to stop the Left.

The theory of world revolution continued to agitate the Russian Communists during the 1920s, but only because it had become a political football in the contest to succeed Lenin in the leadership of the Soviet state. Counterattacking Trotsky's "permanent revolution" with his own "socialism in one country," Stalin created the impression abroad that he was the nationalistic moderate, while Trotsky kept the image of the revolutionary firebrand. In actuality there was little difference between the two, in either their theoretical support of revolution abroad or their practical willingness to accommodate the capitalists.[20]

Naturally, as long as Soviet Russia remained only one of a number of contending great powers it was at the mercy of a potential coalition among the others. Experiencing the great war scare with Britain after the Baldwin government broke off relations in 1927, and the more serious threats posed by the Japanese after 1931 and the Germans after 1933,

Moscow took solace from the theory of inevitable conflict among its various imperialist enemies. This outlook offered the opportunity of playing the balance-of-power game by supporting whichever group of imperialists was most congenial to Soviet security. Such was Stalin's strategy throughout the 1930s.

*

The particulars of Soviet behavior continued to shift with the successive phases of the internal revolutionary process and with the rapid changes in the international situation in the 1930s and 1940s. The "NEP in foreign policy" and the Comintern's "united front" tactics had not been conspicuously successful in holding onto non-Communist allies such as the British Labour Party and the Chinese Nationalists. Consequently, when Stalin began to implement the postrevolutionary dictatorship at home, it was easy for him verbally to reverse the Party's international line. Corresponding to the militant, cultural revolution phase of Stalinism was the so-called "Third Period" in the Comintern and in foreign policy, marked by new revolutionary rhetoric and bitter struggles against democratic socialists and against Trotskyist and Bukharinist deviators from the official Communist line. Commercial relations were not affected, however; the Soviet Union traded more vigorously than ever, swapping grain extorted from starving peasants for the machinery needed to equip the industry being built pursuant to the Five-Year Plan.

Stalin's foreign policy was complicated by the fact that the Soviet Union was not alone as a revolutionary or postrevolutionary state. At the end of the war in 1918 Germany had plunged into revolution, democratic and socialist, tempting the Soviets to think that it too would go Communist and break open the path to world revolution. Instead, the Weimar Republic achieved a temporary stability, rather like a prolonged version of the Russian Provisional Government, only to succumb in the early 1930s to a violent authoritarian movement oddly combining elements of extremist revolution and counterrevolution at the same time. The Soviets contributed unwittingly to the Nazi outcome, first because they served as a foil to frighten the German middle and rural classes, and secondly because they directed the German Communists to concentrate their fire on the Social Democrats, and thereby divided the potential opposition to Hitler.

Hitler's victory targeted the Soviet Union as Germany's prime victim. Together with the political ascendancy of the Japanese militarists after the "Manchurian Incident" of 1931, it discredited Stalin's "Third Period" line and shocked him into yet another tactical reversal. He would avert the new threat to Soviet survival by seeking alliances with democratic governments and parties wherever possible. Thus began the era of "Collective Security," conducted by Foreign Commissar Maxim Litvinov, and the "Popular Front," personified by the new chairman of the Comintern, the Bulgarian Georgi Dimitrov.

Stalin's shift to Collective Security and the Popular Front, starting with the opening of diplomatic relations with the USA in November 1933 and formalized at the Seventh World Congress of the Comintern in July 1935, resembled the "NEP in foreign policy," but there were some fundamentally new elements. The domestic context of Soviet policy was now the postrevolutionary dictatorship, which funneled all key decisions into Stalin's hands personally and thereby permitted much more tactical flexibility. Marxist-Leninist doctrine was no longer a real constraint; Stalin had relegated it to the cynical and mendacious function of justifying these tactical manoeuvres. Changes in the party line became an international joke.

Collective Security and the Popular Front, like earlier Soviet foreign policy tactics, ended in failure when the British and French broke ranks with Stalin and concluded the Munich Agreement with Hitler. Munich implicitly turned Hitler eastward with a free hand to dispose of the Communists, or so Stalin could reasonably have read it.[21] His response was the most cynical maneuver in the entire history of Soviet foreign policy, the non-aggression pact with Germany of August 1939, intended to turn the Nazis back against the West. The pact was evidence of how low ideology had sunk as a policy guide for either the Communists or the Nazis, compared with their security interests and their imperial ambitions. "In fact Stalin and Molotov betrayed the Communist movement," writes the historian N. V. Zagladin from the perspective of glasnost.[22] The Soviet–German deal was so hard to justify in Marxist terms that it might have put an end to Communist ideological influence everywhere, had the shock of it not been widely diminished by Hitler's subsequent treachery and the outbreak of the Great Patriotic War.

In any case, Stalin's new line of 1939 and its involuntary undoing in 1941 did not represent fundamental changes of strategy like 1921 and 1935. The later shifts were only tactical exchanges of alliance partners dictated by calculations of survival and aggrandizement on the part of the postrevolutionary dictatorship. However, these tactics were not executed with the greatest wisdom; having held back while the Germans conquered France, Stalin had no ally on the European continent in 1941. Had Hitler only waged political warfare then with the intuition of his earlier military gambles, there is a good chance that Stalin could have been overthrown.

There is no need to suppose that Stalin's entente with Hitler ran any deeper than the previous one with the democracies, as some authorities have suggested (even to explain the purges). What still remains puzzling is Stalin's stubborn belief that he could appease Hitler and stave off the day of reckoning by abjuring measures of military readiness and disregarding British warnings and his own intelligence reports about the Germans' aggressive intentions. Stalin would cling rigidly to a particular tactical line in the short term until it had blatantly failed, while his long-term strategy was one of opportunistic flexibility. His record thus contradicts the usual attribution to the Soviets of tactical adroitness and strategic implacability.

*

In 1941 most foreign observers, even with their limited knowledge of the murderous impact of Stalinism, gave the Soviet dictator little hope of holding out against the Germans. Or they shared the sentiment expressed by Senator Harry Truman, the future American president, "If we see that Germany is winning we should help Russia and if Russia is winning we ought to help Germany and that way let them kill as many as possible, although I don't want to see Hitler victorious under any circumstances."[23] Churchill, gaining an unexpected ally to share his single-handed defiance of the Nazis, was less equivocal:

> No one has been a more consistent opponent of Communism than I have for the last twenty-five years. I will unsay no word that I have spoken about it. But all this fades away before the spectacle which is now unfolding . . . . Any man or state who fights on against Nazidom will have our aid.[24]

Indeed, among Soviet Russia's Second World War allies much of the memory of the recent past did fade – the Revolution, the ideology, the purges, Stalin's paranoia. Instead, the Allies (Britain perhaps with more reservations than the US) chose to see Stalin's Soviet Union as a state with its own national interests, to be sure, but one that shared Western aspirations for democracy and for a postwar order of international cooperation.

In external appearances Stalin collaborated with this illusion, abolishing the Communist International and directing Communist parties everywhere to back any governments that were fighting against Hitler. In effect, he reverted to the Popular Front line of cooperation with democratic forces. Apart from the Yugoslav and Asian Communists, who acted on their own revolutionary impulses, the language of Marxist class struggle was not heard again until the battle lines had been drawn in the Cold War.

Within the Soviet Union the war did not cause Stalin to relax his grip in the least, though he did give patriotism precedence over Marxism-Leninism in his propaganda. Considering how the country had been racked in the 1930s by collectivization, famine, and the purges, its survival and ultimate victory in the Second World War seem little short of miraculous. In part victory was the fruit of heroic self-sacrifice by people confronted with Nazi atrocities and the fear of national extinction. In part, Stalin may have been right in crediting victory to "the Soviet social order" – the party, centrally planned industrialization, collective farms – that served to squeeze all possible human and material resources into the war effort.[25] In any case, the Soviet Union achieved feats in military industry as well as on the battlefield that nothing in the country's record, pre- or postrevolutionary, anticipated.

Even so, given the wounds and terrors that Soviet society still suffered from when the war began, it is extraordinary that the Stalinist system came through that ordeal so little changed. The experience of the war only confirmed and reinforced the militarization of Soviet society, not, of course, in the literal meaning of rule by the generals, but in a deeper sense recalling the Tsarist polity. Stalinist society was militarized in its mode of government and administration, in the priorities that shaped public policy, and in the spirit of struggle and danger that infused all its dealings with the outside world. All of these characteristics became integral facets of the postrevolutionary dictatorship.

With the war's end – probably even before, once victory became certain – Stalin made a momentous choice. This decision was not a mere change of tactics or even a shift to a new strategy; it turned on a new view of the world. At a moment in history when he could have entered into an unprecedented era of international cooperation, Stalin chose to regard anyone beyond the reach of the Red Army as his potential adversary. To quote George Kennan, "He was, in his own eyes, the enemy of all the world."[26] This is not surprising for the man who had decided, a decade before, to treat the entire society under his control as his enemy. Now the Soviet Union would no longer compete for allies and influence in the familiar pluralistic world of rival nation-states and political movements, nor would it even seriously try to promote revolution by the Western working class or the Eastern colonials. Beyond the zone of Red Army control, the Communist parties, kept in ignorance of Soviet reality, would simply be used as propaganda organs and pressure groups. A present-day Russian nationalist writer maintains, "Until the Soviet Union achieved military-stategic parity with the West, the USSR had no other national goal than that of survival and defense."[27]

Western revisionist historians have popularized the notion that the Cold War was brought on after 1945 by Western – particularly American – affronts to the Soviet Union and a failure to understand Soviet sensitivities. This view perpetuates the illusions about the Soviet Union that prevailed during the Second World War. It ignores the kind of man Stalin had shown himself to be, and the kind of political system he had already put in place before the war and confirmed afterwards, to the deep disappointment of most Soviet citizens. Perhaps Stalin assumed, in his jaundiced view of the imperialists, that since they had got their own share of the Axis sphere in Germany, Italy, and Japan, they would tolerate his Machiavellianism in Eastern Europe. "What can be surprising," he asked rhetorically in 1946, "in the fact that the Soviet Union, in a desire to ensure its security for the future, tries to achieve that these countries should have governments whose relations to the Soviet Union are loyal?"[28] When the West did not acquiesce in his gains, his paranoia took over and led him to construe their objections as part of a counter-revolutionary interventionist plot to destroy the Soviet state.

Awed by the military prowess that the USSR exhibited during the war and its aftermath, the outside world readily acknowledged the Soviets' standing as a "superpower" along with the USA and (briefly) Britain. Analysts spoke of the new "bipolarity" in international relations that emerged with the Cold War. But there was never a true balance; Stalin, having alarmed all the Western powers by fastening his grip on Eastern Europe (the "iron curtain . . . from Stettin to Trieste"), turned virtually the entire outside world against himself, his former allies as well as his former enemies. In population, economic resources, strategic location, military potential, in everything except the number of ground troops kept in uniform after the war, the American-led coalition that Stalin precipitated enjoyed overwhelming superiority.

Such a result, paradoxically, was not unwelcome for Stalin. His guiding passion was to secure his own power by maintaining total control over the USSR and its new satellites, and by legitimizing that control with Marxist-Leninist ideology. This aim entailed cutting foreign contacts to a minimum and tightening all the mechanisms of control – party, police, command economy, ideology and propaganda, and intermittent purges – that he had developed in his prewar consolidation of power. In his paranoid way Stalin assumed the hostility of the outside world as he did that of "class enemies," "bourgeois nationalists," and "cosmopolitans" within the Soviet realm. As is typical of a paranoid, the actual hostility aroused by his heavy-handed responses to these perceived threats, domestic and foreign, only confirmed and justified his suspicions and his security measures. To the end of his days, Stalin rested his power on an ascending spiral of internal repression and external threats.

*

Despite his decision to defy the world, Stalin did not immediately abandon the belief that rivalry among the imperialists would leave him room for maneuver. This was the import of his celebrated "election" speech of February 1946, a statement which the American leadership in particular profoundly misunderstood. Echoing Lenin's analysis of the First World War, Stalin maintained that the Second World War was also "the inevitable result of the development of world economic and political forces on the basis of modern monopoly capitalism." Competition for materials and markets would continue to cause "a splitting of the capitalist world into two hostile camps and war between them."[29]

Stalin's election speech became a benchmark in American–Soviet relations, not for what he said but because of the startling misinterpretation of his meaning. George Kennan, reporting from Moscow in his celebrated "Long Telegram," found the speech just more evidence of the "Kremlin's neurotic view of world affairs," using "trappings of Marxism" in justification of traditional chicanery.[30] British chargé Frank Roberts cabled Foreign Secretary Ernest Bevin at the same time and in the same vein,

> We are faced with a Soviet policy designed to advance Soviet interests at every possible opportunity, regardless of those of its allies . . . . National security is, in fact, at the bottom of Soviet, as of Imperial Russian, policy, and explains much of the high-handed behaviour of the Kremlin and many of the suspicions genuinely held there concerning the outside world . . ., more particularly when they see in London representatives of social democracy and of the Second International . . . . They genuinely despise liberal ideas, tolerance, and the conceptions of right and justice which are the basis of Western thinking . . . . [They] believe that the end justifies the means, and that they are at the head of a chosen people . . . with a chosen system destined to spread throughout the world.

This point Roberts immediately qualified with apposite historical perspective:

> Soviet Russia has reached a similar stage in development as revolutionary France when the First Empire had become solidly established. Although Soviet Russia intends to spread her influence by all possible means, world revolution is no longer part of her programme.[31]

But against the backdrop of heavy-handed Soviet political consolidation in the newly occupied countries of Eastern Europe, Washington construed Stalin's statement as an assertion of the inevitability of war between the Soviet Union and the capitalist world, and hence as a signal of Soviet preparations for an attack. Dean Acheson in his memoirs referred to "Stalin's offensive against the United States and the West, announced in his speech of February 9 1946."[32] Supreme Court Justice

William O. Douglas called the speech "the declaration of World War III."[33]

Marxism has, of course, dwelt at length on the question of the inevitability of war. However, this prediction refers not to war to spread the world revolution, nor even to aggression by the capitalists against the first socialist state, but only to war among the imperialist states of late capitalism. Lenin projected imperialist war theoretically in his *Imperialism, The Highest Stage of Capitalism*, a safe bet since the First World War had already broken out. Again, "imperialist war" was the official Communist view of the Second World War from 1939 to 1941. However, for the Soviet state, despite the "capitalist encirclement," war was never thought subject to the same sort of theoretical inevitability. It was, of course, a historical likelihood, anticipated by Lenin before the Revolution and realized soon after it in the Allied intervention of 1918–1920 (and again in 1941).

Ironically, Stalin's own concern about war with the capitalists came out just a few weeks after his 1946 election speech. Winston Churchill's "Iron Curtain" address, delivered in the USA on 5 March, abruptly gave Stalin to fear that his Manichaean assumptions about the world had become a reality, and that the two leading imperialist rivals, Britain and the United States, were conspiring against the Soviet Union. Reacting quickly in an interview with *Pravda* published on 14 March, Stalin accused Churchill of "a set-up for war, a call to war with the Soviet Union," based on "a racial theory maintaining that only nations speaking the English language are fully valuable nations, called upon to decide the destinies of the entire world." His response to this alleged Anglo-Saxon plan for world domination, reiterated in word and deed throughout the years that followed, was a mirror image of the West's preparations against the threat that it perceived in him.

Officially the Soviets never gave up the imperialist war thesis as long as Stalin lived. In his last major statement Stalin suggested prophetically that Germany and Japan might "rise to their feet again . . . break out of American bondage," so that "the inevitability of wars between capitalist countries remains in force." By contrast, "War with the USSR, as a socialist land, is more dangerous to capitalism than war between capitalist countries." Therefore, though such a war was a hazard, it was not inevitable.[34]

*

The breakup of the wartime alliance and the onset of the Cold War brought about an extraordinarily rapid reversal of assumptions about the Soviet Union on the part of the now leading Western power, the USA. Actually Stalin was behaving more like the kings of old than an astute revolutionary, and initially, under Bevin's leadership, Britain had taken a tougher stand toward him than the US, for balance-of-power reasons more than ideological.[35] America's shocked Wilsonian idealism turned Stalin from a sometimes difficult but well-intentioned ally into the sworn enemy of civilization, a substitute Hitler scheming and plotting to destroy the American way of life pursuant to the doctrinal mandate of Marxist world revolution. As early as September 1946, Truman aide Clark Clifford reported to his chief after a study of Soviet aims, "The key to an understanding of current Soviet foreign policy, in summary, is the realization that Soviet leaders adhere to the Marxian theory of ultimate destruction of capitalist states by communist states."[36] Thus the artificial prolongation of Marxist doctrine as the legitimation of Stalin's dictatorship fed the postwar revival of anti-Communist fervor in the United States.

This turnabout in America, pulling along the rather more pragmatic but also more vulnerable West Europeans, cannot be fully understood outside the context of the domestic political cycle in the US. In general, the state of American relations with the USSR up into the 1980s was governed more by this cycle and by the direction – liberal or conservative – of American politics at any given time than by the actual behavior of the Soviet Union at the corresponding moment. In the 1920s America was conservative, and official relations with the USSR were nonexistent, though the Soviets were attempting to follow the moderate course of the NEP. In the 1930s America was liberal, and relations became much better, though it was the time of the most arduous Stalinization in the Soviet Union. When the Cold War was setting in in the late 1940s, American politics was going into a phase of Thermidorean Reaction, so to speak. The resurgent Republican Party strove in every possible way to undo Roosevelt's New Deal, even by linking it to Soviet Communism (liberal reform = "creeping socialism" = the "first stage of communism" = Stalinist totalitarianism). President Truman, fighting a rearguard action to save both the New Deal and the shreds of wartime cooperation with the Soviet Union, sacrificed the latter. By 1947 he was trying to pre-empt his critics by taking the lead in the struggle against the presumed Communist menace, with the Truman doctrine of military aid to countries pressured by the Soviets; the Marshall Plan; the purge of suspected native Communists from public service; and even the prosecution of the CP-USA for allegedly plotting to overthrow the government. In the words of Secretary of State Acheson, "We made our points clearer than the truth."[37]

George Kennan's "containment" doctrine, fully formulated in his famous "Mr. X" article of July 1947, saw the threat of Soviet power largely as political and economic penetration of regions laid waste by the war. He predicted – too soon, but presciently – an eventual mellowing or even disintegration of the Soviet regime if its expansive ambitions were frustrated.[38] But Kennan found his approach politically obsolete before the ink was dry, as the American leadership jumped to "the panicky conclusion" of "the inevitability of an eventual war between the Soviet Union and the United States."[39] Kennan was left to warn throughout the rest of his career against America's overestimation of the Soviet threat and over-reliance on military means to curb it. Meanwhile postwar social reform movements in Western Europe lost momentum, as Center-Left governments broke with their Communist coalition partners and moved to the right. Efforts at New Dealish curbs on big business in occupied Germany and Japan were abandoned, as these former enemies were adjudged indispensable bastions against the Soviet threat. Stalin's short-lived counteroffensive, extending from the establishment of the Cominform ("Communist Information Bureau") in September 1947, through the Communist coup in Czechoslovakia in February 1948 and strikes against the Marshall Plan in France and Italy, to the Berlin Blockade of July 1948, was a belated reaction to Western mobilization that only strengthened the resolve of his adversaries.

The ideological interpretation of Soviet motivation quickly percolated through the American government as well as the mass media. Responding to the coup in Prague, the National Security Council advised the president, "The ultimate objective of Soviet-directed World Communism is the domination of the world . . . . The USSR is guided by the Communist dogma that the peaceful coexistence of communist and capitalist states is in the long run impossible."[40] By 1950, as codified by Paul Nitze in the now famous National Security Council Directive NSC-68, American policy presumed that the Soviet Union was "animated by a new fanatic faith, antithetical to our own," and that "the Kremlin's design" was "to impose its absolute authority over the rest of the world," with "a premium on a surprise attack against us" if it fell behind in the timetable of global revolution.[41] From this premise the explicit conclusion was drawn that, barring "such a radical change in Soviet policies as to constitute a change in the Soviet system . . ., settlement by negotiation is at this stage impossible."[42] Hence, "Any offer of, or attempt at, negotiation of a general settlement [on our part] could only be a tactic . . ., both to gain public support for the [defense] program and to minimize the immediate risks of war."[43]

The strategic judgement drawn from this reasoning was that the Soviets were determined whenever the opportunity presented itself to launch a blitzkrieg against Western Europe, in order to communize the entire continent and achieve a quantum leap toward the world revolution. Apart from the imputed doctrinal motive, the form of this threat seems to have been conjured up in American minds by the memory of two traumatic episodes, the fall of France in 1940 and the Japanese surprise attack on Pearl Harbor in 1941. The Soviets were presumably preparing for the moment when they too could launch a surprise attack like the Japanese, and overwhelm the West Europeans just as the Germans had routed the French. Since Europe was not deemed militarily capable of resisting this eventuality, the United States had to promise its support, through the vehicle of the North Atlantic Treaty Organization. However, Soviet superiority in ground forces was still presumed to be overwhelming, to be matched in kind only at great cost. Soviet deficiencies in demographics, economics, and technology were overlooked. Stalin's true weakness, evidenced when he backed down from the Berlin Blockade and failed to intervene in Korea, did not affect these calculations.

Obsessed by the specter of blitzkrieg in a hapless Europe, the American government made a very risky decision: it would invoke the threat of nuclear weapons, thought to be an area of overwhelming American superiority, to dissuade the Soviets from overt military adventures, thereby avoiding the cost of underwriting equivalent conventional defenses. Hence the basic doctrine of deterrence, addressing the assumed threat of Soviet aggression with the wishful answer of American nuclear superiority.

The consequences of this reasoning hardly need reiteration, as the Soviets tried to catch up in nuclear technology, and the US, alarmed by the Soviet challenge but reluctant to support a sufficient conventional defense, strove just as hard to stay ahead in the nuclear race. The decision to develop the hydrogen bomb; the interest in tactical nuclear weapons, and the consequent rebuff given to Khrushchev on nuclear testing in the years before the neo-Stalinists began to undermine him; the decision to exclude underground testing from the Nuclear Test-Ban Treaty of 1963; the decision to develop multiple-warhead missiles (the MIRV); and President Reagan's space-based Strategic Defense Initiative, all stemmed from the presumption that the Soviet appetite for expansion could only be curbed by American superiority in nuclear weaponry and other high-tech miracles. The presumed US advantage, it goes without saying, was entered into the power equation by the implicit threat of American first use of nuclear weapons, whatever the risk, if the Soviets should resort even to a conventional attack to implement their presumptive designs.

*

It is unnerving to reflect that the beliefs underlying the nuclear arms race and its potential threat to the survival of civilization were fundamentally mistaken. They were mistaken on both sides: in the American assumption of Soviet revolutionary intent, and in the Soviet fear of Western imperialist intervention. On both sides the error arose from the same source – conclusions drawn from the official Soviet ideology of Marxism-Leninism. The American mistake stemmed from the belief that Marxist mythology still motivated the Soviets in some compelling sense; the Soviet mistake stemmed from Stalin's paranoia reinforced by Marxist mythology.

Khrushchev tried to defuse the whole question of inevitable war when he affirmed the doctrine of peaceful coexistence at the Twentieth Party Congress in 1956 (not in the "secret speech" but in his official report to the congress). Lumping together the two kinds of war distinguished by his predecessors – war among the imperialists and war against the Soviet Union – he rejected the "fatalistic inevitability" of either kind.[44] Unfortunately he rekindled American anxieties soon afterwards when he uttered the unforgettable challenge, "We will bury you."[45] This was not a threat to reduce US cities to rubble, as myriads of nervous politicians and editorialists supposed, but only the old Marxist prophecy that capitalism as a system would collapse while socialism proved its superiority. What Khrushchev evidently said in Russian was, "My vas pokhoronim," "We will conduct your funeral," i.e. bury capitalism in the sense that you bury your relatives after they die a natural death. The following year he boasted in an interview for American television, "I can prophesy that your grandchildren will live under communism."

> We believe that our socialist system will be victorious, but that does not mean under any conditions that we want to impose that system on anyone. We simply believe that the people of each country themselves will come to realize that that system is best for them.[46]

Khrushchev's successors made the same point – that their professed belief required no military action to make the predictions of Marxism come true. Maintaining that the "revolutionary war" theory had been rejected with Lenin's defeat of Trotsky and the "Left Communists" back in 1918, Gorbachev asserted at the Twenty-Seventh Party Congress in February 1986, "Socialism has never, of its own free will, linked its future with military solutions to international problems . . . . We are firmly convinced that 'pushing' revolution from outside, especially by military means, is futile and impermissible."[47] Former Ambassador to Washington Anatoly Dobrynin in a subsequent remark put it bluntly: "The USSR . . . as a state did not set itself the aim of overthrowing capitalism in other countries."[48] Such statements can, of course, be dismissed as propaganda that in no way inhibited the Soviet Union from the aggressive pursuit of its interests; the point is that such actions would and did take place in disregard of ideology, not because of it.

*

While the mutual fears and recriminations of the Cold War were intensifying in the late 1940s and early 1950s, Stalin settled down behind his East European glacis to a stance of rhetorical defiance *cum* practical caution *vis-à-vis* the North Atlantic alliance. As Marshall Shulman noted in his pioneering study of the Cold War, Stalin adopted "an essentially defensive strategic outlook in response to the adverse trend in world power developments in the postwar world," while hoping that Soviet industrial progress and an economic crisis of capitalism would eventually change the balance.[49] Following the failure of the Berlin Blockade of 1948–49, he switched to "a quasi-Right line," gave up on proletarian revolution, and tried to use the Communist-controlled peace movement, with all its nasty anti-Western propaganda, to keep the Western powers off balance.[50] "The aim of this movement," Stalin asserted in 1952, "is not to overthrow capitalism and establish socialism . . . . The present-day peace movement differs from the movement of the time of the First World War for the conversion of the imperialist war into civil war since the latter movement went further and pursued socialist aims."[51]

Throughout the rest of the Cold War era, up to the mid-1970s, the Soviet Union took no risky actions in Europe apart from emergency intervention to maintain control in its East European bloc – East Berlin in 1953, Hungary in 1956, Berlin again with the Wall in 1961, Czechoslovakia in 1968. The Western reaction to these moves was loud but purely rhetorical. The only serious Cold War confrontations from the late 1940s to the early 1970s took place on the periphery of the Soviet realm where Moscow or its surrogates tried to probe further in places where the post-Second World War line of demarcation was blurred by partitioned countries or revolutionary guerrilla movements.

On this periphery there were two critical exceptions to the rule of Communist caution – the North Korean invasion of South Korea in 1950, and the Cuban Missile Crisis of 1962. As the evidence now indicates, Stalin condoned the idea of the attack in Korea, perhaps to probe the American ring of containment, perhaps to avoid being upstaged by the Chinese, though strictly speaking he neither initiated the aggression nor rescued it (leaving the latter task to the Chinese).[52] Yet the Korean War, coming soon after the Communist victory in China and coinciding with the peak of conservative politics in the US, appeared to validate the worst American fears about Moscow's revolutionary expansionism. It led directly to the unprecedented peacetime militarization of American economic life and political thinking, not to mention the rearmament of West Germany, and was thus counterproductive for Soviet security interests.[53] Other Soviet actions, in Eastern Europe and in Cuba, repeatedly reinforced the most pessimistic American assumptions and the corresponding pursuit of military superiority. Ex-President Eisenhower, though he had protested against the overgrowth of the military-industrial complex, still warned, "Communists embrace every kind of tactic to gain their fundamental objective, the domination of the earth's peoples."[54]

Throughout the 1950s and 1960s – thanks to the vigorous American response, many would claim – Communist power nowhere advanced beyond the power vacuum left by enemy occupation in the Second World War, with the exception of Cuba. (Cuba was really only a windfall that landed in the Soviet camp after Castro's advent to power in 1959, and confronted Moscow with the need to protect it from the United States or else lose revolutionary face.) Stalin may indeed have been contained at certain points by fear of Western reactions, but he had no interest in promoting revolution for its own sake beyond the reach of his personal control. George Kennan wrote in 1960, "Unless other states were very small, and contiguous to Russia's borders, so that there were good prospects for controlling them by the same concealed police methods he employed in Russia, Stalin did not want other states to be communist."[55] Unlike his successors, Stalin made little or no effort to forge revolutionary links with Third World countries, apart from the brief rash of futile Communist uprisings in the former war zone of South-East Asia in 1948. Not counting his satellites and his uneasy Chinese confrères, Stalin had no true allies, large or small, a lack Khrushchev and his successors tried to remedy at considerable expense and with dubious success in the Middle East.

Stalin's skepticism about the reliability of uncontrolled Communist governments was borne out by threats from within the bloc to the Soviet monopoly of ideological legitimacy. The first crack was the defection of Tito's Yugoslavia in 1948, an experience that may have contributed to Stalin's apprehension about relations with Mao Tse-tung's new Communist regime in China. We know now that the embrace of Stalin and Mao was less than totally trusting. China's revolution was fresh and militant, particularly *vis-à-vis* the United States, which had succeeded in containing Chinese Communism – in Korea, Taiwan, Indo-China – rather more tightly than it had the Soviets. The Chinese wanted to take on the US directly; the Soviets wanted to keep tension from rising to the danger point. So the two major Communist powers were pursuing different interests and different policies, which each wanted to legitimize by reference to the same body of Marxist-Leninist doctrine. Neither could tolerate the other's claim to primary ideological authority – hence the inevitable schism between them, reminiscent of the Great Schism between the churches of Rome and Constantinople in the eleventh century. A common doctrine claimed by two power centers came to serve not as a bond between them, but as a battleground.

Khrushchev probably started the actual schism when he undertook his anti-Stalin campaign in 1956 without consulting the Chinese. De-Stalinization also meant the rupture of unquestioning Soviet discipline over the international Communist movement wherever it was not reinforced by the presence of Soviet troops. The "polycentrism" touted by Italian Communist leader Palmiro Togliatti widened the crack between the Stalinist heritage and Marxist legitimation: "The Soviet model," fraught with perils of "bureaucratic degeneration," "cannot and must not any longer be obligatory."[56] Thenceforth the international Communist movement survived only on accumulated momentum, ceasing in most places to be either revolutionary in its own terms or a reliable support for Soviet policy. Soviet intervention in Czechoslovakia in 1968 dispersed most residual Communist loyalty, and set the stage for the short-lived reformist movement of Eurocommunism.

*

Weaknesses and hesitations on the part of the Soviet bloc made little impression on the other superpower after the shock of the Korean War. Once on the path of Cold War confrontation, driven along by domestic political forces and economic interests, the United States found it almost as convenient as did Stalin. "The Cold War was a major organizing principle of American life, politically and culturally and in other ways as well," notes the Columbia University historian Alan Brinkley. "The Cold War also gave an enormous boost to American exceptionalism and triumphalism, the idea that America was carrying the banner of freedom in a world in which freedom was threatened."[57]

Immediately after Stalin's death the Malenkov government signaled a willingness to emerge from isolation and establish more normal relations with the West. Churchill, in one of his last acts as prime minister, urged a positive Western response, and went so far as to assume the co-chairmanship with the Soviets of the 1954 Geneva conference that ended the French phase of the Vietnam War. But the American leadership of President Eisenhower and Secretary of State John Foster Dulles, wedded to Cold War imagery of "rolling back" the Communists, came around only with great reluctance. Not until 1955 did the first and only four-power summit conference take place, when Eisenhower, Anthony Eden, Edgar Faure of France, and Khrushchev and his new prime minister Nikolai Bulganin met in Geneva. The early shoots of detente planted at this inconclusive gathering withered in the blast of the Hungarian and Suez crises the following year, and even when the climate warmed again sufficiently to permit Khrushchev to visit the United States in 1959, Americans received him with suspicion. They recalled the "bury you" remark, and laughed off his call for "universal and complete disarmament." Arms control negotiations, politically unavoidable, fell chronically afoul of the inspection issue: the Americans wanted more because they were afraid of being tricked, and the Soviets wanted less because they were afraid of being found out. At the same time, Soviet exploits in rockets, bombs, and earth satellites shocked the Americans out of their technological complacency and set the stage for the fall-out shelter panic of the early 1960s.

Khrushchev is remembered by most in the West as a boorish and erratic blusterer, but this was the post-1960 Khrushchev, after his calls for peaceful coexistence and arms reductions had been snubbed, and after the neo-Stalinists in the Soviet leadership had begun to close in on him. In the years from 1960 to 1962 Khrushchev was indeed a threatening figure, breaking up the 1960 summit meeting in Paris, manufacturing a crisis in Germany and throwing up the Berlin Wall, breaking his own unilateral nuclear test moratorium by exploding a 100–megaton H-bomb (the largest ever), and trying to establish a nuclear beachhead in Cuba. The West took no note at the time that this behavior might have been imposed by the neo-Stalinists or (more likely) carried on by Khrushchev to outmaneuver his internal foes. Nor was much consideration given to the backdrop of Moscow's dissension with China, a fact that the US government long refused to accept, since it upset the simplistic identification of Marxism and Soviet policy.

By the early 1960s the American political weathervane was finally shifting again in the liberal direction. For a brief moment this movement coincided with a Soviet opening, when the neo-Stalinist leader Frol Kozlov fell ill and Khrushchev had a short reprieve. The outcome was the nuclear test ban treaty of 1963. However, the treaty was restricted to atmospheric testing, because the Pentagon wanted to continue underground testing to maintain its lead in the tactical nuclear weapons that were supposed to deter a Soviet ground attack in Europe.

Khrushchev's overthrow in 1964, surprisingly, changed neither Soviet policy nor American responses, which lends substance to the view that the "harebrained schemes" of the early 1960s were Khrushchev's own initiatives. In the teeth of the Vietnam War and the Czechoslovakian crisis the Americans and the Soviets pressed toward detente and arms control, reaching the high point of the Strategic Arms Limitation Treaty (SALT I) and the Anti-Ballistic Missile (ABM) Treaty concluded by the Nixon and Brezhnev governments in 1972. The treaties were a source of great self-satisfaction to the Soviet leadership, which could now claim, while still touting peaceful coexistence, that it had caught up in the arms race and had forced the Americans to recognize strategic parity between the two superpowers.

*

Flushed with their success in achieving a semblance of equal and amicable relations with the West, the Brezhnev team gambled these gains in the mid-1970s in a change of international strategy almost as basic as Stalin's shift to isolationism in 1945. The new line was a vigorous political offensive throughout the Third World, inspired by the hope of wresting one developing country after another away from dependence on the capitalists and making them allies of the socialist camp. This strategy was probably more opportunistic than premeditated, a response to new openings for influence on the lines of the Cuban alliance of the 1960s. It was made feasible by the cover of nuclear parity (deterring the deterrent), a neo-isolationist mood in the US after its failure in Vietnam, progress in Soviet long-range air and naval forces, and the windfall of petrodollars earned by Soviet oil exports after the 1973 price explosion. Moreover, the push in the Third World acquired some urgency as a way to offset lost Soviet influence with the Chinese and among the Western Left. On the downside, the new forward strategy prompted America's reversion to the worst Cold War fears and recriminations in superpower relations.

The immediate occasion for the change in Soviet behavior was revolution in Africa, including the overthrow of the ancient Ethiopian monarchy, military revolts in several former British and French colonies, and above all the guerrilla victories in Portugal's colonies, ratified by the Communist-influenced revolutionary government in Lisbon in 1974–75. Generally these movements were led either by Communists or by nationalists who identified the Soviet Union with their own anti-imperialist aspirations and were happy to accept Soviet aid, protection, and political models. Particularly galling to the US was the introduction of Cuban troops as Soviet surrogates to support a number of these regimes, most decisively in Angola.

Considering the rudimentary development of these newly revolutionary countries, it would have been preposterous for the Soviets to apply to them the ideology of the proletarian revolution and socialism. Instead, the new pro-Moscow one-party systems were blessed as "governments of socialist orientation," led by "vanguard parties," one circle of grace short of the "socialist" governments of Cuba and Vietnam under self-professed Communist parties. Vietnam, where the US had struggled so long, it thought, to contain Chinese expansion, proved to be another windfall for Soviet influence, though for Moscow this did not turn out to be an opportunity to carry revolution further, but only a transfer of the responsibility for containing China. Other anti-Western countries were classified by Soviet policy-makers in a descending hierarchy of Communist influence – "revolutionary democracies" like Libya, "national democracies" like Algeria, and "bourgeois democracies" like India that were willing to cooperate with Moscow as independent allies. The "socialist orientation" category was extended wherever opportunity arose – to South Yemen in 1978, to Afghanistan after the radical revolution later that year, to Nicaragua after the Sandinista revolution of 1979. Moscow tried to cement these relations with arms, economic subsidies, military missions, police infiltration, and political cadres trained at Lumumba University or other Soviet indoctrination programmes for Third Worlders. At the same time, the Soviets seized upon the opportunity to establish air and naval bases and a direct military presence as they strove to replicate the United States' global security system.

These Soviet adventures prompted growing alarm in the United States, where they were seen not as the pursuit of parity but as part of the grand revolutionary design. A new conservative swing of the American political pendulum was already calling detente into question. Soviet intervention in Afghanistan in 1979 after the pro-Communist modernizers got into trouble with tribal guerrilla resistance intensified the renewed East–West confrontation. Soviet aid and comfort for the Sandinistas, amplifying the challenge to US hegemony in the New World that had begun with Cuba, was especially annoying to the Americans. All this helped set the stage for Ronald Reagan and the "evil empire."

The USSR paid a heavy price at home for its ephemeral successes in power politics in the 1970s. A large share of Soviet manpower, industrial potential, and gross domestic product – the exact fraction is still in dispute – had to be dedicated to the arms race and overseas aid programmes. The most sanguine estimate is 15 per cent for defense out of an economy generating half the value of the American, but the percentage may have gone to 25, depending on methods of estimating it. Roughly speaking, the Soviet military-industrial complex was extracting an arms and aid effort comparable in absolute terms to the American effort, out of a much more modest economy, leaving it to Soviet consumers to bear the shortfall. It was the virtue of the "command-administrative system" of militarized socialism to be able to compel these priorities. Yet that system could not keep up in the high-tech world of computers and electronics, let alone ordinary consumer goods and services. The Soviet Union's quantitative military effort might be comparable to that of the USA, but the qualitative gap and the deficiency in public morale could not be overcome. Thus the prospect of unending military competition with the USA undermined the confidence of the neo-Stalinist leadership, and helped ready the USSR for the experiments of perestroika. Shevardnadze writes,

It was clear to all that the old methods of confrontation and the elevation of ideology above politics and law were no longer suitable. By remaining stuck in the old positions, we would not stop the arms race, which was bleeding our already anemic country, or reestablish cooperation with the West, or cease our involvement in regional conficts, primarily in Afghanistan, or normalize relations with China. We had to build new relations with the Third World, to search for a new world economic order, and to prevent the dangers of global crises.

To achieve this, we had to rebuild confidence, convince the world of the absence of a Soviet threat, and reassure our partners that our intentions were pure and sincere.[58]

*

Like perestroika internally, Soviet foreign policy in the Gorbachev era falls into two distinct stages, first its softening, up to the upheavals of 1989, and then the collapse of the Soviet Union's world position. In the first phase, Gorbachev was still able to direct the Soviet Union as a superpower, steering it away from the counterproductive confrontations of the late Brezhnev and Andropov years, reducing tensions, slowing down the arms race, and restraining competition in the Third World. In his book, *Perestroika*, written in 1987, he expressed deep alarm over the nuclear threat to human survival, and concluded that war was out of date as an instrument of national policy. He abruptly abandoned the rhetoric of Marxist-Leninist legitimation, placing "universal human values" ahead of the so-called class struggle, and advancing the nebulous ideal of a "common European home." Soviet military doctrine began to be overhauled on the basis of the principle of defensive "sufficiency." All this became known as "the New Thinking."[59]

At first the New Thinking came up against ingrained Western skepticism and a recalcitrant faction in Washington that regarded the whole new line as a trick to disarm the West. At the Reykjavik Summit in 1986 Gorbachev offered extraordinary reductions in arms and a total abolition of nuclear missiles, the one element of power where the Soviet Union truly enjoyed parity with the West, only to find President Reagan still stubbornly attached to the "Star Wars" defense-in-space. For a time arms control moved very slowly, against an American defense establishment reluctant to acknowledge that Soviet power was in headlong decline. Internally, Gorbachev's conciliatory line strengthened his political base by making him seem indispensable, though some demurred. The Soviet military were upset because Moscow had made most of the arms concessions, notably in the Intermediate-Range Nuclear Forces Treaty signed in December 1987, and in conventional arms reductions. Owing to conservative worries on both sides, the crucial step in arms control – the Strategic Arms Reduction Treaty, cutting intercontinental missiles by a third – was not concluded in all its details until the eve of the 1991 coup attempt.

A nagging issue that could no longer be covered up under glasnost was the Soviet involvement in Afghanistan. This fruitless war against the American-backed rebels proved to be a turning point both in Soviet fortunes in the Third World and in the political ability of the Soviet government to expend more blood and treasure in such ventures. Afghanistan became the Soviet Vietnam. The mode of escape from the quandary was similar to the exit the US chose in Vietnam – "Afghaniza-tion," so to speak – and the outcome was equally unsuccessful. The US and the Soviet Union agreed at Geneva in April 1988 to mutual non-intervention, and the last Soviet troops under General Boris Gromov were pulled out early in 1989, though this did not immediately put an end to the fighting or to surreptitious outside aid by each side. The Malta Summit meeting of Gorbachev and President George Bush in December 1989, culminating in a joint press conference, really ratified the end of the Cold War. "We don't consider you an enemy any more. Things have changed," said Gorbachev. "We stand at the threshold of a brand new era of US–Soviet relations," said Bush.[60]

By this time the second phase of perestroika was having its impact on Soviet foreign policy. Soviet influence and the will and ability to commit resources to the service of national power declined precipitously. This was no mere reaction to momentary difficulties, like the "post-Vietnam syndrome" in the US. It was an epochal collapse of national will, directly prompted by the last stage in the Soviet Union's revolutionary develop-ment. Returning to the principles and priorities of the moderate revolu-tion, Soviet society would no longer support the use of force either to hold unwilling components of the revolutionary realm, or to pursue great-power aims beyond the bloc. The mood that glasnost opened up was quite literally reminiscent of 1917, when the nation questioned its dubious participation in the First World War and saw the more self-conscious national minorities try to assert their independence. The parallel holds even for the minority of die-hard Russian nationalists who resisted these threats to the country's status in both epochs.

In 1989 Gorbachev's premises of normalized great-power behavior were overtaken by the forces that glasnost had released. In the words of the Italian sovietologist Vittorio Strada, "Gorbachev . . . drew up a Brest-Litovsk peace with the West, essentially putting an end to the Cold War."[61] Stephen Sestanovich of the Center for Strategic and International Studies in Washington called it "a diplomacy of decline."[62] Yielding its entire East European security zone and disbanding the Warsaw Pact, the Soviet Union executed the greatest strategic contrac-tion that any country has ever peacefully accepted. Napoleon's empire was ended only by military defeat; Hitler's and the contemporary Japanese likewise. The only nearly comparable instance of voluntary withdrawal is Britain's relinquishment of the Empire after the Second

World War. Some of the circumstances of the Soviet retreat were pitiful, almost humiliating: to be paid by the united German government to support Soviet troops in East Germany until housing could be found for them back home. Meanwhile, Moscow's function as a rallying point for unregenerate foreign Communists and Third World nationalists was rapidly disappearing, as the Soviets gave up trying to mobilize revolutionaries abroad against the West. Soviet clients everywhere faced the question of redefining themselves and fighting for their political lives.

The impact of the failed August Coup on Soviet foreign relations was almost anti-climatic, so rapidly had the projection of Soviet power faded away. The retreat from world competition was a top issue on the agenda of the plotters, but in this respect as in domestic matters their attempt to turn the clock back only broke the spring and let it whirl ahead. The most common popular response was relief that the country would no longer be paying the price for its superpower aspirations. Even the reduced power of the old Union was fractionated, as the individual Soviet republics claimed sovereign powers. Virtually all that remained of the superpower legacy was the nuclear arsenal.

*

The reasons for the sudden collapse of Soviet power and of the fear it had instilled in the outside world are easy to elucidate. To begin with, the Soviet regime was not cast in a rigid, immutable form by the Revolution, and its foreign policy was always subject to development and maneuver as internal and external circumstances changed. The dramatic transformation in its international relations in the late 1980s and early 1990s was inherent in the end of the long revolutionary process and the country's attainment of the moderate revolutionary revival. This made it possible to abandon the cover of revolutionary rhetoric, to stop frightening the outside world, and to recognize that concessions and conciliation may often do more for one's security than armed might and scowling threats.

The Communist menace had always loomed larger in the minds of its adversaries than in its real capabilities and intentions. Moreover, while the menace was very real for the unfortunates who fell directly into the Soviet imperial zone, the "communist" element ceased early on to be anything more than ideological window-dressing and a tactical tool. The "rubbery consistency" of doctrine, Kennan wrote, "permits it to be used as an infinitely flexible rationalization for anything whatsoever that the regime finds it advantageous to do."[63] Gorbachev's abandonment of ideologically couched confrontation, irreversibly confirmed by the failure of the August Coup, brought the moderate revolutionary revival fully into foreign policy and finally washed away the revolutionary basis of antagonism between the Soviet Union and the rest of the planet.

All along, Soviet power had been much more modest than super-power appearances suggested. Abandoning the power politics of one state among many, Stalin claimed the status of a superpower on the basis of his relative strength in the war-devastated world of 1945. The coalescence of all those whom Stalin threatened, and the rapid recovery of the European industrial countries and Japan, hopelessly turned the balance of power against the Soviet Union. Only by maintaining the principles and priorities of a wartime regime, a war economy, and military occupation of its satellites, could it try to keep up as a super-power, and even so the gap widened. As in Tsarist Russia, Stalinist military priorities came into conflict with the modern society and econ-omy that had been developed to sustain those priorities. Shevardnadze has underscored the consequences:

> We became a superpower largely because of our military might. But the bloated size and unrestrained escalation of this military might was reducing us to the level of a third-rate country, unleash-ing processes that pushed us to the brink of catastrophe.[64]

Late in the day, Gorbachev himself said of the military, "If this is not half of society, then it's at least a third of it . . . . We cannot live a normal life in our supermilitarized economy."[65] As he realized, the human base could not be made to function adequately by despotic methods. Soviet parity as it was achieved in the 1970s was a shell, based largely on nuclear weapons plus a ground arsenal that the Americans or the Europeans could easily match if they chose those spending priorities. There was not much economic yolk in the Soviet military egg.

Gorbachev's generation saw that it was impossible to go on dealing with the world in the old way, although the people who ran the institutions of force and coercion – the army, the police, and the party bureaucracy – were not easily persuaded of the need for fundamental change. The August Coup, drawing on this foot-dragging sentiment, was the last gasp of Soviet superpower politics, and its failure dealt the *coup de grâce* to those yearnings. Discrediting most of the leadership, the Communist Party, and the idea of the Union, the coup attempt des-troyed all effective bonds among the Soviet republics that were not their voluntary choice, and *ipso facto* eliminated any pretense by Moscow to superpower status. Further, the coup and its aftermath, along with the concurrent economic breakdown, turned Soviet concerns and energies so exclusively inward that foreign ambitions became inconceivable. Once the citadel of international revolutionary defiance of capitalism, Soviet Russia became a humble supplicant at the capitalists' table.

*

The loss of superpower status brought on a frenetic reaction within the

Soviet Union itself. While reformers and democrats welcomed the end of enmity between the USSR and the capitalists, both traditional Communists and Russian nationalists were grievously afflicted by it. No one would have thought before perestroika and the breakup of the Union that Russia in any guise would readily have abandoned its imperial interests and its superpower rank. For the Communist apparatchiki, the threat of peace was similar to that faced by the American military-industrial complex, though more severe: the totalitarian system that provided their jobs and privileges had lost its justification. For the nationalists, the great Soviet retreat was a painful blow to their sense of power, virtue, and special role in the world. In desperation, both of these currents came together in the August Coup. Its failure ended their serious aspirations to restore the Union as a superpower.

Nevertheless, the breakup of the Union does not mean the exclusion of its constituent parts from any future role in world politics. The Union did not totally disintegrate; it was rather a question of the Muscovite center losing its peripheral appendages. The Russian Federation, though shorn of its imperial gains of three centuries, is still a significant power, a huge country with a population double its nearest European competitor, Germany. It is poor neither in land nor in trained talent nor in natural resources nor even in capital plant; its poverty, rooted in the Stalinist system of centralization and secrecy, is one of mismanagement of assets and skewing of priorities. Given time to work its way out of the economic crisis of perestroika, whether through market or statist methods or (more likely) some combination of them, Russia will inevitably claim its position as a major power – not a superpower with the aspirations and reach of the former Soviet Union, but nevertheless one of the leading members of the world community, politically, economically, and culturally.

8

IS THERE SOCIALISM AFTER COMMUNISM?

2 July 1990. Nearly 5,000 delegates from all over the country assemble in the Kremlin's magnificent Finnish-built Palace of Congress for what will turn out to be the last congress of the Communist Party of the Soviet Union.

Following tradition, General Secretary Gorbachev takes the podium to deliver a two-and-a-half-hour keynote speech. Breaking with tradition, he packs his address full of criticism of the past as well as hope for a new kind of future:

> The Stalinist model of socialism is being replaced by a civil society of free people . . . . Production relations that served as a source for the alienation of the working people from property and the results of their labour are being dismantled, and conditions are being created for free competition among socialist producers.

He tries to put the best possible face on the troubles of perestroika: "We inherited an extremely heavy legacy . . ., the militarization of the economy." If the upheaval in Eastern Europe is the "collapse of socialism," then "We answer with a counterquestion – what kind of 'socialism'? Essentially a variant of the Stalinist authoritarian bureaucratic system."[1]

Prime Minister Ryzhkov, coming next with his customary report on the economy, is less dramatic and more pragmatic: "The former structure of social production . . . had been exhausted. The structure became an obstacle," requiring "a turn in the economy toward a social orientation," though "the first steps of the reform still retained a touch of the old approaches and exaggerated the role of centralized planned regulation."[2] Ryzhkov is followed by ideology chief Vadim Medvedev, who criticizes only the "mediocre work" of the old regime, and warns of some of the "new public groups" who "began to feel burdened by any limits, including the socialist framework, and thus began feeding extreme radicalist sentiments."[3]

The mood is sharper with Alexander Yakovlev, the acknowledged architect of perestroika: the Party is to blame for "the system of societal

167

stagnation engendered by the regime of personal power." Furthermore, "For seventy years we too often allowed ourselves to ignore everything we didn't like. Even today, to be quite frank, we frequently continue to trick ourselves and to be hypocritical." Perestroika is "behindhand . . . by about fifty years." He never uses the word "socialism."[4] Neither does Eduard Shevardnadze in his report on foreign policy, except to deny that the "collapse of socialism" in Eastern Europe was a defeat for Soviet security; he prefers to hail "the thoroughgoing democratization of society, the humanization of domestic legislation, the return of rights to citizens . . ., the right of believers to worship according to their faith and conscience."[5] At a private meeting with agitated conservative delegates, Yakovlev is asked which path he chooses, "toward socialism or toward communism?" He reportedly answers, "I have made my choice. I am in favor of joint-stock capital. All small enterprises must immediately be sold to private individuals." He mentions a manuscript he has written on Marxism, for which "if I publish those pages *now*, I'll be hanged from the nearest tree." He adds, "Marx created a theory of class struggle . . . which alas, we must reject."[6]

Yegor Ligachev, the acknowledged leader of Communist conservatism who has been relegated to the shadows of agricultural policy for the past two years, speaks on the second day of the congress. He is still unyielding on his principles: "Our restructuring began . . . with the goal of making the fullest use of the potential of socialism." Privatization hardly promotes this aim. "Socialist values incorporate universal human values." Moreover, "We are also unjustified in consigning the class approach to oblivion . . . . That is where the underestimation of the workers' and peasants' movement comes from." Finally, "There are forces in our country that are fighting against the socialist system, against the Communist Party . . . . All kinds of reckless radicalism, improvization and shifts in position have brought us little during the five years of restructuring."[7] Answering delegates' questions later on, Ligachev asserts,

I am for genuine scientific socialism as Lenin envisioned it. By the way, I don't accept it when it is said that at the end of his life Lenin decisively changed his viewpoint on socialism. He did not change his viewpoint on socialism. He only changed his views on the ways and means of building socialism. I understand restructuring as the provision of an adequate material and spiritual life for people and real participation by the working people in the management of society.

I want to say once again that I am against private property, for I am sure it will set us back both politically and socially. I am resolutely against mass unemployment, and I would like to repeat once again: Let whoever is pushing the country toward free-market relations be the first of the Soviet unemployed.[8]

KGB Chief Vladimir Kriuchkov is even more firmly attached to the old thinking – "commitment to Lenin, October, the socialist choice." He warns against "assertions that everything is good in the West and everything is bad in our country . . . . Can we allow the negative aspects that exist in the world of capital" – he cites unemployment, crime, drugs, lack of access to medical care and education – "to be transferred to our life?" He sees a new polarization of rich and poor in the Soviet Union, and warns, "If we don't come to our senses in time, given the present pace at which social distortions are intensifying, won't we or our children end up in the maelstrom of a new version of the October Revolution?" Despite the recent repeal of the Communist Party's constitutional privileges, he affirms, "We [of the KGB] see the Party as the political force that is marching in the vanguard of the struggle for progress."[9]

In contrast to the set speeches of the past, discussion of the leaders' reports at the congress opens up the broadest debate ever seen in the Soviet Union since the October Revolution. While conservatives rise to the defense of the Party and hope to keep reform gradual and socialist, deputy prime minister and economic reform chief Leonid Abalkin warns, "The socialist choice has begun to lose its attractive force among the country's population, to be called into doubt." He attempts to save the ideal by radically divorcing it from the Soviet past: "There is not one but several, very different, models of socialism. The downfall or defeat of one of these models does not mean the collapse of the very idea and principle of the socialist choice." On the contrary:

> We must clearly understand that it was not socialism that we were building, and that we were not living under a socialist society. Otherwise we will have to admit that a society in which the food problem has not been solved and the housing problem has not been solved, a society that lacks the democratic institutions of a state based on the rule of law, can be called socialist. Finally, a society cannot be considered socialist in which the working person is alienated and separated from property and from economic and political power.[10]

Boris Yeltsin, newly elected as chairman of the Russian Republic's Supreme Soviet, takes the floor to castigate the party apparatus for resisting change and clinging to power at all costs:

> The country cannot be given orders any longer . . . . It will support only a political organization that does not summon them to a distant prospect of communism beyond the clouds but that,

through its daily deeds, defends the interests of everyone and helps make them and our own country advanced, rich, and happy.[11]

On the next to last day of the congress he announces his resignation from the Party, and with every television camera on him defiantly walks out of the hall.

Yeltsin's speech is followed by Viacheslav Shostakovsky, rector of the Higher Party School in Moscow and a noted exponent of reform, even though he is responsible for the advanced training of party officials. Shostakovsky offers the most profound critique of Communist principles ever heard from a leader of the movement:

> About the socialist choice. Yes, the people followed the Bolsheviks' slogans in 1917. But seventy-three years later, we are repeating these slogans again and again: land to the peasants, factories to the workers, power to the soviets, peace to the peoples. We have not fulfilled these slogans. The land has ended up with the state; thus, it has ended up without a proprietor. The factories belong to the departments. Power belongs to the Party, and generally speaking, there is no peace among the peoples. I would like to recall one more slogan from October: "Bread to the hungry." It is taking on a kind of new, tragic urgency.

This outcome, Shostakovsky contends, is due not just to leadership errors but to "flaws and miscalculations in the design itself," particularly in failing to provide incentives for labor and then "replacing economic interest with a system of noneconomic compulsion and a system of repression . . . . Everything we have," he asserts, "was created through the heroic labor, including military labor, of our peoples. But it was created in spite of the system, a system of a social Chernobyl and of total control . . ., mismanagement, aimlessness, and spiritual emptiness." He concludes, "The Party is guilty as a system."[12]

"We remain committed to socialist values," Gorbachev maintains in his closing remarks to the congress. "But believe me, the success of the Party depends on whether it understands that this is already a different society." He is openly upset that the congress has deleted the word "market" from the name of the Party's commission on economic reform. "Hasn't our entire history shown the futility of attempts to break out of the plight that both the state and citizens are in through mending and patching the command-administrative system?" He calls for "a regulated market economy" providing "a high level of social safeguards," while admitting

> alarm concerning manners and morals that are becoming widespread and are in no way compatible with the ideals of humane

socialism. This is not only a legacy of the past [the old villain traditionally blamed for Soviet ills] but also the result, I repeat, of the "explosive" nature of the freedom that society has suddenly received.

The Party, he says, must

assimilate anew universal human values, not as something that is alien in a class sense, but as something that is normal for normal human beings . . ., worked out over centuries and millennia . . . . The ideology of socialism will be shaped in the process of the country's inclusion in the overall progress of civilisation.

Though he credits Marx and Lenin for their dialectical method of thinking, "We will not allow everything created by these classical thinkers to be turned into another 'short course,' " i.e. a Stalin-type catechism. "Adherence to dogma is a special impediment . . . . The CPSU's monopoly on power and administration has come to an end."[13]

Later, speaking on behalf of his candidacy for re-election as general secretary, Gorbachev rejects the charge that the economic reform is "in effect, a restoration of capitalism," and tries to embrace both worlds:

I take my stand firmly on the positions of the socialist choice. I am convinced that this system possesses immense untapped possibilities. Within the framework of using this potential, we can do a great deal, conducting radical transformations, returning man to power through democracy and returning to him the means of production. I will never link myself to those who want to push our country toward a restoration of capitalist ways.[14]

*

The Twenty-Eighth Party Congress was the last stand of Soviet socialism as an authoritative ideology. In the ensuing months, as political authority dissolved, the economy deteriorated, and the Union disintegrated, hardly a shred of old belief survived. By the time of the August Coup, socialism was not to be mentioned even by the plotters themselves. Even before, at the last plenum of the Central Committee, in July 1991, Gorbachev had persuaded the Party to forswear the historical verities of Marxism-Leninism.

Released from outworn dogma by glasnost, democratization, and the collapse of Communist authority, thinkers and populace alike in the former satellites and Soviet republics heaved deep sighs of collective relief and undertook to throw every idea and institution connected with the Old Regime into the dustbin of history. One can well sympathize with this mood of rejection, even if it did not encourage objective

171

appraisal of the circumstances in which the formerly Communist societies found themselves. In particular, by identifying "socialism" with the barrack regime of Stalinism, Eastern reformers narrowed the range of alternative social systems before them, and persuaded themselves that the Western utopia of *laissez-faire* private enterprise was the only economic model they could follow.

However, this exclusion of options was a purely political deduction, not based on a full consideration of what kind of social structure is likely to emerge after the specific revolutionary upheaval and postrevolutionary evolution that the Soviet Union and its satellites have gone through. Judgements about the sort of system that would or should eventually come after the dismantling of Stalinist "Communism" generally depend on one belief or another about the natural course of history. Most Soviet and foreign critics of the Stalinist legacy and the inadequacies of perestroika implicitly take the position that free-market capitalism along with political democracy is the final condition of modern humanity, the "end of history," to cite Francis Fukuyama, formerly of the American State Department.[15] Socialism, in this view, was a long, grim, misguided experiment finally discredited by the sickness of the system that glasnost revealed. This is the conviction of the paradoxically labeled "left" or "radical" reformers in the Soviet Union, as well as the overwhelming reaction in the West, even among socialists themselves.

To pose the question whether socialism can nevertheless follow Communism does not mean that the Marxian vision of socialism evolving into "communism" might simply be thrown into reverse. In distinction to "socialism" with all its possible variants, Marx's ultimate "communism" (small c) was a myth, a future utopia projected imaginatively and believed by Marxists with varying degrees of conviction, but never really acted upon, let alone realized. Therefore we cannot speak seriously of returning from that blissful state to socialism or anything else. The point is what comes after the actual Stalinist system, that totalitarian-bureaucratic postrevolutionary dictatorship practicing militarized state socialism, ordinarily called "Communism" by outsiders. Can it or will it be followed by some other form of social organization that could still be called socialism?

Three competing views about socialism in the future have stood out in the former Soviet bloc since Gorbachev came to power in 1985. The first phase of perestroika, up to 1989, was marked by the effort to develop an alternative model of socialism, democratic, decentralized, and market-oriented, drawing on the NEP or some of the more radical ideas of 1917 for its inspiration. Gorbachev himself consistently defended this position. The alternative that seized the foreground after 1989 took its guidance from Western democratic theory and classical economics, and rejected everything associated with "socialism" and "planning." A third approach was that of the Soviet conservatives, who used the freedom of glasnost to defend their old setup, hoping to confine perestroika to minor improvements in the postrevolutionary system of centrally planned state socialism.

These alternative visions all rest on the same basis of past experience and present reality, in other words the subject of all that has gone before in this book. From this basis three fundamental questions arise that must be answered in any vision of the Soviet and East European future. What actually was the nature of the Soviet system that the East is reacting against? What are the universal trends that may affect the evolution of Eastern societies from this point on? And what are the policy options? None of these matters can be addressed clearly until the ideological stereotypes that have governed thinking in this realm, anti-Communist as well as Communist, have been set aside.

*

In the joint interview that he held with Gorbachev in September 1991, two weeks after the collapse of the August Coup, Yeltsin exclaimed, "I think this experiment which was conducted on our soil was a tragedy for our people." Gorbachev did not gainsay him: "The historical experience which we have accumulated has allowed us to say, in a decisive fashion, that that model has failed which was brought about in our country."[16] This is the conventional wisdom in the outside world as well: that a "Marxist experiment" suddenly "failed" after it had been forcibly carried on in the Soviet Union for seventy-three years.

Several essential points are missing from these capsule characterizations. First of all, they do not show any sense of what a revolution is and how it rolls ahead regardless of individual intentions. No single, enduring model of conscious policy guided the process. There were elements of revolutionary experiment under Lenin, to be sure, but some failed in the early months, and the rest were swept away by Stalin's postrevolutionary dictatorship. Stalin's regime was not a continuation of the "experiment" or even a new "experiment"; it was a feverish annihilation of experiment, camouflaged by retention of the revolutionary language.

Secondly, the idea of a "Marxist experiment" lends too much credence to the regime's claims of ideological legitimacy. The propaganda of Stalinist and neo-Stalinist Marxism led most people inside and outside the former Soviet Union to believe that the Soviet system really was socialism-on-the-road-to-communism as prophesied by Marx and Lenin. This assumption about the framework of Marxist theory is still shared by radical Eastern reformers, die-hard Communists, and most Westerners, despite all their other differences. However, it ignores the step-by-step realities of Soviet history (blanketed by Stalinist falsifications) and the critique of Communism carried on ever since the beginning by non-Bolshevik Marxists. The plain fact is that the mythic Marxian futurology had absolutely no validity as a description of the evolving Soviet system. Gorbachev said almost as much in presenting his de-revolutionized program to the Communist Central Committee in July 1991, shortly before the coup:

> No doubt the comrades have noticed that communism is barely mentioned in the Program. It must be admitted that our experience, and others' as well, gives us no reason to believe that this goal is realistically attainable in the foreseeable future.

Still, he clung to the word in its more innocuous sense: "The communist idea – that the free development of each person is a condition for the free development of all – has been and continues to be an attractive guideline for mankind."[17]

To say that Marxism has finally failed in the Soviet Union, and that it is only now being rejected, makes sense only on the most superficial plane of verbal symbols. As we have seen, the Stalinist dictatorship and planned economy drew very little if anything from Marx. In fact, Marx and Engels had little practical guidance to offer anyone about running a dictatorship of the proletariat and planning a socialized economy, other than vague statements about "administration of things" and prophecies of a level of abundance that would transcend individual greed. They had nothing to say about planning under socialism to overcome the economic backwardness of a country like Russia. Even Lenin complained, "It did not even occur to Marx to write a single word on this topic and he died without leaving any precise citation, any irrefutable instruction."[18]

Soviet economic planning was in fact entirely *ad hoc*. As Rita di Leo observes, the system never produced "a Soviet Lord Keynes" to formulate a general theory of planning.[19] Lenin got most of his ideas on planning from a couple of books he read about the German war economy in the First World War – *Kriegssozialismus*, as it was known – "the ultimate in modern large-scale capitalist techniques, planning, and organization . . . to direct the whole economic life of a nation . . . *from one central agency*."[20] The Communists' first experience with planning was the system of War Communism, compounded of utopianism, desperation, and military methods adopted during the Civil War – a military success but an economic disaster. During the NEP the Gosplan economists pioneered the development of true planning concepts, all to no avail when Stalin swept them aside in 1928–29. Stalin's planning reverted to the War Communism experience, as recent Soviet critiques have emphasized, when he turned the whole saga of economic development into a new form of warfare. What failed in the 1970s and 1980s, therefore, was not Marxism but a unique system of militarized state socialism in the Russian imperial tradition, flying the purloined banner of Marxism.

*

Notwithstanding the mythic element in Marxism and its manipulation under Stalinism, the proposition that capitalism is not the end of history but instead leads naturally into socialism still bears some examination. Socialist and labor movements arose in the mid-nineteenth century for good reason, as a response to the growing power of private capital and the gap between rich and poor in industrializing countries. These movements were not content with mere redistribution of income; they also developed a powerful ethical component of community, brotherhood, and internationalism as well as rejection of the profit motive. Up to the Russian Revolution, "socialism" was a generic term, defined more by its ethical spirit than by any particular program. By no means did the concept accord an automatic monopoly of truth or virtue to the Marxist version. Now, in a world governed by disillusionment or pragmatism, the ethic of socialism has largely been forgotten, or dismissed as merely quaint.

Socialism in both its economic and ethical respects was a core idea in the Russian Revolution. The Bolshevik takeover was not just the work of a few power-hungry conspirators acting in isolation; rather, it represented the fanatical extreme of a broad spectrum of socialist movements, in Russia and internationally. Otherwise it would never have had the domestic support and international impact it did, and never would have created the dilemmas it did for the Left in other countries. One could go so far as to maintain that the "Great October Socialist Revolution" was a natural sequel (though a perverse one, skewed by Russian circumstances) to the American and European democratic revolutions of the eighteenth and nineteenth centuries. The socialist revolution attacked economic inequality where the earlier upheavals had largely confined themselves to addressing political inequality.

Even under perestroika, Gorbachev still insisted that socialism was the natural condition of humanity after it had passed through capitalism. In his book he rejected "the view that socialism is an accident of history and one long overdue for the ash-heap," and added, "An escape into the past is no reply to the challenges of the future."[21] Of course, Gorbachev and his supporters agreed that Stalinism was an abominable distortion of the socialist idea. Said Yuri Krasin of the Party's Academy of Social Sciences, "Historically, state socialism was objectively necessary," i.e., for the industrialization of Russia, but "no references to historical necessity can justify the Stalinist deformations of state socialism that exaggerated the state's role, placed it above civil society, and erected a bureaucratic barrier to the development of democracy and popular sovereignty."[22] The reformers ceased to believe literally in the Marxist prophecy of utopian communism as the outgrowth of socialism, but proposed instead to manage a moderated and decentralized version of socialism through democratic government. Thus, despite the deficiencies in its material record, the Gorbachevians believed that their reformed socialism still put them ahead of Western society on the scale of historical progress.

Modern capitalism has meanwhile changed profoundly since all these socialist theories and movements first took aim at it. It bears little resemblance to the free-market, *laissez-faire* ideal of Adam Smith that envisages a universe of small enterprises engaging in pure competition with one another. For both technical and financial reasons capital has become intensely concentrated in large corporations and conglomerates, often operating on a multinational basis. Inescapably bureaucratic in its structure, corporate capitalism has called forth a new ruling class, the meritocracy of administrators and experts, largely displacing the traditional "bourgeoisie."

Marx missed this social transformation, but he anticipated the basic trend toward capitalist concentration more clearly than any other thinker of his time. Left unchecked, capitalist concentration would and did result in monopoly and oligopoly with the power to control the theoretically free market. Marx merely erred about how long it would take for the concentration of capital to run its course. Only intervention by the state through regulatory and antitrust policies could curb the trend, while small enterprises, agriculturalists, and labor clamored for protection by the "countervailing power" of government, in J. K. Galbraith's phrase. Certain physical characteristics of the modern economy unforeseen by Adam Smith, above all the unique networks of transportation, communication, and energy supply, as well as the "externalities" of health, safety, and environmental degradation, also set limits to the free market and invited government intervention. Thus the free market, caught between the power of capital and the responses of the state, was doomed either way to become at best a manipulated market.

Marx also highlighted the "contradiction" between the social organization of production in large, complex units on the one hand, and the legal context of private property, management, and appropriation of profit on the other. Except as mediated by trade unionism, the relation between owners and employees ran directly counter to the political principles of the democratic state. Until the rise of socialism and its American counterpart of "progressivism" (or "liberalism" in its twentieth-century sense), the democratic state naively assumed the

176

Jeffersonian-Jacobin ideal of dispersed property ownership as the basis of individual independence, and failed to address inequality of power and condition in the economic sphere. But as time went on it faced a growing contradiction between its political principles and the realities of industrial society. Thus, "democratic capitalism" is an oxymoron, and "capitalist democracy" is a *non sequitur*. The Soviet experience has cautioned us that socialism, like capitalism, is not necessarily democratic; but democracy, to be consistent, must somehow come to terms with the aims of socialism. This will not be easy. As the Russian political scientist Lilia Shevtsova has noted, "In practice the criteria of democracy in politics and in economics are different and, what is more, may contradict one another."[23]

*

Fifteen or twenty years ago it was fashionable to talk about the theory of convergence between Soviet and Western societies. "Convergence" enabled outsiders to see ordinary Soviet citizens not as revolutionaries crouching in their barracks but as normal people working for large organizations and living their private lives as small families. It recognized the modernization of the Soviet economy and of Soviet urban life, as well as the infiltration of Western fashions and Western mass culture, and speculated about the democratizing effect all this might have on the Soviet political system, while Western economic organization was becoming larger in scale and more bureaucratic in form. Needless to say, Brezhnevian ideologists rejected the theory of convergence and its suggestion of the diminution of Soviet revolutionary zeal as bourgeois psychological warfare. American conservatives, with their eyes on political differences and international rivalry, likewise condemned the convergence idea, as a notion that might induce the West to let down its guard. In actuality the theory was true and even banal in some respects (the social and economic dimension), and altogether wrong – for the time being – in the political realm. But this discrepancy reflected the growing dialectical incompatibility within the Soviet system between its evolving social-economic base and its rigid political superstructure. Once the latter was shaken apart by Gorbachev's reforms, politics became the realm of the most rapid Soviet–Western convergence, while the economic system still suffered from the constraints of neo-Stalinism and the hazards of desocializing.

Where the theory of convergence was most accurate, up to Gorbachev, was in reflecting the physical modernization of Soviet life to parallel the Western model, even if at a distinctly lower quantitative level of creature comforts. Fyodor Burlatsky asserted, midway in perestroika,

177

I am profoundly convinced that the present scientific and technological revolution is having a similar effect on all social systems and all civilizations, giving rise to a number of problems that are common to them all . . . . New forms of economic management are emerging in both the capitalist and the socialist world.[24]

While the socialized USSR was becoming more industrialized, the industrialized West was becoming more socialized, as the scale of the work unit widened, managers displaced owners in controlling positions, and the competitive market of the nineteenth century gave way to monopolistic takeovers and mountainous state regulation.

Marx's vision of the *de facto* socialization of the process of production has proven to be highly accurate if a little premature. In terms of the social structure – Marx's "relations of production" – the outcomes have been parallel in both the Communist and Western systems: the managerial revolution of salaried bureaucrats and experts, public or private, who gain access to power through university degrees rather than through capital accumulation. Thus, when it came to the class character of the convergent postindustrial society, East as well as West, Marx turned out to be totally wrong.

The events of 1991 appeared to jump beyond convergence, as the Soviet successor republics acclaimed Western models both in democracy and in capitalism. Still, the underlying bureaucratic reality in social and economic organization on both sides was unrelieved. Below the level of government, Max Weber would be at home in either system.

Industrial growth and concentration eventually develop another, self-limiting dialectic, again unanticipated by Marx. This is the familiar tendency to bureaucratic centralism, rigidity, and inertia, the "routinization" that Weber wrote about, in corporate as well as public entities. In this respect, the effect of the Bolsheviks' revolutionary socialism was to jump ahead to a premature bureaucratic centralism in society and economy, far beyond what Russia's natural development had generated and ahead even of the most advanced capitalist countries. The resulting "command-adminstrative system" then became a brake on progress when Soviet society was still at a much less mature level than the major Western countries when they too hit a growth ceiling in the 1970s and 1980s.

Despite the lessons taught by Lord Keynes, late twentieth-century capitalism has continued to suffer from another condition heavily emphasized by Marx, namely the trade cycle and the insufficiency of attractive investment opportunity. While the Western world enjoyed a steady surge of growing productivity and living standards between the Second World War and the 1970s (stimulated in the USA by military spending and aided everywhere by the urbanization of redundant agriculturalists), capitalism never cured the problem of economic fluctuations and underutilization of resources that left social needs unmet while millions of people remained unemployed. By the end of the 1970s most capitalist economies had reached a limit in the standard of living and public life that they could deliver. Meanwhile the processes of capital investment and concentration were internationalized to a degree heretofore undreamed of, and multinational corporations became virtually independent of any government. In this context, economic reform in the East offered an exciting new opportunity for restless capital from the West, provided the interested firms were big enough to ride out the uncertainties of the transition.

In the face of the powerful trend toward what some Marxists used to call "organized capitalism," how could the West (or its leaders and theoreticians) continue to espouse the free-market doctrine and even try to export that model to the East? Marx and Engels had the answer even in their own day. As we have already noted in the analogy with Marxist ideology under Stalin, classical economics was itself "ideology" or "false consciousness," an idealization of reality to legitimize the interests of the capitalist ruling class. Unlike the "false consciousness" of Communist ideology, governmentally dictated and imposed, free-market ideology is broadly based in civil society, and needs no censorship to shield its claims. Now that the moderate revolutionary revival has freed the Eastern reformers from imposed Marxism-Leninism, they have voluntarily embraced the opposite false consciousness as their guide in reconstructing their societies.

*

No one, East or West, disputes the fact that the Stalinist economic model – call it a form of socialism, or not – went badly awry. There is less agreement on the reasons for the trouble and what aspects of the old system were to blame. Theories attempting to explain the failure tend to reflect ideological standpoints about the normal and desirable development of modern society.

The conventional wisdom today, Eastern as well as Western, is that the "command-administrative system," mistakenly identified with Marxism, broke down because it was inherently unable to mobilize people and resources to meet a country's needs and sustain its growth. This view does not account for or even recognize the extraordinary period of growth that the Soviet and East European economies experienced from the end of the Second World War until the mid-1970s, even if that growth was conducted wastefully and was skewed toward the industrial base of military power. The problem of stagnation was not intrinsic to the old system, but lay in certain specific factors that

179

impeded its operation under contemporary conditions of economic maturity and the high-tech explosion.

To begin with, the Stalinist command economy, though highly centralized and bureaucratic, was never truly based on planning. As we have noted, Stalin liquidated economic planning as a science at the very moment that he was putting the command system into place and launching his industrialization drive with orders to aim at the highest targets. Instead of genuinely planning, he governed the economy by military commands – assault that objective, destroy that enemy. No matter that resources were insufficient to reach all his goals – Stalin would shift allocations in midstream to accomplish his real priorities (which were military in substance as well as in method), and shoot the commanders who fell short. Backdating the First Five-Year Plan and then declaring it completed three years and eight months from its official implementation underscore the function of the document as exhortation and propaganda rather than as a real plan.

It is true that planning of a sort developed under Gosplan and the central industrial ministries using the so-called "method of balances" to assign targets and allocate supplies to enterprises, though Soviet economists more recently have complained that they had no true theory of economic planning. As one American businessman observed, "It was as though the whole economy were run by the Pentagon." Burlatsky blamed "precapitalist Russian tradition" for encouraging "the notion of a strong state authority that controls everyone and everything."[25] By the 1980s the faults in these methods were glaring. Not surprisingly, the system worked best in the military-industrial complex, favored by the government's priorities, where normal economic considerations of cost, efficiency, labor, productivity, and environmental damage were no object. Everywhere else the original defects of the system caused it more and more to fall short of the progress that the country's human and natural resources seemed to make feasible.

Thanks to its bureaucratic structure and military style, the Stalinist regime suffered not only from poor planning at the top but from ludicrously inept management down below. One might speak of a culture of management, disrupted first by revolution and civil war, partially restored with Lenin's emphatic encouragement during the NEP, then disrupted even more severely by the class-enemy campaigns of the early 1930s and by the purges of mid-decade. The new industrial and political leadership installed by Stalin at the level of district chief and enterprise director had no conception of how to operate except by receiving and transmitting commands. They were conditioned by a climate of authoritarianism, violence, fear, evasion of responsibility, and personal nest-feathering, which reached down to the lowest level of supervisor–worker relations. These habits have persisted right up to the present, often without regard to minimal standards of honesty, efficiency, clientele satisfaction, or human decency.

Worst of all was the veil of secrecy that the totalitarian state threw over all its economic operations. Secrecy gave cover to the stupidity, irrationality, and sheer corruption that prevailed among the post-purge generation of Stalinists. Secrecy not only walled the Soviet economy off from the outside world but isolated different enterprises and institutions from each other, and thereby worsened the country's technological lag. The center could not get reliable information even before it falsified its aggregate statistics. No one controlled the waste of capital, energy, human talent, and the carrying capacity of the environment. In the Stalinist and neo-Stalinist mind, resources were unlimited and the priority of military power was unquestioned. The American economist Robert Campbell comments, "The state and its agents have proved to be feckless stewards in managing [socialist] property."[26] Without a political context of freedom and responsibility where correctives and criticism could operate to promote more rational economic policies, the secret, incompetent, and obsessive management of the Soviet economy at all levels was bound to fail even the regime's own objectives.

*

Gorbachev and his personal advisors had concluded well before his accession to power that the top-heavy, secrecy-ridden structure of the Soviet economy had to change if the country were to escape stagnation, sustain its power in the world, and push ahead toward modern life. People such as Abel Aganbegian, Anatoly Butenko, and Tatiana Zaslavskaya, condemning the "command-administration system" as the "braking mechanism," looked back to the NEP and its model of market socialism, whereby enterprises would have both the incentive and the opportunity to respond to demand for their product, improve efficiency, raise wages, and better serve the public and the state. For agriculture and services the reformers were prepared to invoke the NEP's toleration of individual enterprise, though they balked at the outright restoration of private ownership of land and means of production – hence their attraction to the euphemisms of "leasing" and "cooperatives." By the 1990s Gorbachev was redefining socialism as a "mixed economy." Even the Soviet conservatives, exemplified by the last pre-coup prime minister, Valentin Pavlov, went along with that formula.[27]

More radical reformers who surfaced after the first year or two of perestroika saw Gorbachev's approach as a series of half-measures still contaminated by the centralism of the old order. Convinced by the winds of free enterprise theory blowing in from the West that there was no "third way" between socialism and capitalism, they embraced the pure market model calling for privatization of practically all enterprise. In East-Central Europe, where socialism was identified with national oppression, this feeling impelled newly democratic governments to opt for the free-market shock treatment, despite the immediate hardship and ultimate multinational penetration that this approach invited.

The "no third way" argument, though understandably attractive to people reacting against the Stalinist legacy, suffers from the well-known "fallacy of the excluded middle." It is a purely semantic conclusion that rests on postulating two verbal abstractions, capitalism and socialism, and neglecting the wide range of real situations around either term that offer a multitude of policy choices. Michael Ellman asserts, "It is simply not true" that "planning and the market are two mutually exclusive categories," as both Marxists and free-enterprisers have maintained.[28] Sir Karl Popper, noting the potential abuses of capitalism as well as of "holistic" Communist systems, has warned, "What people in the Soviet Union must absolutely abandon is any ambition to build a perfect society. This cannot be done either on the Left or on the Right."[29]

In the absence of Marxist diatribe, little critical evaluation of the free-market economic model has been advanced among its Eastern admirers. A number of important distinctions between the kinds and levels of economic activity under "real existing capitalism" remain blurred. The free-market model confuses decentralization (which could accommodate planning and directed economy within small governmental units), marketizing (which could accommodate publicly owned enterprise operating according to the laws of supply and demand), and privatization (which has very different implications, centralist or decentralist, at different levels). These three categories are now hopelessly mixed up in Soviet and East European thinking.

Conspicuously overlooked is the discrepancy in the Soviet-type economy between its postcapitalist and precapitalist sectors – the overblown military-industrial complex and the smothered realm of agriculture and services. In industry, the Soviet model not only incorporated modern organizational developments but even jumped ahead to the extreme logic of bureaucratic centralism. Privatization here is an attempt to reverse this logic and turn the structure back to a form less mature than present industrial reality. In the precapitalist sectors, by contrast, privatization does fit the reality of the "forces of production," though it requires major efforts to dismantle the artificial, bureaucratic "relations of production" that were imposed according to the Stalinist model. Stalinist policies have uprooted most of the population from precapitalist self-sufficiency, but have not allowed market-based commodity production to meet everyday needs.

The embrace of unqualified free-market economics by most of the new East European governments and by many ex-Soviet reformers prompts a number of questions. Why, to begin with, have they adopted a purist conception of the market which has been the subject of a century of controversy in the West, and is now extensively qualified in practice everywhere that it prevails in theory? Understandably, there is a strong reaction against any and all of the policies of the totalitarian regimes from which the former subjects of Communism have just escaped, reinforced by the identification of anything called socialism with the oppressive heritage of Stalinism. Furthermore, classical market theory has been riding high, above all in Britain and the United States, as the ideology – i.e., false consciousness – legitimizing unregulated corporate capitalism. "In my view," J. K. Galbraith wrote in 1990, "some, and perhaps much, of the advice now being offered the Central and Eastern European states proceeds from a view of the so-called capitalist or free-enterprise economies that bears no relation to their reality," but instead offers "casual acceptance of – even commitment to – human deprivation, unemployment, inflation, and disastrously reduced living standards," as "essential therapy."[30] Yet the post-Communist reformers are taking this philosophy seriously as a guide to policy, even in the unprecedented task of dismantling the command economy.

In their reaction against any form of central economic authority, the reformers have failed to appreciate that the *laissez-faire* doctrine, formulated even longer ago than Marxism, is equally outdated under the conditions of modern industrialism and the global economy. Ignored in the new Eastern orthodoxy are old debates in the West as to whether the "free" market achieved the wisest allocation of investment; the clumsy record (ever since seventeenth-century mercantilism) of pursuing public purposes through state protection or subsidy of private interests; the clear trend from individual proprietorship to corporate operation even in those sectors (trade, services, agriculture) dearest to the individualist ideology; and the damage done to long-run business rationality by the free-wheeling operations of billionaire buccaneers, not to mention the long struggle for trade-union rights and the welfare state. The Eastern reformers assume without reflection that pure capitalist economics will carry them along the developmental track of Germany and the USA, when they may be more likely to find themselves bogged down in a Latin-American-style morass of corruption above and desperation below. Cornelius Castoriadis writes, "The mythology of the market and the prevalence of 'liberal' rhetoric over the last ten years make people forget that 'market mechanisms' – though undoubtedly much less wasteful than a bureaucratic command economy – are themselves in a big mess. Just look around."[31]

*

How do the prospects for socialism and capitalism in the East appear in the context of the moderate revolutionary revival, the ultimate phase of the revolutionary experience following the Stalinist post-revolutionary dictatorship that the world thought of as "Communism"? Unfortunately, the concept of the moderate revolutionary revival does not offer a precise determination of the new organization and direction of society. It is as variable and uncertain as the elements that come and go in the original moderate stage of any revolution. In the Russian case this precedent notably leaves the economic destiny of the country undecided.

All post-Communist governments and parties adhere at least verbally to the democratic part of the ideal of 1917, while the socialist component remains subject to wide-ranging debate. Some of the ultra-nationalist elements in Eastern Europe may lean toward private property plus dictatorship on the model of the Russian Whites or Western Fascism. These political variations underscore the point that the moderate revolutionary revival has no predetermined content – it may incorporate some of the more radical aims and achievements of the revolution, as Social Democrats and Gorbachevians would do, with their talk of the "social market" and a "safety net"; or it may subscribe to a model minimally adapted from prerevolutionary society, as represented by the democratic free-marketeers; or it may at some point or other give way to a new authoritarian regime. The critical difference in the Soviet instance of the moderate revolutionary revival is the fact that the postrevolutionary dictatorship against which the new reformers were reacting had survived for an abnormally long time and had enforced a verbal identity with the Revolution and its socialist ideal. This background was decisive in the reformers' reluctance to accept any economic arrangements associated even verbally with that experience, and in their search for a foreign model that would distinguish their new regimes both politically from the older Tsarist past and economically from the newer Communist past.

*

Surprisingly, neither the Eastern reformers nor their Western advisors appear to have given much thought to non-statist alternatives to capitalist enterprise. Some of these ideas, including anarchism and workers' control of factories, are familiar positions in the corpus of socialist theory, and were well known in 1917, inappropriately utopian as they may appear under present circumstances. Other non-capitalist forms, pragmatically tested and better suited to a market context, are actually well developed in the West – the cooperative movement, especially in Northern Europe, and non-profit organizations, especially in the US (voluntary hospitals and private universities, for example). A third non-capitalist form includes entities created by the state but independently controlled, ranging from local school districts in most American states to research organizations (the Smithsonian Institution) and public broadcasting systems (BBC, CBC, PBS). Marie Lavigne of the Centre Nationale des Recherches Scientifiques in Paris observes, "The combination of public ownership and private management methods that is a distinctive feature of the French industrial system is still unknown in the USSR, even as a concept."[32] To be sure, directly state-owned and controlled enterprise, prominent in the economies of Latin Europe and Latin America, has been plagued with inefficiency and deficits, but this may be more a cultural and political problem than an economic one, depending on such factors as a society's standards of efficiency and honesty and the political power of free labor movements. In any case, there is no reason in principle why any and all of these alternative forms of organization cannot coexist in a system of economic pluralism, particularly if they are kept accountable by market relations.

The most compelling argument adduced by the free-market advocates is the familiar proposition that political democracy cannot exist without a market economy and private ownership. In fact, this contention has never been tested. In 1917 Russia the thin shoots of democracy were mowed down by the Bolshevik Revolution *before* the market economy was eradicated. It is certainly false to suppose that a capitalist economy guarantees democracy – witness every right-wing dictatorship from Mussolini to Pinochet. In Russia the Communist dictatorship was actually tightened simultaneously with the introduction of the market socialism of the NEP, while political democratization ran well ahead of economic marketizing and privatizing under perestroika. The practical question now facing the former Soviet republics as well as the former East European satellites is how far and how fast they feel the democracy-market principle requires them to marketize and privatize their economies in order to consolidate their new democracies. We know that the market is not a sufficient condition for democracy, and we do not know to what extent it may be a necessary condition. Economic conclusions drawn from the purist extreme may prove to be as dangerous to democracy as centrist inaction or conservative obstructionism.

Beyond question, a complex modern economy cannot do without a certain basis of market relationships, even if the state has to interfere to keep them operative. Privatization is another matter. Whether privatization is rational or irrational, progressive or retrogressive, depends both on the kind of economic activity in question and on a country's overall level of economic development. In the Soviet Union and Eastern Europe, nationalization of small-scale enterprise including services, retailing, and agriculture was highly inappropriate to begin with. In these areas privatization (or other local forms of ownership such as

185

cooperatives and small municipalities) is for the time being inescapable, though it should be noted that in the most advanced countries, capitalist concentration is transforming those presumably individualist sectors through centralized trade and service chains and large-scale agri-business. In large-scale industry, natural resource extraction, and the transportation and communication infrastructure, privatization may prove to be an artificial and irrational effort to turn back the clock of economic change. As such experiments as the British government's sale of public utilities illustrate, privatization at this level is truly an attempt to unscramble eggs. Moreover, as practiced in the East today, it threatens to squander the national patrimony painfully accumulated under Stalinist socialism. The Hungarian free-market economist János Kornai has been prompted to warn against "the offensive and irresponsible liquidation of state ownership," and observes, "The labor and the sacrifices of this country's population were embodied in the state's wealth."[33] Privatization proceeds in the name of a grand theory but it is more likely to redound to the benefit of interests powerful enough (often multinational) or shady enough (emerging from the old black market or from the *nomenklatura*) to take advantage of it.

No matter, says Grigory Yavlinsky, the leading Soviet theorist of privatization: "The privatisation process is no longer a matter for debate; it is simply under way . . . . An urgent reaction from the state . . . was needed."[34] Then he adds an unusual notion of economic justice, "a new conception of social protection in which the decisive role is played by the individual's right to earn as much as he can and by the state's protection of the weak to an extent corresponding to the efficiency of the economy as a whole." Yavlinsky's view only highlights the analogy between privatization of large-scale enterprise and attempts to restore the feudal privileges of the aristocracy when the bourgeois revolutions of the seventeenth and eighteenth centuries began to recede.

*

Whatever the theoretical merits of privatizing and marketizing, early gestures in this direction did little to improve actual economic performance, certainly not in the Soviet Union. The great paradox of perestroika is the astounding progress of political reform, leading to the total demise of the Communist dictatorship, coupled with an utter disaster in economic reform. For this contrast there is no commanding explanation, despite all the theories, Left, Right, and Center, that have been offered in search of an answer. One might refer to the dialectical contradiction in the neo-Stalinist regime where the rigid political system had fallen out of step with socioeconomic advance. In this situation, political democratization, in tune with the logic of history, was a progressive release, whereas the drive to decentralize and privatize the economy ran counter to the basic organizational trends of modern society and proved more disruptive than constructive. Besides, in Russia this kind of economic reform ignored the economic culture of passivity that sixty years of the command economy had only reinforced.

Rapid clearing of the rubble of the command economy is nonetheless urged by the marketizing-privatizing school as a *sine qua non* to arrest and reverse the collapse of the former Communist economies. However, the recipe derives more from imported ideology than from concrete analysis of the collapse and its causes. East and West, people were talking about free-market remedies for the Soviet economic collapse well before the collapse became a reality; they confused stagnation and a fall in the growth rate with absolute deterioration of economic performance. Stagnation had set in by the late 1970s, occasioning great frustration and eventually the reforms of perestroika. Absolute deterioration (as distinct from the diversion of goods to unconventional channels) did not commence until about 1990, five years into perestroika and democratization.

Without holding any brief for the old economic system, one must confront the *prima facie* case, *post hoc ergo propter hoc*, that the economic collapse was brought on by perestroika, not the other way around. As long-suffering Soviet citizens constantly complained, perestroika dismantled the old economic mechanism without putting anything in its place. The Gorbachevian reformers targeted the old central planning system as the culprit in stagnation, and campaigned against the party bureaucracy that served as a backup authority to intervene in economic problems as they arose either at the center or locally. They underestimated the country's cultural resistance to market economics and the deficiency of managerial personnel capable of acting in a market environment. They failed to appreciate either the indirect planning methods of the NEP or the remediable faults of the Stalinist command economy. They failed to foresee that it would be much harder to convert the long-established Stalinist economy to a market system at this juncture than it had been to shift from the raw experiments of War Communism to the market socialism of the NEP.

What alternative approach to economic planning might there be, retaining the mechanism of central direction but correcting its deficiencies? It would be the opposite of Stalinist practice in every respect. First, it would not try to dictate in those areas of consumer-oriented economic activity best left to individuals or very small enterprise. Secondly, it would reject the priority for heavy industry and military production, no longer excused by the international situation. It would recognize that it is difficult to scale back or reconvert the current excess capacity in producer goods industry, but it is easy to stop expanding it and, for example, to divert construction work into housing and roads. Thirdly, it would emphasize indirect controls such as finance and taxation, in the spirit of French indicative planning, or in James Millar's words, rely on "central management" in preference to "central planning."[35] Fourthly and most importantly, it would no longer operate under cover of official secrecy and falsified statistics, but instead in the open conditions of glasnost. It would have to have a realistic system of prices and foreign exchange values, and a balanced budget. Beyond these considerations, there is no reason in principle why an East European country could not operate the complex of its large-scale industry and infrastructure just as a capitalist multinational conglomerate operates all its subsidiary branches and enterprises. Given the problems bequeathed by the old economy, notably in transportation, distribution, and the food supply, intelligent planning would seem a much quicker and more effective remedy for the effects of stupid planning, than to wait for the slower and less certain workings of an artificial free market and international profit-seekers.

In addition to its empirical inappropriateness today, the free-market ideology even as professed in the West suffers from a critical methodological flaw. This is to judge the performance of the economy as a whole according to the economics of the individual capitalist firm. Under pure capitalism, of course, if a firm constantly runs deficits and cannot cure them, it goes bankrupt, discharges its employees, and liquidates its assets. In practice, in all capitalist countries, if a firm is "too big to fail" the government will intervene to rescue it. Bankruptcy makes sense in the individual case and from the standpoint of the creditors of the particular firm, but it does not necessarily make sense from the standpoint of the national economy. A country cannot go out of existence because it is "unprofitable."

The real economic challenge for any nation is to achieve the wisest possible deployment of its resources, not the annihilation of those units which are not being used to the satisfaction of the bookkeeper's definition of a profit. Thus, a socialized factory may be producing at a "loss" because of the relationship of prices, wages, technology, and efficiency, which therefore requires a state subsidy, but this does not mean that the plant in question is not contributing to the gross domestic product. It may make sense to transfer the capital and workers involved to some more rewarding line of production, but it makes no sense at all in the national perspective to close the plant down and give up its product while its unemployed workers are left producing nothing at all. The only justification for this self-punishing approach is the pious hope that private entrepreneurs in a free-market situation can move faster and more effectively to re-employ the idle capital and labor than can state planners.

The ultimate limit to free-market principles in the East and especially in Russia is cultural more than economic. The long-standing historical circumstances shaping popular Russian economic attitudes include the centralized authoritarian state, bureaucratic administration and feudalistic control instead of bargaining in the economic and political marketplace, and constant pressures for national defense and expansion. Work, in the Russian experience, is exploitation, and trade is parasitic, particularly if carried on by non-Russians; initiative and self-improvement are acts of defiance that your neighbors or the state will punish. Perestroika, supported by the intelligentsia as representatives of an alternative culture, did not just repudiate Stalinism; it challenged all of the slavish old Russian cultural traits as they affected both economics and politics. The conservative Russian nationalist opposition still embodies these attitudes. Modernization has weakened this culture in the urban sector at least, but it will remain a factor to be reckoned with despite the failure of overt conservation in the August Coup.

Where, through this thicket of theory and practice, lies the most rational path for a society emerging from a prolonged revolutionary experience and a deeply entrenched system of barracks socialism? The belief is widely held both in the former Soviet republics and abroad that the "Left," "socialism," Marxism, and "social experiments," have all been suddenly discredited by the malfunctioning of the economic system inherited from Stalinism. Actually the record of Stalinism is no more relevant now in judging these economic alternatives than it was fifty years ago, if one understands the Stalinist model as a particular Russian postrevolutionary perversion of socialism. If anything, the final collapse of the Stalinist model should leave the world freer to consider radical reform and social experiment, unburdened by the need to explain away the Soviet record or to fend off fears that an agenda of change might advance the threat of Soviet power. The unresolved problem is how to reconcile the principles of democracy and the realities of the modern economy. The answer would be a good definition of socialism for the present day. If this proposition involves contradictions, they stem not from a particular ideological scheme but from the inherent clash between modern industrial society and its professed values.

The most logical direction for the ex-Soviet republics and the former satellites, reflecting the realities of the modern economy, the legacy of the postrevolutionary experience, and the limitations of national culture, is the mixed economy. Gorbachev himself came to this conclusion by the late 1980s and tried repeatedly to articulate it. "The matter at hand is nothing other than the creation of a mixed economy. Plus the free development of all types of ownership," he told the July 1991 plenum.[36]

The mixed economy, in other words a social-democratic system, is the basic trend in Western societies, though they differ widely in their specific approaches, in their verbal professions about it, and in their distance from the goal. Embracing all forms of enterprise – individual, cooperative, private capitalist, private non-profit, worker-controlled, municipal, and state, each at the most appropriate level – the mixed economy would reflect the social ideals of 1917 and give the heirs of the Revolution some economic guideposts from their own history. It would incorporate the negative lessons of the Communist experience – that force is no substitute for stable finances and personal incentives, that the state cannot plan everything, that officials and managers behave stupidly and corruptly when they are protected by dictatorship, that there is more to economic life than the support of national military prowess. But it would also retain the useful heritage of the Communist period, in the industrial and educational base that it built up, in the planning system appropriately reformed, in the principles of individual economic security, and in the absence of concentrations of private economic power that could corrupt the new democratic political process and foil pursuit of the public interest.

With this kind of economic solution, the moderate revolutionary revival offers the ex-Soviet republics the chance – perhaps thrown away already in some of the former satellites – to construct with minimal resistance, for the whole world to see and judge, a new model of democratic and pluralist socialism. So in this limited sense, however labeled, there can be socialism after Communism, though it cannot be either the socialism that Marx projected onto the escalator of history, or the socialism that Stalin built on the bones of his unnumbered victims.

NOTES

INTRODUCTION

1 George Bush, Address to the United Nations General Assembly, 23 September 1991, quoted in *The New York Times*, 24 September 1991.

1 PERESTROIKA I: BACK TO THE FUTURE

1 M. S. Gorbachev, Speech at the Joint Session of the Soviet of the Union and the Soviet of Nationalities, 11 April 1984, *Pravda*, 12 April 1984 (*Current Digest of the Soviet Press* [hereafter cited as CDSP], 9 May 1984, p. 8).
2 Seweryn Bialer, *The Soviet Paradox: External Expansion, Internal Decline*, New York, Knopf, 1986, p. 109.
3 Gorbachev himself described these misfortunes in a speech to a meeting of cultural leaders, 28 November 1990, *Pravda* and *Izvestiya*, 1 December 1990 (CDSP, 2 January 1991, pp. 1–2).
4 Zdeněk Mlynář, "My Classmate Mikhail Gorbachev," *L'Unità*, 9 April 1985.
5 Mlynář interview, quoted in Hedrick Smith, *The New Russians*, New York, Random House, 1990, p. 47.
6 Lev Yudovich, "Gorbachev, New Chief of Russia, May Make a Tougher Adversary," *The Wall Street Journal*, 12 March 1985.
7 Zhores A. Medvedev, *Gorbachev*, New York, Norton, 1986, p. 93. Medvedev reasons that the first secretary of Stavropol was well placed to become favorably known to the higher-ups because the province contained a number of their favorite vacation resorts.
8 Yuri Andropov, Speech to the Central Committee of the CPSU, 22 November 1982, *Pravda*, 23 November 1982 (CDSP, 22 December 1982, p. 4).
9 See Robert V. Daniels, "Stalin's Rise to Dictatorship, 1922–29," in Alexander Dallin and Alan F. Westin (eds), *Politics in the Soviet Union*, New York, Harcourt, Brace & World, 1966, pp. 4–5, 36, and "Political Processes and Generational Change," in Archie Brown (ed.), *Political Leadership in the Soviet Union*, London, Macmillan, 1989, pp. 109–114.
10 ibid., pp. 113–114.
11 See Archie Brown, "The Soviet Succession: From Andropov to Chernenko," *The World Today*, April 1984, pp. 136–137.
12 Aganbegian interview, quoted in Angus Roxburgh, *The Second Russian Revolution*, London, BBC Books, 1991, p. 33.
13 See Dusko Doder, *Shadows and Whispers: Power Politics inside the Kremlin from Brezhnev to Gorbachev*, New York, Random House, 1986, p. 214; Martin

Walker, *The Waking Giant: Gorbachev's Russia*, New York, Pantheon Books, 1986, p. 32; Michel Tatu, *Mikhail Gorbachev: The Origins of Perestroika*, Boulder Colo., East European Monographs, 1991, p. 62.

14 M. S. Gorbachev, Speech to the Central Committee of the CPSU, 10 December 1984, *Pravda*, 12 December 1984.

15 See Rowland Evans and Robert Novak, "Gorbachev's Mandate," *The Washington Post*, 1 November 1985, citing "a well-placed political source in Poland."

16 Hedrick Smith reports the story that the plug was literally pulled on Chernenko's life-support systems at a moment chosen when some of the conservative Politburo members were away from Moscow. Smith, *The New Russians*, p. 77.

17 Richard Owen, *Comrade Chairman: Soviet Succession and the Rise of Gorbachev*, New York, Arbor House, 1987, p. 211; see also Doder, *Shadows and Whispers*, p. 267, and Tatu, *Gorbachev*, pp. 67–68.

18 Yegor Ligachev on Moscow Television, 1 July 1988. See Dusko Doder and Louise Branson, *Gorbachev: Heretic in the Kremlin*, New York, Viking Penguin, 1990, p. 63.

19 Boris Yeltsin, *Against the Grain: An Autobiography*, New York, Summit Books, 1990, pp. 183–189.

20 Recorded and translated by CNN; text in *The New York Times*, 26 December 1991.

21 M. S. Gorbachev, "On Convening the Regular 27th Congress and the Tasks Connected with Preparing and Holding It," *Pravda*, 24 April 1985 (CDSP, 22 May 1985, pp. 3–4).

22 M. S. Gorbachev, Report to the Plenum of the Central Committee of the CPSU, "On Restructuring and the Party's Personnel Policy," 27 January 1987, *Pravda*, 28 January 1987 (CDSP, 11 March 1987, p. 8).

23 Doder and Branson, *Gorbachev*, pp. 132–133; Eduard Shevardnadze, *The Future Belongs to Freedom*, New York, The Free Press, 1991, p. 174.

24 Zhores A. Medvedev, *The Legacy of Chernobyl*, New York, Norton, 1990, p. 50.

25 M. S. Gorbachev, Address on Soviet Television, 14 May 1986, *Pravda* and *Izvestiya*, 15 May 1986 (CDSP, 18 June 1986, pp. 18–19).

26 Shevardnadze, *The Future Belongs to Freedom*, pp. 175–176.

27 M. S. Gorbachev, *Perestroika: New Thinking for Our Country and the World*, New York, Harper & Row, 1987, p. 81.

28 Vitaly Tretiakov, "Gorbachev's Enigma," *Moscow News*, 3 December 1989, p. 10.

29 Notes of the meeting, evidently authentic, were circulated unofficially – "Talk of M. S. Gorbachev with Members of the Writers' Union of the USSR" (June 1986), *Arkhiv Samizdata*, no. 7585. A much abbreviated account was published in *Pravda*, 21 June 1986.

30 Fyodor Burlatsky, remarks at Soviet press conference, Reykjavik, Iceland, 12 October 1986, *Radio Liberty Research*, RL 396/86.

31 M. S. Gorbachev, Speech at a conference of the Khabarovsk Territory Party Organization, *Pravda*, 2 August 1986.

32 A. N. Yakovlev, Speech to a meeting of intellectuals in Dushanbe, Tadzhikistan, *Pravda*, 10 April 1987.

33 Sergei Voronitsyn, "New Center Created for the Study of Public Opinion," *Radio Liberty Research*, RL 183/86, 7 May 1986.

34 M. S. Gorbachev, reported in *Literaturnaya Gazeta*, 5 November 1986.

35 See M. S. Gorbachev, Address to a meeting of media executives, "Deepen Perestroika with Practical Deeds," *Pravda*, 15 July 1987; Thomas Remington,

"A Socialist Pluralism of Opinions: Glasnost and Policy-Making under Gorbachev," *The Russian Review*, July 1989, pp. 278–279.

36 Gorbachev, Talk with members of the Writers' Union, p. 5.

37 M. S. Gorbachev, Speech at a meeting of media executives, *Pravda*, 14 February 1987 (CDSP, 18 March 1987, p. 6).

38 See, e.g., *Ogonyok*, no. 43, 1988.

39 See, e.g., Ye. K. Ligachev, Speech at a conference of mass media executives, *Pravda*, 17 September 1987.

40 Gorbachev, Talk with members of the Writers' Union, p. 5.

41 Andrei Sakharov, quoted in *The Washington Post*, 1 February 1987.

42 M. S. Gorbachev, Concluding remarks at the Plenum of the Central Committee of the CPSU, 28 January 1987, *Pravda*, 30 January 1987.

43 Academician T. I. Zaslavskaya, "Questions of Theory: Restructuring Sociology," *Pravda*, 6 February 1987.

44 Walter Laqueur, *The Long Road to Freedom: Russia and Glasnost*, New York, Scribner's, 1990, p. 78.

45 Walter Joyce, "The Law of the State Enterprise," in Walter Joyce, Hillel Ticktin, and Stephen White (eds), *Gorbachev and Gorbachevism*, London, Frank Cass, 1989, p. 81.

46 Gorbachev, *Perestroika*, p. 253.

47 M. S. Gorbachev, Speech to the Polish Sejm, 11 July 1988, *Pravda*, 12 July 1988, quoted in Astrid von Borcke, "Gorbachev's *Perestroika*: Can the Soviet System be Reformed?" in Susan L. Clark (ed.), *Gorbachev's Agenda: Changes in Soviet Domestic and Foreign Policy*, Boulder, Colo., Westview Press, 1989, p. 43.

48 Yeltsin, *Against the Grain*, pp. 190–191.

49 I. T. Frolov, Report to the section on ideological work, 28th CPSU Congress, 5 July 1990, *Pravda*, 7 July 1990 (CDSP, 5 September 1990, p. 17).

50 See Doder and Branson, *Gorbachev*, pp. 304–311.

51 Nina Andreyeva, "I Cannot Forgo Principles," *Sovetskaya Rossiya*, 13 March 1988. High-level inspiration and editing of the Andreyeva letter were demonstrated by Giulietto Chiesa, *L'Unità*, 23 May 1988.

52 "The Principles of Restructuring: The Revolutionary Nature of New Thinking," *Pravda*, 5 April 1988 (CDSP, 4 May 1988, p. 3); conversation with Vitaly Korotich, 15 February 1992.

53 Letter to the Editor from Y. Borokhovich, *Sovetskaya Kultura*, quoted in *The Washington Post*, 1 May 1988.

54 Leon Trotsky, Letter to the Central Committee and the Central Control Commission, 8 October 1923, excerpts in Trotsky, *The New Course*, New York, New International, 1943, pp. 153–155; full text published in *Izvestiya TsK*, no. 5, 1990, pp. 165–173.

55 Interview of Ye. Z. Razumov, "Important Stage of Preparations for the Conference," *Pravda*, 13 June 1988 (CDSP, 6 July 1988), p. 1).

56 See Baruch A. Hazen, *Gorbachev's Gamble: The 19th All-Union Party Conference*, Boulder, Colo., Westview Press, 1990, pp. 16–21.

57 M. S. Gorbachev, Report to the 19th All-Union CPSU Conference, "On Progress in the Implementation of the Decisions of the 27th CPSU Congress and the Tasks of Deepening Restructuring," 28 June 1988, *Pravda*, 29 June 1988 (CDSP, 27 July 1988, p. 15).

58 M. S. Gorbachev, Speech at the conclusion of the 19th All-Union CPSU Conference, *Pravda*, 2 July 1988.

59 See Edward L. Keenan, "Muscovite Political Folkways," *The Russian Review*, April 1986; Robert V. Daniels, "Russian Political Culture and the

Postrevolutionary Impasse," *The Russian Review*, April 1987.
60 See Ben Eklof, *Soviet Briefing: Gorbachev and the Reform Period*, Boulder, Colo., Westview Press, 1989, pp. 66–79.
61 Gorbachev, *Perestroika*, p. 108.
62 V. Krivosheyev, "August, 1968," *Moscow News*, 28 August 1988.
63 Roy A. Medvedev and Giulietto Chiesa, *Time of Change: an Insider's View of Russia's Transformation*, New York, Pantheon Books, 1989, pp. 228–229.
64 Vadim A. Medvedev, "The Contemporary Conception of Socialism," *Pravda*, 5 October 1988.
65 Anatoly Sobchak, *For a New Russia: The Mayor of St. Petersburg's Own Struggle for Justice and Democracy*, New York, The Free Press, 1992, p. 16.
66 Joel C. Moses, "Democratic Reform in the Gorbachev Era," *The Russian Review*, July 1989, p. 269.
67 Frolov, Report to the 28th CPSU Congress (CDSP, 5 September 1990, p. 17).
68 Quoted in Len Karpinsky, "Mikhail Gorbachev: A Revolutionary Rethink Necessary," *Moscow News*, 3 November 1991.
69 Robert G. Kaiser, *Why Gorbachev Happened: His Triumphs and His Failures*, New York, Simon & Schuster, 1991, pp. 10, 19–20, 415, 420.
70 Cornelius Castoriadis, "The Gorbachev Interlude," in Ferenc Féher and Andrew Arato (eds), *Gorbachev: the Debate*, Atlantic Highlands, NJ, Humanities Press International, 1989, p. 61.
71 Owen, *Comrade Chairman*, p. 240.
72 Kaiser, *Why Gorbachev Happened*, p. 413.
73 Gorbachev, Report to the 28th CPSU Congress, p. 12.
74 Yeltsin, *Against the Grain*, p. 139.

2 PERESTROIKA II: DEATH ON THE OPERATING TABLE

1 Statement by the Soviet Leadership, *Pravda* and *Izvestiya*, 20 August 1991; Resolution no. 1 of the State Committee on the State of Emergency in the USSR, *Pravda* and *Izvestiya*, 20 August 1991; Appeal to the Soviet People by the State Committee on the State of Emergency, 18 August 1991, *Pravda* and *Izvestiya*, 20 August 1991 (all in *Current Digest of the Soviet Press* [CDSP], 18 September 1991, pp. 1–5).
2 Excerpts from the press conference of the State Committee on the Emergency Situation, *The New York Times*, 20 August 1991.
3 Reported by First Deputy Prime Minister Vitaly Doguzhiev to the Supreme Soviet, 28 August 1991. Radio Free Europe/Radio Liberty *Report on the USSR*, 6 September 1991, p. 94.
4 M. S. Gorbachev, Press conference, 22 August 1991, *Pravda*, 23 August 1991 (CDSP, 25 September 1991, pp. 21–22); *The Washington Post*, 26 August 1991; Mikhail Gorbachev, *The August Coup: The Truth and the Lessons*, New York, HarperCollins, 1991, pp. 19–21.
5 ibid., pp. 21, 23.
6 Broadcast by NBC News, 25 August 1991; text in *The New York Times*, 26 August 1991, and in Gorbachev, *The August Coup*, pp. 91–93.
7 Excerpts of transcript of investigative hearing, 22 August 1991, *Der Spiegel*, 7 October 1991, pp. 199, 202.
8 ibid., pp. 199, 201.
9 ibid., pp. 199–200, 204–205; various interviews by Foreign Minister Alexander Bessmertnykh, cited in Stuart H. Loory and Ann Imse, *Seven Days That Shook the World*, Atlanta, Turner Publications, 1991, pp. 72–74.
10 *Der Spiegel*, 7 October 1991, p. 203.

11 Quoted in I. Sichka, "How We Flew to Foros to Pick up the President," *Komsomolskaya Pravda*, 23 August 1991 (CDSP, 25 September 1991, p. 14).
12 See, e.g., Stephen Foye, "A Lesson in Ineptitude: Military-backed Coup Crumbles," RFE/RL *Report on the USSR*, 30 August 1991, p. 8.
13 Interview of Maj. Gen. Viktor Karpukhin in *Sovetskii Sport*, cited in Loory and Imse, *Seven Days*, p. 82.
14 Sergei Zalygin, quoted in *The New York Times*, 16 September 1991.
15 Boris Yeltsin, Ivan Silayev, and Ruslan Khasbulatov, "To the Citizens of Russia," *Megapolis-Express*, 19 August 1991 (CDSP, 18 September 1991, pp. 6–7).
16 Giulietto Chiesa, *Cronaca del golpe rosso*, Milan, Baldini & Castoldi, 1991, p. 16.
17 ibid., p. 18.
18 Quoted in Loory and Imse, *Seven Days*, p. 84.
19 Karpukhin interview, cited ibid., p. 94.
20 Sichka, "How We Flew to Foros," CDSP, 25 September 1991, p. 15.
21 M. S. Gorbachev, Remarks to the press, 21 August 1991, *Pravda*, 23 August 1991 (CDSP, 25 September 1991, p. 6).
22 Gorbachev, *The August Coup*, p. 38.
23 M. S. Gorbachev, Report on the draft of the new CPSU Program, to the plenary session of the CPSU Central Committee, 25 July 1991, *Pravda* and *Izvestiya*, 26 July 1991 (CDSP, 28 August 1991, p. 3).
24 Dusko Doder and Louise Branson, *Gorbachev: Heretic in the Kremlin*, New York, Viking, 1990, p. 415.
25 John Morrison, *Boris Yeltsin: From Bolshevik to Democrat*, London and New York, Penguin Books, 1991, p. 290.
26 Vladimir Bukovsky, "Born Again and Again," *The New Republic*, 10 September 1990, p. 41.
27 Boris Yeltsin, interview in *Newsweek*, 30 December 1991, p. 21; Moscow Television, quoted in Morrison, *Boris Yeltsin*, pp. 231–232.
28 M. S. Gorbachev, "Political Report of the CPSU Central Committee to the Twenty-Eighth CPSU Congress and the Party's Tasks," 2 July 1990, *Pravda*, 3 July 1990 (CDSP, 8 August 1990, p. 3).
29 Boris Kagarlitsky, *The Dialectic of Change*, London, Verso, 1990, p. 271.
30 Gorbachev, Report to the 28th CPSU Congress (CDSP, 8 August 1990, p. 2).
31 Brookings Institution roundtable on the 19th Conference of the CPSU, 11 August 1988, in Ed A. Hewett and Victor H. Winston (eds), *Milestones in Glasnost and Perestroyka: The Economy*, Washington, Brookings Institution, 1991, p. 245.
32 Yu. D. Masliukov, Report to the 28th CPSU Congress, 3 July 1990, *Pravda*, 5 July 1990 (CDSP, 22 August 1990, pp. 13–14).
33 CIA data cited in Gertrude E. Schroeder, "The Soviet Economy on a Treadmill of Perestroika: Gorbachev's First Five Years," in Harley D. Balzer (ed.), *Five Years That Shook the World: Gorbachev's Unfinished Revolution*, Boulder, Colo., Westview Press, 1991, pp. 32–35.
34 M. S. Gorbachev, *Pravda*, 28 February 1991, quoted in Stephen White, *Gorbachev and After*, Cambridge, Cambridge University Press, 1991, p. 129.
35 János Kornai, *Economics of Shortage*, 2 vols, Amsterdam and New York, North Holland, 1980.
36 Tatiana Zaslavskaya, interview in *Komsomolskaya Pravda*, 30 October 1990 (CDSP, 5 December 1990, p. 26).
37 V. A. Ivashko, press conference, 12 July 1990, *Izvestiya*, 13 July 1990 (CDSP, 3 October 1990, p. 21).

38 "Appeal to the Soviet People," CDSP, 18 September 1991, p. 4.
39 Anders Åslund, *Gorbachev's Struggle for Economic Reform*, updated and expanded edition, Ithaca, NY, Cornell University Press, 1991, p. 191; cf. Schroeder, "The Soviet Economy," p. 36.
40 ibid.; M. S. Gorbachev, Speech to a meeting of enterprise executives, 7 December 1990, *Pravda* and *Izvestiya*, 10 December 1990 (CDSP, 9 January 1991, p. 9).
41 Frances Foster-Simons, "Towards a More Perfect Union? The 'Restructuring' of Soviet Legislation," *Stanford Journal of International Law*, no. 2, 1989, p. 363.
42 Gertrude E. Schroeder, "Anatomy of Gorbachev's Economic Reform," *Soviet Economy*, no. 3, 1987, repr. in Hewett and Winston, *Milestones*, pp. 218, 224.
43 ibid., p. 218.
44 Hewett and Winston, editors' note, *Milestones*, p. 163.
45 Åslund, *Gorbachev's Struggle*, pp. 191–192, 196.
46 *A Study of the Soviet Economy*, Paris, International Monetary Fund et al., 1991, vol. 1, pp. 241–242.
47 Åslund, *Gorbachev's Struggle*, p. 225.
48 All quoted in V. Badov et al., "Economic Reform at a Turning Point," *Pravda*, 6 November 1989 (CDSP, 6 December 1989, p. 11).
49 N. I. Ryzhkov, Speech to the 2nd Congress of People's Deputies, 19 December 1989, *Pravda*, 20 December 1989.
50 M. S. Gorbachev, "On the CPSU Central Committee's Draft Platform for the 28th Party Congress," Report at the plenary session of the CPSU Central Committee, 5 February 1990, *Pravda* and *Izvestiya*, 6 February 1990 (CDSP, 14 March 1990, p. 4).
51 Åslund, *Gorbachev's Struggle*, p. 221.
52 Press conference of the USSR President, *Pravda*, 23 August 1991 (CDSP, 25 September 1991, p. 24).
53 Eduard Shevardnadze, *The Future Belongs to Freedom*, New York, The Free Press, 1991, p. 211.
54 ibid., pp. xvii–xviii.
55 Reported by a Gorbachev aide, *Time* Magazine, 2 September 1991, pp. 51–52.
56 Quoted ibid., p. 53.
57 KGB investigative report by Anatoly Aleinikov, cited in Loory and Imse, *Seven Days*, p. 57.
58 "Gorbachev Goes and Stays – Interview with the First and Last President of the USSR," 18 December 1991, *Komsomolskaya Pravda*, 24 December 1991 (CDSP, 22 January 1992, p. 8).
59 Draft Program of the Communist Party of the Soviet Union, "Socialism, Democracy, Progress," *Pravda*, 8 August 1991, pp. 3–4; M. S. Gorbachev, Report on the draft of the new CPSU Program, to the plenary session of the CPSU Central Committee, 25 July 1991, *Pravda* and *Izvestiya*, 26 July 1991 (CDSP, 28 August 1991, pp. 4–5).
60 Quoted in Loory and Imse, *Seven Days*, p. 26.
61 Quoted in *The Washington Post*, 27 December 1991.
62 Yeltsin et al., "To the Citizens of Russia," *Megapolis-Express*, 19 August 1991 (CDSP, 18 September 1991, p. 6).
63 M. S. Gorbachev, quoted in Len Karpinsky, "Mikhail Gorbachev: A Revolutionary Rethinking Necessary," *Moscow News*, 3 November 1991, p. 5.
64 Recorded and translated by CNN; text in *The New York Times*, 26 December 1991.
65 Alexander Yakovlev, quoted in *The Washington Post*, 16 September 1991.
66 Dmitri Furman, "What Can the Democrats Hope For?" *Nezavisimaya Gazeta*, 8

October 1991.
67 Anatoly Sobchak, *For a New Russia: The Mayor of St. Petersburg's Own Story of the Struggle for Justice and Democracy*, New York, The Free Press, 1992, p. 175.

3 SEEDS OF ITS OWN DESTRUCTION

1 Fyodor Burlatsky, "Khrushchev: Sketches for a Political Portrait," *Literaturnaya Gazeta*, 24 February 1988 (translated in Isaac J. Tarasulo (ed.), *Gorbachev and Glasnost: Viewpoints from the Soviet Press*, Wilmington, Del., Scholarly Resources Books, 1989, p. 45).
2 Recounted by Michel Tatu in "La chute de Khroutchev," *Le Monde*, 8–9 October 1989, citing the recollections of Politburo member Pyotr Shelest and a transcript of Khrushchev's statement in N. A. Barsulov, "How N. S. Khrushchev was 'Put Down,' " *Obshchestvennye nauki*, no. 6, 1989. See Roy A. Medvedev in *Argumenti i Fakty*, no. 27, 1988, cited in Werner Hahn, "Who Ousted Nikita Sergeyevich?" *Problems of Communism*, May–June 1991, p. 110; Thomas Sherlock, "Khrushchev Observed," Radio Free Europe/Radio Liberty *Report on the USSR*, 8 June 1990, p. 14.
3 "Report of M. Suslov at the Plenum of the Central Committee of the CPSU and Charges against Khrushchev" (reconstructed version published in samizdat), *Politicheskii Dnevnik*, no. 1, 1965 (translated in Robert V. Daniels (ed.), *A Documentary History of Communism*, revised edn, Hanover, NH, University Press of New England, 1984, vol. 1, pp. 350–354). See also Roy A. Medvedev, *Khrushchev*, Garden City, NY, Anchor Press/Doubleday, 1983, pp. 237–244; Michel Tatu, *Power in the Kremlin: From Khrushchev to Kosygin*, New York, Viking Press, 1969, pp. 408–417.
4 Sergei N. Khrushchev, *Khrushchev on Khrushchev: An Inside Account of the Man and His Era*, Boston, Little, Brown, 1990, p. 151.
5 ibid., pp. 159–160.
6 Informational Communiqué of the Plenum of the Central Committee of the CPSU, *Pravda*, 16 October 1964.
7 Gennady Voronov, interview in *Izvestiya*, 18 November 1988, quoted in Hahn, "Who Ousted Nikita Sergeyevich?" p. 112.
8 Sergei Khrushchev, *Khrushchev*, p. 154; Mark Frankland, *Khrushchev*, Harmondsworth, Penguin Books, 1966, p. 206.
9 Fyodor Burlatsky, "Brezhnev and the End of the Thaw: Reflections on the Nature of Political Leadership," *Literaturnaya Gazeta*, 14 September 1988 (Tarasulo, *Gorbachev and Glasnost*, p. 50).
10 Robert M. Slusser, *Stalin in October: The Man Who Missed the Revolution*, Baltimore, Johns Hopkins University Press, 1987, p. 255.
11 Sheila Fitzpatrick, "Stalin and the Making of the New Elite, 1928–1939," *Slavic Review*, September 1979, pp. 377–402.
12 Cf. Jerry Hough, *Soviet Leadership in Transition*, Washington, Brookings Institution, 1980, pp. 37–60.
13 T. H. Rigby, "The Soviet Leadership: Towards a Self-Stabilising Oligarchy," *Soviet Studies*, October 1970, p. 175.
14 P. A. Rodionov, "How Did Stagnation Begin? Notes of a Historian of the Party," *Znamia*, no. 8, 1989, p. 184.
15 Robert V. Daniels, "Participatory Bureaucracy and the Soviet Political System," in Norton T. Dodge (ed.), *Analysis of the USSR's 24th Party Congress and 9th Five-Year Plan*, Mechanicsville, Md., Cremona Foundation, 1971.
16 Medvedev interview, quoted in Hedrick Smith, *The New Russians*, New York, Random House, 1990, p. 23.

17 Reports of the USSR Central Statistical Administration, "On Results of Fulfillment of the State Plan for Development of the USSR National Economy," for 1965, *Pravda*, 3 February 1966, and for 1975, *Pravda*, 1 February 1976.
18 See, e.g., Marshall I. Goldman, *USSR in Crisis: The Failure of an Economic System*, New York, Norton, 1983, p. 33.
19 Martin Walker, *The Walking Giant: Gorbachev's Russia*, London, Michael Joseph, and New York, Pantheon Books, 1986, p. 66.
20 M. S. Gorbachev, Report to the Plenum of the Central Committee of the CPSU, "On the Tasks of the Party in the Radical Reconstruction of the Administration of the Economy," *Pravda*, 26 June 1987.
21 See note 17.
22 James R. Miller, *The Soviet Economic Experiment*, Urbana, University of Illinois Press, 1990, p. 191.
23 Zdeněk Mlynář, *Can Gorbachev Change the Soviet Union? The International Dimensions of Political Reform*, Boulder, Colo., Westview Press, 1990, pp. 19–20.
24 See, e.g., Tatiana Zaslavskaya, "Report on the Necessity of a Deeper Study in the USSR of the Social Mechanism of the Development of the Economy," *Arkhiv Samizdata*, AS 5043, 26 August 1983 (translated as "The Novosibirsk Report," *Survey*, spring 1984, pp. 88–92, 106).
25 Nikolai Shmelev and Vladimir Popov, *The Turning Point: Revitalizing the Soviet Economy*, New York, Doubleday, 1989, p. 75.
26 Joseph Stalin, "The Tasks of Business Executives" (Speech delivered at the First All-Union Conference of Managers of Socialist Industry, 4 February 1931), in J. Stalin, *Problems of Leninism*, Moscow, Foreign Languages Publishing House, 1953, p. 458. Stalin actually borrowed the phrase from the economist S. G. Strumilin ("The Industrialization of the USSR and the Epigones of Populism," *Planovoye Khoziaistvo*, no. 7, 1927, p. 11).
27 See Cyril E. Black, *The Modernization of Japan and Russia: A Comparative Study*, New York, The Free Press, 1975.
28 See Hedrick Smith, "The Russian Character," *The New York Times Magazine*, 28 October 1990, pp. 30ff.
29 Yu. V. Andropov, Speech to the Central Committee of the CPSU, 23 November 1982, *Pravda*, 23 November 1982 (*Current Digest of the Soviet Press* [CDSP], 22 December 1982, p. 4).
30 D. Filtzer, "Labour," in Martin McCauley (ed.), *Khrushchev and Khrushchevism*, London, Macmillan, 1987, pp. 119, 137. See also Terry L. Thompson, *Ideology and Policy: The Political Uses of Doctrine in the Soviet Union*, Boulder, Colo., Westview Press, 1989, pp. 48–49, 55–58.
31 Rita di Leo, *L'economia sovietica tra crisi e riforme* (1965–1982), Naples, Liguori, 1983, pp. 147, 160–161. See also Aaron Vinokur and Gur Ofer, "Inequality of Earnings, Income and Wealth," in James R. Millar (ed.), *Politics, Work, and Daily Life in the Soviet Union*, Cambridge, Cambridge University Press, 1987, pp. 197–198.
32 Eduard Shevardnadze, *The Future Belongs to Freedom*, New York, The Free Press, 1991, p. xiv.
33 Aleksei N. Kosygin, Report on the Directives of the 24th CPSU Congress for the Five-Year Plan for the Development of the USSR National Economy in 1971–75 (6 April 1971), in *Current Soviet Policies*, vol. 6, Columbus, Ohio, American Association for the Advancement of Slavic Studies, 1973, pp. 132–133.
34 Tatiana Zaslavskaya in her "Novosibirsk Report" of 1983 (p. 88) puts econ-

omic growth for 1966–1970 at 7.5 per cent annually; for 1971–75, 5.8 per cent; for 1976–1980, 3.8 per cent; and for 1981–82, 2.5 per cent, with population growth at 0.8 per cent per annum. See also Anders Åslund, *Gorbachev's Struggle for Economic Reform: The Soviet Reform Process, 1985–88*, Ithaca, NY, Cornell University Press, 1989, p. 15.

35 Second Congress of USSR People's Deputies, verbatim report, *Izvestiya*, 18 December 1989 (CDSP, 14 February 1990, p. 23).

36 Zaslavskaya, "Novosibirsk Report," p. 89.

37 ibid., p. 106.

38 ibid., p. 92.

39 ibid., p. 96.

40 Walker, *The Waking Giant*, p. 175.

41 Boris Kagarlitsky, *The Dialectic of Change*, London, Verso, 1990, p. 296.

42 V. G. Afanasiev, *The Scientific and Technological Revolution: Its Impact on Management and Education*, Moscow, Progress Publishers, 1975, p. 294.

43 Alexander Vucinich, *Empire of Knowledge: The Academy of Sciences of the USSR, 1917–1970*, Berkeley, University of California Press, 1984, p. 294.

44 L. A. Gordon and V. V. Komarovsky, "The Dynamics of the Social-Occupational Composition of Generations," *Sotsiologicheskie issledovaniya*, no. 3, 1986, quoted ibid., p. 55.

45 Afanasiev, *Scientific and Technological Revolution*, pp. 295–297.

46 Zaslavskaya interview, *Argumenty i fakty*, 28 March 1987, p. 5.

47 Smith, *The New Russians*, p. 95.

48 See "A. Volsky" [Jan Machajski], *Umstvennyi rabochii*, Geneva, 1905, repr. New York, Inter-Language Literary Associates, 1968.

49 See Robert V. Daniels, *Trotsky, Stalin, and Socialism*, Boulder, Colo., Westview Press, 1991, pp. 103–104.

50 See, e.g., Adolf Berle and Gardner Means, *The Modern Corporation and Private Property*, New York, Macmillan, 1933; Alfred D. Chandler, Jr., *The Visible Hand: The Managerial Revolution in American Business*, Cambridge, Mass., Belknap Press, 1977.

51 Bruno Rizzi, *La Bureaucratisation du monde*, Paris, Hachette, 1939; James Burnham, *The Managerial Revolution*, New York, John Day, 1941.

52 Milovan Djilas, *The New Class: An Analysis of the Communist System*, New York, Praeger, 1957.

53 Svetozar Stojanović, "Marxism and Democracy: the Ruling Class or the Dominant Class?" *Praxis International*, July 1981; Antonio Gramsci, "Notes on Italian History," in Quentin Hoare and G. N. Smith (eds), *Selections from the Prison Notebooks of Antonio Gramsci*, London and New York, International Publishers, 1972, pp. 104–105.

54 Jerry F. Hough, *How the Soviet Union is Governed*, Cambridge, Mass., Harvard University Press, 1979, pp. 547–548, 571–572.

55 Tatiana Zaslavskaya, *The Second Socialist Revolution: An Alternative Soviet Strategy*, London, Tauris, and Bloomington, Ind., Indiana University Press, 1990, p. 3.

56 Burlatsky, "Brezhnev," p. 61.

57 Abel Aganbegian, *The Economic Challenge of Perestroika*, Bloomington, Ind., Indiana University Press, 1988, p. 15.

58 James Millar, "The Little Deal: Brezhnev's Contribution to Acquisitive Socialism," *Slavic Review*, winter 1985, repr. in Millar, *The Soviet Economic Experiment*, Urbana, University of Illinois Press, 1990.

59 Vladimir Shlapentokh, *Public and Private Life of the Soviet People: Changing Values in Post-Stalin Russia*, New York and Oxford, Oxford University Press,

1989, pp. 153–155.
60 Mylnář, *Can Gorbachev Change the Soviet Union?*, p. 15.
61 Conversation with Giulietto Chiesa, April 1984.
62 Goldman, *USSR in Crisis*, p. 1.
63 Shevardnadze, *The Future Belongs to Freedom*, p. 37; M. S. Gorbachev in *Pravda*, 1 December 1990, quoted in Marshall I. Goldman, *What Went Wrong with Perestroika?*, New York and London, Norton, 1991, p. 83.

4 WAS STALINISM COMMUNIST?

1 Stalin, Report to the 17th Congress of the CPSU (B) on the Work of the Central Committee (26 January 1934), in J. V. Stalin, *Problems of Leninism*, Moscow, Foreign Languages Publishing House, 1953, pp. 596–597, 628–629.
2 ibid., pp. 630, 641.
3 *Semnadtsatyi syezd VKP(b): Stenograficheskii otchet*, Moscow, Partizdat, 1934, p. 147.
4 ibid., p. 125.
5 ibid., p. 188.
6 Lenin, "Continuation of Notes," 24 December 1922, in Lenin, *Pismo syezdu*, Moscow, State Press for Political Literature, 1956; English translation by Max Eastman, *The New York Times*, 19 November 1926.
7 Dmitri Volkogonov, *Triumf i tragediya: Politicheskii portret I. V. Stalina*, Moscow, Novosti, 1989, book 1, part 2, pp. 77–78, citing the recollections of Anastas Mikoyan; Anton Antonov-Ovseyenko, *The Time of Stalin*, New York, Harper & Row, 1981, pp. 80–85; Roy A. Medvedev, *Let History Judge: The Origins and Consequences of Stalinism*, revised and expanded edition, New York, Columbia University Press, 1989, pp. 330–333. Medvedev reports (p. 333) that in 1957 a secret party commission re-examined the actual ballots of 1934 and found them 267 short of the total announced at the congress.
8 Ogonyok, 13 December 1987, quoted in Robert Conquest, *Stalin and the Kirov Murder*, New York and Oxford, Oxford University Press, 1989, p. 48.
9 Nikita Khrushchev, Secret Speech on the "Cult of the Individual" delivered at the 20th Congress of the CPSU, 25 February 1956, in *The Anti-Stalin Campaign and International Communism*, New York, Columbia University Press, 1956, p. 23. (Original published in *Izvestiya TsK*, no. 1, 1989.)
10 Editorial note to Round Table, "The 'Stalinist Model of Socialism': Establishment, Development, Collapse (1920s–1980s)," *Voprosy Istorii KPSS*, no. 12, 1990, p. 37.
11 Hannah Arendt, *The Origins of Totalitarianism*, New York, Harcourt, Brace, 1951.
12 Conversation with V. P. Danilov, 21 May 1989.
13 Moshe Lewin, *The Gorbachev Phenomenon: A Historical Explanation*, Berkeley, University of California Press, 1988, p. 3.
14 Karl Marx, *Critique of the Gotha Program*, in Marx, *Selected Works*, New York, International Publishers, n. d., vol. 2, p. 566.
15 V. I. Lenin, *State and Revolution*, in Lenin, *Selected Works*, Moscow, Foreign Languages Publishing House, 1950–52, vol. 2, book 1, pp. 295–297.
16 Emil Durkheim, *Socialism and Saint-Simon*, 1928, London, Routledge & Kegan Paul, 1959, p. 19.
17 Stalin, "On the Draft Constitution of the USSR" (Report delivered at the Extraordinary 8th Congress of Soviets of the USSR, 25 November 1936), *Problems of Leninism*, pp. 683–684.
18 See e.g., Victor Afanasiev, *Fundamentals of Scientific Communism*, revised edn,

Moscow, Progress Publishers, 1981, p. 123. The equivalent term in Eastern Europe was "real existing socialism."

19 See Alfred G. Meyer, *Marxism: The Unity of Theory and Practice*, Cambridge, Mass., Harvard University Press, 1954, pp. 91–100.

20 V. I. Lenin, "The Crisis Has Matured," 7 [20] October 1917, in Lenin, *Collected Works*, Moscow, Progress Publishers, 1964, vol. 26, p. 85.

21 Lenin, Letter to the Members of the Central Committee, 24 October [6 November] 1917, in Lenin, *Selected Works*, Moscow, Foreign Languages Publishing House, 1951, vol. 2, book 1, pp. 197–198.

22 See, e.g., V. S. Lipitsky, "The Socialism of the Promised Land," *Voprosy Istorii KPSS*, no. 12, 1990, pp. 69–70. Cf. J. Martov, *The State and the Socialist Revolution*, New York, International Review, 1938, pp. 33–34.

23 Lenin, "What is to be Done?" *Selected Works*, vol. 1, book 1, p. 233.

24 Mikhail Heller and Alexander Nekrich, *Utopia in Power: The History of the Soviet Union from 1917 to the Present*, New York, Summit Books, 1986, p. 267.

25 Georg Lukács, "Reflections on the Cult of Stalin," in E. San Juan (ed.), *Marxism and Human Liberation: Essays on History, Culture, and Revolution by Georg Lukács*, New York, Dell, 1973, pp. 66–69.

26 M. S. Gorbachev, Report on the draft of the new CPSU Program, to the plenary session of the CPSU Central Committee, 25 July 1991, *Pravda* and *Izvestiya*, 26 July 1991 (*Current Digest of the Soviet Press* [CDSP], 28 August 1991, pp. 4–5).

27 See Marx and Engels, *The German Ideology*, New York, International Publishers, 1947, pp. 39–41; Engels to Franz Mehring, 14 July 1893, in Marx and Engels, *Selected Correspondence, 1846–1895*, New York, International Publishers, 1942, pp. 511–512; Melvin Rader, *Marx's Interpretation of History*, New York, Oxford University Press, 1979, p. 42; Robert V. Daniels, *Trotsky, Stalin, and Socialism*, Boulder, Colo., Westview Press, 1991, pp. 177–179.

28 Robert C. Tucker, *Stalin as Revolutionary, 1879–1929: A Study in History and Personality*, New York, Norton, 1973, pp. 85, 90.

29 Notes by Kamenev of talk with Bukharin, 11 July 1928, Trotsky Archive, Harvard University, document T1897.

30 Lenin, "On the Slogan of the United States of Europe" (25 August 1915), *Sochineniya*, 3rd edn, Moscow, Marx-Engels-Lenin Institute, 1928–1937, vol. 18, pp. 232–233.

31 See Lev Kamenev, Speech at the 15th Party Conference, November 1926, *Pravda*, 5 November 1926.

32 Stalin, "The October Revolution and the Tactics of the Russian Communists" (December 1924), *Problems of Leninism*, p. 124.

33 Michal Reiman, *The Birth of Stalinism: The USSR on the Eve of the "Second Revolution,"* Bloomington, Indiana University Press, 1987.

34 Alec Nove, "Was Stalin Necessary?" *Encounter*, April 1962.

35 Alexander Erlich, *The Soviet Industrialization Debate, 1924–1928*, Cambridge, Mass., Harvard University Press, 1960.

36 Platform of Bukharin, Rykov, and Tomsky, presented to the Politburo 9 February 1929, quoted in Stalin, "The Right Deviation in the CPSU(B)" (Speech delivered at the plenum of the Central Committee and the Central Control Commission of the CPSU(B), 16 April 1929), *Problems of Leninism*, p. 289.

37 See esp. N. I. Bukharin, "Notes of an Economist," *Pravda*, 30 September 1928, translated in Bertram D. Wolfe, *Khrushchev and Stalin's Ghost*, New York, Praeger, 1957.

38 Resolution of the Second All-Union Conference of Marxist-Leninist Scientific

Research Institutions, "On Contemporary Problems of the Philosophy of Marxism-Leninism" (April 1929), *Pod Znamenem Marksizma*, no. 5, 1929, pp. 7–8.

39 Robert C. Tucker, "Stalinism as Revolution from Above," in Tucker, *Stalinism: Essays in Historical Interpretation*, New York, Norton, 1977.

40 Leon Trotsky, "What Happened and Why" (1929), in *Writings of Leon Trotsky*, New York, Pathfinder Press, vol. 1, 1975, p. 47; Trotsky, "The Danger of Bonapartism and the Opposition's Role" (1928), in Naomi Allen (ed.), *Leon Trotsky: The Challenge of the Left Opposition*, New York, Pathfinder Press, 1975–1981, vol. 3, p. 274.

41 Alexander Tsipko, "The Roots of Stalinism," essay no. 4, *Nauka i Zhizn*, February 1989 (CDSP, 26 April 1989, p. 15).

42 Yu. V. Andropov, Speech at the plenary session of the CPSU Central Committee, *Pravda*, 16 June 1983 (CDSP, 20 July 1983, p. 6).

43 See, e.g., Holland Hunter, "The Overambitious First Soviet Five-Year Plan," *Slavic Review*, June 1973.

44 Michael Ellman, *Socialist Planning*, Cambridge, Cambridge University Press, 1989, p. 27.

45 G. Warren Nutter, *Growth of Industrial Production in the Soviet Union*, Princeton, NJ, Princeton University Press, 1962, p. 285; Martin L. Weitzman, "Industrial Production," in Abram Bergson and Herbert S. Levine (eds), *The Soviet Economy: Toward the Year 2000*, London, George Allen & Unwin, 1983, p. 179.

46 Stalin, Report to the 17th Congress, *Problems of Leninism*, p. 634.

47 For a more extensive exposition of this argument, see Daniels, *Trotsky, Stalin, and Socialism*, pp. 137–168.

48 See Heller and Nekrich, *Utopia in Power*.

49 Alexander Yakovlev, "Pages of History: The Tragedy of December 1934," *Pravda*, 28 January 1991 (CDSP, 27 March 1991, p. 18).

50 Tsipko, "The Roots of Stalinism," essay no. 1, *Nauka i Zhizn*, November 1988 (CDSP, 5 April 1989, p. 3).

51 See, e.g., J. L. Talmon, *The Origins of Totalitarian Democracy*, Boston, Beacon Press, 1951.

52 Otto Latsis, "Treating Thermidor as Brumaire," *Znamia*, May 1989, p. 187.

53 Viktor Yerefeyev, quoted in *The New York Times*, 26 December 1991.

5 THE LONG AGONY OF THE RUSSIAN REVOLUTION

1 V. I. Lenin, Theses for a Report at the October Conference of the Petrograd Organization (ca. 1 [14] October 1917), Lenin, *Collected Works*, New York, International Publishers, 1932, vol. 21, book 2, p. 62; Letter to the Central Committee, Moscow Committee, Petrograd Committee, and the Bolshevik Members of the Petrograd and Moscow Soviets (ca. 3 [16] October 1917), ibid., p. 69; "Advice from an Outsider" (8 [21] October 1917), ibid., p. 99.

For details of the revolutionary days and an explication of the role of accident in the Bolshevik victory, see Robert V. Daniels, *Red October: The Bolshevik Revolution of 1917*, New York, Scribner's, 1967, and Boston, Beacon Press, 1984. John Reed's *Ten Days That Shook the World*, New York, Boni & Liveright, 1919, and Vintage Books, 1960, is graphic for setting and atmosphere but unreliable on the particulars of times and places.

2 Contrary to legend, Kerensky did not ride in the American Embassy car – that one followed with some of his staff. See V. I. Startsev, "Kerensky's Flight," *Vechernyi Leningrad*, 12 October 1966.

3 S. Uralov, "A Small Page of October," *Proletarskaya Revoliutsiya*, no. 10, 1924, p. 277.
4 Proclamation of the Military-Revolutionary Committee, 25 October [7 November] 1917, Lenin, *Collected Works*, Moscow, State Press, 1964, vol. 26, p. 236.
5 Leon Trotsky, Speech to the Petrograd Soviet, 25 October [7 November] 1917, quoted in N. N. Sukhanov, *The Russian Revolution, 1917: A Personal Record*, London, Oxford University Press, 1955, p. 627.
6 Quoted in Daniels, *Red October*, p. 175.
7 Lenin, "Report on the Tasks of the Soviet Power," to the Petrograd Soviet, 25 October [7 November] 1917, Lenin, *Collected Works*, vol. 26, pp. 239–240.
8 Leon Trotsky, *The History of the Russian Revolution*, Ann Arbor, University of Michigan Press, 1932, vol. 3, p. 311.
9 "Decree on the Formation of a Workers' and Peasants' Government," in Robert V. Daniels (ed.), *A Documentary History of Communism*, updated revised edn, Hanover, NH, University Press of New England, 1988, vol. 1, pp. 80–81.
10 Lenin, *Selected Works*, Moscow, Foreign Languages Publishing House, 1951, vol. 2, book 1, pp. 339–343.
11 ibid., pp. 328–333.
12 Daniels, *Documentary History of Communism*, vol. 1, pp. 82–83.
13 J. Christopher Herold (ed.), *The Mind of Napoleon: A Selection from His Written and Spoken Words*, New York, Columbia University Press, 1956, p. 64.
14 Alexander Yakovlev, Speech at the 28th Party Congress, July 1990, *Pravda*, 4 July 1990 (*Current Digest of the Soviet Press* [CDSP], 15 August 1990, p. 6).
15 Engels to Vera Zasulich, 23 April 1885, Karl Marx and Friedrich Engels, *Selected Correspondence, 1846–1895*, New York, International Publishers, 1942, pp. 437–438.
16 Crane Brinton, *The Anatomy of Revolution*, New York, Prentice-Hall, 1938, 1952.
17 Maria Chegodayeva, "October 25, Old Style," *Moscow News*, 18 November 1990.
18 Nikolai Shmelyov, "Loans and Debts," *Novyi Mir*, no. 6, 1987, translated in Robert V. Daniels (ed.), *The Stalin Revolution*, Lexington, Mass., D. C. Heath, 1990, p. 239.
19 Michal Reiman, *Lenin, Stalin, Gorbačev: Kontinuität und Brüche in der sowjetischen Geschichte*, Hamburg, Junius, 1987, p. 139.
20 Alexander Yakovlev, "The Great French Revolution and the Present Day," *Sovetskaya Kultura*, 15 July 1989 (CDSP, 13 September 1989, p. 15).
21 "What Kind of Socialism Are We Rejecting? What Kind of Socialism are We Striving for?" (condensed transcript of a discussion organized by the journal *MEMO*, 1989), in Steve Hirsch (ed.), *MEMO 2: Soviets Examine Foreign Policy for a New Decade*, Washington, Bureau of National Affairs, 1991, p. 136.
22 Reported in *Izvestiya*, 21 March [3 April] 1917, translated in Robert P. Browder and Alexander F. Kerensky (eds), *The Russian Provisional Government: Documents*, Stanford, Cal., Stanford University Press, 1961, vol. 3, pp. 1219–1220.
23 See Massimo L. Salvadori, *Karl Kautsky and the Socialist Revolution, 1880–1930*, London, New Left Books, 1979, pp. 261ff.
24 Theses on the Present Moment presented by the group of Left Communists at a meeting with the Central Committee, *Kommunist*, no. 1, April 1918, pp. 7–8.
25 Yakovlev, "The Great French Revolution," p. 15.

26 M. S. Gorbachev, Remarks at meeting with Erich Honecker and members of the Politburo of the Socialist Unity Party, *Pravda*, 9 October 1989 (CDSP, 12 November, 1989, p. 20).

27 See M. S. Gorbachev, Report to the 19th Party Conference, 28 June 1988, *Pravda*, 29 June 1988 (CDSP, 27 July 1988, pp. 19–20).

28 Yakovlev, "The Great French Revolution," p. 14.

6 THE END OF REVOLUTIONARY EMPIRE

1 M. S. Gorbachev, Press conference in Berlin, 7 October 1989, quoted in *Le Monde*, 8–9 October 1989.

2 M. S. Gorbachev, Speech at ceremonial meeting on the 40th anniversary of the German Democratic Republic, *Pravda*, 7 October 1989 (*Current Digest of the Soviet Press* [CDSP], 1 November 1989, p. 19).

3 Quoted in *The Washington Post*, 8 October 1989.

4 Quoted in *The New York Times*, 9 October 1989.

5 *The New York Times*, 19 November 1989.

6 Quoted in interview of Georgi Shakhnazarov, Angus Roxburgh, *The Second Russian Revolution: The Struggle for Power in the Kremlin*, London, BBC Books, 1991, p. 157.

7 Quoted in *The New York Times*, 19 November 1989.

8 Timothy Garton Ash, "The German Revolution," *New York Review of Books*, 21 December 1989, p. 14.

9 New Forum manifesto of 12 September 1989, quoted in *The New York Times*, 16 October 1989.

10 Quoted in *The New York Times*, 10 October 1989.

11 Markus Wolf, quoted in *The New York Times*, 19 November 1989, p. 27.

12 Christof Hein, "Crisis Diary," *The New York Times Magazine*, 17 December 1989, p. 77.

13 Quoted in *The New York Times*, 19 November 1989.

14 Quoted in Don Oberdorfer, *The Turn – From the Cold War to a New Era: The United States and the Soviet Union, 1983–1990*, New York, Poseidon Press, 1991, p. 363.

15 Interview of Erich Honecker by Heinz Junge, *The European*, 2 November 1990.

16 *The Washington Post*, 10 November 1990, citing "several former East German Central Committee members."

17 E. A. Shevardnadze, Report to the 28th CPSU Congress, 3 July 1990, *Pravda*, 5 July 1990 (CDSP, 22 August 1990, p. 12).

18 See Alfred G. Meyer, *Leninism*, Cambridge, Mass., Harvard University Press, 1957, p. 158.

19 Winston Churchill, in *Hansard's Debates*, 10 February 1920, quoted in William Manchester, *The Last Lion: Winston Spencer Churchill*, Boston, Little, Brown, vol. 1, 1983, p. 688.

20 Report by M. S. Gorbachev, President of the USSR, to the Supreme Soviet, 16 November 1990, *Pravda* and *Izvestiya*, 17 November 1990 (CDSP, 19 December 1990, pp. 1, 4).

21 Quoted in *The New York Times*, 6 February 1991.

22 Quoted in *The Americana Annual: 1989*, Danbury, Conn., Grolier, 1989, p. 227.

23 See Federigo Argentieri (ed.), *La fine del blocco sovietico*, Florence, Ponte alle Grazie, 1991, editor's postscript, p. 227.

24 See Charles Gati, *The Bloc That Failed*, Bloomington, Indiana University Press, 1990, p. 168.

25 Adam Michnik, "The Two Faces of Eastern Europe," *The New Republic*, 12

November 1990, p. 25.
26 M. S. Gorbachev, Interview in *Der Spiegel*, 25 March 1991, pp. 174–175.

7 THE END OF THE COMMUNIST MENACE

1 *The New York Times*, 24 November 1985, citing an unnamed White House official.
2 *Newsweek*, 25 November 1985, p. 32; *Pravda*, 19 November 1985 (*Current Digest of the Soviet Press* [CDSP], 18 December 1985, p. 1).
3 Quoted in *Newsweek*, 2 December 1985, p. 31.
4 Interview of Gorbachev aide Andrei Alexandrov-Agentov, cited in Don Oberdorfer, *The Turn – from the Cold War to a New Era: The United States and the Soviet Union, 1983–1990*, New York, Poseidon Press, 1991, p. 154.
5 "After Geneva," *Pravda*, 23 November 1985 (CDSP, 18 December 1985, p. 8).
6 *American Foreign Policy Current Documents, 1985*, Washington, US Department of State, p. 427.
7 Quoted in *Newsweek*, 2 December 1985, p. 32.
8 Quoted in *The New York Times*, 22 November 1985.
9 A. Krasnov and Yu. Nikolaev, "On the Swings of the New Thinking," *Sovetskaya Rossiya*, 15 June 1991 (CDSP, 17 July 1991, p. 7).
10 Decree on Peace, 26 October [8 November] 1917, Lenin, *Selected Works*, Moscow, Foreign Languages Publishing House, 1952, vol. 2, book 1, p. 330.
11 "Manifesto of the Communist International to the Proletarians of the World," *The Communist International*, 1 May 1919.
12 Piero Melograni, *Lenin and the Myth of World Revolution*, Atlantic Highlands, NJ, Humanities Press International, 1989.
13 Robert Lansing, Memorandum of November 1917 embodying his advice to President Wilson, text in *War Memoirs of Robert Lansing*, Indianapolis, Bobbs-Merrill, 1935, p. 341.
14 Winston Churchill, in *The Weekly Dispatch*, 22 June 1919, quoted in Martin Gilbert, *Winston S. Churchill*, Boston, Houghton-Mifflin, 1975, vol. 4, p. 903.
15 Churchill, Speech to constituents in Dundee, 28 July 1920, quoted in William Manchester, *The Last Lion*, Boston, Little, Brown, 1983, vol. 1, p. 676. Not to be found in the "Complete Speeches." (See note 24.)
16 Professor Alexei Velidov has recently researched this story and traces it to a right-wing fabrication in the city of Saratov in March 1918, intended to discredit the local anarchists. "The 'Decree' on the Nationalisation of Women: The Story of a Mystification," *Moscow News*, 11 March 1990.
17 Senator Henry Myers, *Congressional Record*, 66th Congress, 2nd session, 20 April 1920, p. 6208.
18 J. Edgar Hoover, Lecture prepared for delivery at the Conference of Methodist Ministers, Garrett Institute, Evanston, Ill., 26 November 1947, and Remarks before the Military Chaplains' Association of the United States, Washington, DC, 5 May 1954, quoted in J. Edgar Hoover, *On Communism*, New York, Random House, 1969, pp. 91–92.
19 Edward Hallett Carr, *The Bolshevik Revolution*, London, Macmillan, 1953, vol. 3, pp. 271–272.
20 See Robert V. Daniels, *The Conscience of the Revolution: Communist Opposition in Soviet Russia*, Cambridge, Mass., Harvard University Press, 1960, pp. 248–252, 295–299.
21 See, e.g., Keith Robbins, *Munich 1938*, London, Cassell, 1968, pp. 334–335; Williamson Murray, *The Change in the European Balance of Power, 1938–1939: The Path to Ruin*, Princeton, NJ, Princeton University Press, 1984, pp. 237–

238, 264; N. V. Zagladin, *Istoriya uspekhov i neudach sovetskoi diplomatii*, Moscow, Mezhdunarodnye Otnosheniya, 1990, pp. 107–108. Most Western writers on Munich neglect the Soviet angle.

22 Zagladin, *Istoriya*, p. 113.

23 Harry S. Truman, quoted in *The New York Times*, 24 June 1941.

24 Winston Churchill, Broadcast of 22 June 1941, in Robert Rhodes James (ed.), *Winston S. Churchill: His Complete Speeches, 1897–1963*, London, Chelsea House, 1974, vol. 6, pp. 6429–6430.

25 Stalin, Speech of 9 February 1946, *Pravda*, 10 February 1946.

26 George F. Kennan, *Russia and the West under Lenin and Stalin*, Boston, Little, Brown, 1960, p. 254.

27 Alexander Prokhanov, *Detente*, no. 9–10, 1987, p. 26.

28 Stalin, Speech of 9 February 1946, *Pravda*, 10 February 1946.

29 ibid.

30 The Chargé in the Soviet Union (Kennan) to the Secretary of State, 22 February 1946, *Foreign Relations of the United States, 1946* (FRUS), Washington, Government Printing Office, vol. 6, pp. 699–700.

31 Frank Roberts to FO, 14, 17 and 18 March 1946, FO 371 56763 N4065/4156/4157/38, Public Record Office, London; published in Kenneth M. Jensen (ed.), *Origins of the Cold War: The Novikov, Kennan, and Roberts "Long Telegrams" of 1946*, Washington, United States Institute of Peace, 1991, pp. 40, 43, 48–49, 51–53.

32 Dean Acheson, *Present at the Creation: My Years in the State Department*, New York, Norton, 1969, p. 194.

33 Quoted in Walter Millis (ed.), *The Forrestal Diaries*, New York, Viking, 1951, pp. 134–135.

34 Stalin, *Economic Problems of Socialism in the USSR*, Moscow, Foreign Languages Publishing House, 1952, pp. 39–40.

35 See Fraser J. Harbutt, *The Iron Curtain: Churchill, America and the Origins of the Cold War*, Oxford, Oxford University Press, 1986.

36 Clark Clifford, "American Relations with the Soviet Union: A Report to the President by the Special Counsel to the President," September 1946, published as an appendix in Arthur Krock, *Memoirs*, New York, Funk & Wagnalls, 1968, p. 431.

37 Acheson, *Present at the Creation*, p. 375.

38 George F. Kennan ("X"), "The Sources of Soviet Conduct," *Foreign Affairs*, July 1947.

39 George F. Kennan, *Memoirs, 1925–1950*, Boston, Little, Brown, 1967, p. 364.

40 NSC–7, FRUS, 1948, vol. 1, part 2, pp. 546–547.

41 NSC–68, FRUS, 1950, vol. 1, pp. 237, 264.

42 ibid., p. 273; State Department policy paper, "Negotiations with the Soviet Union," 20 April 1950, FRUS, 1950, vol. 4, p. 1156.

43 NSC–68, FRUS, 1950, vol. 1, pp. 273–274.

44 N. S. Khrushchev, Report of the Central Committee to the 20th Party Congress, 14 February 1956, *Current Soviet Policies*, published by *The Current Digest of the Soviet Press*, Columbus, Ohio, vol. 2, 1957, pp. 36–37.

45 The original occasion for this outburst was a reception at the Polish embassy in Moscow, 18 November 1956, when the NATO ambassadors were walking out in protest against Khrushchev's remarks about the Suez crisis. Charles Bohlen, *Witness to History*, New York, Norton, 1973, p. 437.

46 CBS, "Face the Nation," 2 June 1957; text in *The New York Times*, 3 June 1957.

47 M. S. Gorbachev, Political report of the Central Committee to the 27th Congress of the CPSU, *Pravda*, 26 February 1986.

48 Anatoly Dobrynin, Speech at a Moscow scientific conference, 27 May 1986, reported in *Radio Liberty Research*, no. 218/86, 30 May 1986, p. 5.
49 Cf. Marshall D. Shulman, *Stalin's Foreign Policy Reappraised*, Cambridge, Mass., Harvard University Press, 1963, pp. 250–251. Shulman's was a contrarian view at the time (cf., e.g., Robert C. Tucker, "The Stalin Heritage in Soviet Policy," in *The Soviet Political Mind: Studies in Stalinism and Post-Stalin Change*, New York, Prueger, 1963), but it stands up well in the context of the present analysis.
50 Shulman, *Stalin's Foreign Policy*, p. 264 and passim.
51 Stalin, *Economic Problems of Socialism*, p. 41.
52 See Strobe Talbott (ed.), *Khrushchev Remembers*, Boston, Little, Brown, 1970, pp. 367–368.
53 See Walter LaFeber, *America, Russia, and the Cold War, 1945–1984*, New York, Knopf, 1985, pp. 105–110, 125–126.
54 Dwight D. Eisenhower, *Waging Peace, 1956–1961: The White House Years*, Garden City, NY, Doubleday, 1965, pp. 624–625.
55 Kennan, *Russia and the West*, p. 253.
56 Togliatti interview, "Nine Questions on Stalinism," *Nuovi Argomenti*, 16 June 1956; translated in *The Anti-Stalin Campaign and International Communism*, New York, Columbia University Press, 1956, pp. 138–139.
57 Quoted in *The New York Times*, 2 February 1992.
58 Eduard Shevardnadze, *The Future Belongs to Freedom*, New York, The Free Press, 1991, p. xi.
59 M. S. Gorbachev, *Perestroika: New Thinking for Our Country and the World*, New York, Harper & Row, 1987, pp. 140–141, 146–147.
60 Quoted in Oberdorfer, *The Turn*, pp. 381, 383.
61 Vittorio Strada, "The Ruined Dream of Mikhail Sergeyevich," *Corriere della Sera*, 20 August 1991.
62 Stephen Sestanovich, "Gorbachev's Foreign Policy: a Diplomacy of Decline," *Problems of Communism*, vol. 37, no. 1 (January–February 1988), p. 1.
63 Kennan, *Russia and the West*, p. 273.
64 Shevardnadze, *The Future Belongs to Freedom*, p. 54.
65 "Mikhail Gorbachev: A Revolutionary Rethinking Necessary," *Moscow News*, no. 44, 3–10 November 1991, p. 5.

8 IS THERE SOCIALISM AFTER COMMUNISM?

1 M. S. Gorbachev, "Advance Further along the Path of Restructuring," Political Report of the CPSU Central Committee to the 28th CPSU Congress and the Party's Tasks, *Pravda*, 3 July 1990 (*Current Digest of the Soviet Press* [CDSP], 8 August 1990, pp. 3, 11).
2 N. I. Ryzhkov, Report to the 28th Congress of the CPSU, *Pravda*, 4 July 1990 (CDSP, 15 August 1990, pp. 1, 3).
3 V. A. Medvedev, Report to the 28th Congress of the CPSU, *Pravda*, 4 July 1990 (ibid., p. 5).
4 A. N. Yakovlev, Report to the 28th Congress of the CPSU, *Pravda*, 4 July 1990 (ibid., pp. 6–8).
5 E. A. Shevardnadze, Report to the 28th Congress of the CPSU, *Pravda*, 5 July 1990 (CDSP, 22 August 1990, pp. 12–13).
6 There are four versions of this exchange: a "bulletin" distributed by the conservatives, quoting the remark about capital; a purported stenographic transcript of the meeting, published together with the "bulletin" in *Komsomolskaya Pravda*, 10 July 1990; an account in *Izvestiya*, 10 July 1990; and

Yakovlev's own brief comment on the floor of the congress, 7 July 1990, *Pravda*, 11 July 1990 (all in CDSP, 19 September 1990, pp. 17–18, 21–23). The main dispute among these versions is how hypothetically the "hanging" was meant.

7 Ye. K. Ligachev, Report to the 28th Congress of the CPSU, *Pravda*, 5 July 1990 (CDSP, 22 August 1990, pp. 11, 12).

8 Replies by Ye. K. Ligachev, 28th Congress of the CPSU, 7 July 1990, *Pravda*, 11 July 1990 (CDSP, 19 September 1990, p. 18).

9 V. A. Kriuchkov, Report to the 28th Congress of the CPSU, *Pravda*, 5 July 1990 (CDSP, 22 August 1990, pp. 14–16).

10 L. I. Abalkin, Speech to the 28th Congress of the CPSU, 4 July 1990, *Pravda*, 7 July 1990 (CDSP, 29 August 1990, p. 18).

11 B. N. Yeltsin, Speech to the 28th Congress of the CPSU, 6 July 1990, *Pravda*, 7 July 1990 (CDSP, 12 September 1990, p. 12).

12 V. N. Shostakovsky, Speech to the 28th Congress of the CPSU, 6 July 1990, *Pravda*, 8 July 1990 (ibid., p. 14).

13 M. S. Gorbachev, Speech on the results of the discussion of the CPSU Central Committee's Political Report, 28th Congress of the CPSU, 10 July 1990, *Pravda*, 11 July 1990 (CDSP, 26 September 1990, pp. 17–19).

14 Reported in "Chronicle of the Congress, Day Nine," *Pravda*, 11 July 1990 (ibid., p. 19).

15 Francis Fukuyama, "The End of History," *The National Interest*, summer 1989.

16 ABC News, 6 September 1991; excerpts of text in *The New York Times*, 7 September 1991.

17 M. S. Gorbachev, Report on the draft of the new CPSU Program, *Pravda*, 26 July 1991 (CDSP, 28 August 1991, p. 5).

18 Lenin, *Sochineniya*, vol. 33, p. 249, quoted in Leon Smolinski, "Lenin and Economic Planning," *Studies in Comparative Communism*, January 1969, p. 99.

19 Rita di Leo, *L'economia sovietica fra crisi e riforme (1965–1982)*, Naples, Liguori, 1983, p. 21.

20 Lenin, *Sochineniya*, vol. 23, p. 202, quoted in Smolinski, "Lenin and Economic Planning," p. 99.

21 Mikhail Gorbachev, *Perestroika: New Thinking for Our Country and the World*, New York, Harper & Row, 1987, p. 136.

22 "What Kind of Socialism Are We Rejecting? What Kind of Socialism Are We Striving For?" (condensed transcript of a discussion organized by the journal *MEMO*, 1989), in Steve Hirsch (ed.) *MEMO 2: Soviets Examine Foreign Policy for a New Decade*, Washington, Bureau of National Affairs, 1991, p. 124.

23 ibid., p. 133.

24 ibid., pp. 129–130.

25 ibid., p. 130.

26 Robert W. Campbell, *The Socialist Economies in Transition: A Primer on Semi-Reformed Systems*, Bloomington, Ind., Indiana University Press, 1991, p. 193.

27 V. S. Pavlov, Speech to the USSR Supreme Soviet, "On the Structure of the USSR Cabinet of Ministers and Basic Guidelines for its Activity," *Pravda* and *Izvestiya*, 21 February 1991 (CDSP, 27 March 1991, pp. 18–19).

28 Michael Ellman, *Socialist Planning*, Cambridge, Cambridge University Press, 1989, p. 324.

29 Interview of Sir Karl Popper by George Urban, Radio Free Europe/Radio Liberty *Report on the USSR*, 31 May 1991, p. 21.

30 John Kenneth Galbraith, "The Rush to Capitalism," *The New York Review of Books*, 25 October 1990, p. 51.

31 Cornelius Castoriadis, "The Gorbachev Interlude," *New Politics*, winter 1988,

reprinted in Ferenc Fehér and Andrew Arato (eds), *Gorbachev: The Debate*, Atlantic Highlands, NJ, Humanitites Press International, 1989, p. 75.

32 Marie Lavigne, *Financing the Transition in the USSR: The Shatalin Plan and the Soviet Economy*, New York, Institute for East–West Security Studies, 1990, p. 26.

33 Janos Kornai, *The Road to a Free Economy – Shifting from a Socialism System: The Example of Hungary*, New York and London, Norton, 1990, pp. 187, 189.

34 Interview of Grigory Yavlinsky, "I Had No Right to Deprive People of Hope," *Nezavisimaya Gazeta*, 13 April 1991 (CDSP, 5 June 1991, p. 3).

35 James R. Millar, *The ABCs of Soviet Socialism*, Urbana, University of Illinois Press, 1981, p. 184.

36 M. S. Gorbachev, Report on the draft of the new CPSU Program, *Pravda*, 26 July 1991 (CDSP, 28 August 1991, p. 3).

INDEX

Abalkin, Leonid 47, 48, 169
Abuladze, Tenghiz 18
Academy of Sciences 25, 26
Acheson, Dean 150, 152
Afanasiev, Viktor 69
Afghanistan 24, 66, 136, 161–163
Africa 160
Aganbegian, Abel 11, 44, 73, 181
agriculture: under Brezhnev 61, 65;
    and Gorbachev 5, 8, 9; and
    perestroika 24, 46; *see also* collective
    farms; peasants
Albania 130
Alexander I 66
Algeria 160
Aliev, Geidar 11, 24
Allilueva, Nadezhda 76
All-Union Communist Party (of
    Bolsheviks) *see* Communist Party of
    the Soviet Union
anarchists 109, 143, 184, 205n16
anarcho-syndicalism 111
Andreyeva, Nina 21–22, 49
Andropov, Yuri 9–10, 17, 18; and
    circular flow of power 10–11, 60;
    and economy 14, 45, 63, 90; and
    foreign relations 162; succession to
    5–6, 12
Angola 160
Anti-Ballistic Missile (ABM) Treaty
    159
anti-Communism 142–144
"Anti-Party Group" 59
anti-Semitism 19, 38, 71
apparatus, party: under Brezhnev 43,
    60; and "circular flow of power" 11,
    14; decline of 27, 35, 58; and
    Gorbachev 7–9, 14, 22, 23, 113–114;

and Stalinism 77, 85, 105; Trotsky
    on 22; and Yeltsin 36–37, 169; *see
    also* bureaucracy
Arbatov, Georgi 66
Arendt, Hannah 77, 78
Armenia 40, 126, 133, 134
arms and arms control 137, 158–159,
    161, 162; *see also* nuclear weapons
Ash, Timothy Garton 118
Åslund, Anders, quoted 44, 47, 48
August Coup (August Putsch, 1991)
    1, 29–35, 41, 51, 53–55, 115, 189;
    and foreign relations 164, 166; and
    socialism 171; and Union 125, 133
Austria 93, 124, 132
Azerbaidzhan 40, 133, 134; *see also*
    Baku

Bakatin, Vadim 31, 49
Baker, James 53
Baklanov, Oleg 29, 30, 33
Baku, city of 126
Baldwin, Stanley 144
Balkans 124, 132; *see also* Eastern
    Europe
Baltic region 27, 37–38, 40, 49, 52; and
    August Coup 31; independence of
    122, 132, 134; separatism in 126,
    133, 134; Soviet takeover of 123; *see
    also* Lithuania; Riga; Vilnius
Belorussia (Belarus) 38, 52, 123, 133,
    134
Beria, Lavrenty 59
Berlin, East, city of 117, 118, 156
Berlin Blockade 153, 154, 156
Berlin Wall 119, 129, 156, 159
Bessarabia 123
Bevin, Ernest 150, 152

108; on world revolution 141; on
workers 82; *see also* Marxism-
Leninism
Leningrad 26, 27, 46, 54, 134; *see also*
Petrograd; St. Petersburg
Leninism *see* Marxism-Leninism
Lewin, Moshe, quoted 78
Liberman, Yevsei 65
Libya 160
Ligachev, Yegor: and conservative
Communists 19, 21; and Gorbachev
11, 13, 24; retires 39; on socialism
168–169; and Yeltsin 21, 23, 37
Lithuania 41, 126; *see also* Vilnius
Litvinov, Maxim 146
Lukács, György 83
Lukianov, Anatoly 20, 50
Lumumba University 161
Lutheran Church 118
Lysenko, Trofim 93

Machajski, Jan 70
Major, John 33
Malenkov, Georgi 59, 158
Malinovsky, Rodion 56
Malta, summit meeting at 163
"managerial revolution" 178; *see also*
New Class
Mao Tse-tung 54, 79, 157
market economy: and democracy 185;
in Eastern Europe 128, 131;
Marxism on 83; and perestroika
166, 169, 170; and radical reform
181–182, 184; and socialism 172,
181; as utopia 53, 176, 179, 183,
188–189; *see also* perestroika;
privatization
Marshall Plan 152, 153
Martov, Yuli 35
Marx, Karl: on capitalism 91, 176; and
convergence 178; on "ideology" 83,
179; and socialism 95, 174, 190; *see
also* Marxism
Marxism: in China 80; and Gorbachev
17, 171; and laws of history 62, 67,
69–70, 78, 98; predictions of 80–83,
86, 94, 95, 173; rejection of 168, 189;
and revolution 81, 108; and
revolutionary ideal 82, 87, 108, 147,
173, 174–176; and Russia 78, 80, 97,
109–110; and socialism 80, 110, 172,
175, 182; and Stalinism 71, 86, 92,

93, 179; and war 151; *see also*
ideology; Marxism-Leninism
Marxism-Leninism: abandonment of
50–51, 114, 171; meaning of 80–81,
83; and Stalin 75, 85–86, 92, 94–96,
106, 147
Masliukov, Yuri 42
Masur, Kurt 119
Mazowiecki, Tadeusz 129
media 15–17, 29–32, 100, 118; *see also*
glasnost
Medvedev, Roy 24, 36, 60
Medvedev, Vadim 24, 25, 47, 167
Medvedev, Zhores 9, 15, 191n7
Melograni, Piero 141
Menshevik-Internationalists 109
Mensheviks 51, 81, 89, 90, 100, 109;
see also Martov
meritocracy 70–71, 82, 176; *see also*
"New Class"
Michnik, Adam 132
Middle East 157
Mikhailov, V. M. 85
Mikoyan, Anastas 57, 76
militarization: in economy 58, 90–92,
174, 179, 180, 190; and national
power 140, 165; and Second World
War 148; and socialism 84, 112, 161,
175; and War Communism 104,
111; *see also* military-industrial
complex
military: and August Coup 32–33;
under Brezhnev 62; under
Gorbachev 127, 162, 165;
Khrushchev and 56; in Revolution
98–100, 102–103; and Second World
War 94; under Stalin 59, 71; *see also*
militarization; Red Army
military-industrial complex: Soviet
161, 180; U.S. 166
Military-Revolutionary Committee 99,
100
Millar, James 61–62, 73, 188
minorities *see* nationalities
Minsk Agreement 52, 134
Mlynář, Zdeněk 7, 62, 74
"moderate revolutionary revival":
concept of 112, 116, 120, 124; and
end of Communism 184, 190; and
foreign policy 139, 163, 164; and
perestroika 113–115, 125, 133, 184
modernization: in Eastern Europe